Revitalizing Urban Neighborhoods

STUDIES IN GOVERNMENT
AND PUBLIC POLICY

Revitalizing Urban Neighborhoods

Edited by
W. Dennis Keating,
Norman Krumholz, and
Philip Star

 University Press of Kansas

© 1996 by the University Press of Kansas
All rights reserved

Published by the University Press of Kansas (Lawrence, Kansas 66049), which was organized by the Kansas Board of Regents and is operated and funded by Emporia State University, Fort Hays State University, Kansas State University, Pittsburg State University, the University of Kansas, and Wichita State University

Library of Congress Cataloging-in-Publication Data

Revitalizing urban neighborhoods / edited by W. Dennis Keating, Norman
   Krumholz, and Philip Star.
     p.   cm. — (Studies in government and public policy)
   Includes bibliographical references and index.
   ISBN 0-7006-0789-7 (cloth)   ISBN 0-7006-0790-0 (pbk.)
   1. Urban renewal—United States.   I. Keating, W. Dennis (William
Dennis) II. Krumholz, Norman.   III. Star, Philip.   IV. Series.
HT175.R48 1996
307.3'416'0973—dc20   96-18180

British Library Cataloguing in Publication Data is available.

Printed in the United States of America

10 9 8   7 6 5 4 3 2 1

The paper used in this publication meets the minimum requirements of the American National Standard for Permanence of Paper for Printed Library Materials Z39.48-1984.

Dedication

We dedicate this book to Robert Mier, professor of urban planning, author, and leading expert on economic and social issues, who died in 1995. More than most planners and academics, Robert Mier personified the social theoretician in action. As a professor, he helped build the capacity of many neighborhood-based organizations in Chicago through the Center for Urban Economic Development at the University of Illinois at Chicago. Subsequently, Mier served as commissioner of Economic Development for Chicago mayor Harold Washington's administration, during which time he wrote the acclaimed "Chicago Works Together: The 1984 Development Plan." The plan combined Mier's concerns for neighborhood-based development and social justice in ways that were both practical and politically sensitive. It remains the strongest indication thus far that some American cities are willing to harness economic development for their disadvantaged residents.

Contents

Preface

The neighborhood has long been an important center for addressing urban problems. Over the course of the last century, urban neighborhood-based initiatives have taken up such issues as bad housing, racial and class conflict, neighborhood disinvestment and decline, and the cause and consequences of poverty in urban America. At the turn of the century, settlement houses attempted to improve conditions for the urban poor. Today, efforts to revitalize urban neighborhoods include activities by hundreds of community-based development corporations, dozens of large-scale, comprehensive neighborhood improvement projects, and the Clinton administration's Empowerment Zone program. Through it all, the neighborhood has been the locus of activity. Neighborhood initiatives are both a strategy and a metaphor for how America deals with its most significant urban problems.

The editors of this book, W. Dennis Keating, Norman Krumholz, and Philip Star, have had a long involvement with neighborhood initiatives in Cleveland. Krumholz, who was Cleveland's planning director during the 1970s and a member of President Carter's National Commission on Neighborhoods, developed many neighborhood initiatives from city hall. When he left his position with the city, it was to set up the Cleveland Center for Neighborhood Development (CND) at Cleveland State University, a technical assistance provider for Cleveland neighborhoods. When Krumholz left CND, Keating served as interim director until the new director, Phil Star, was chosen. Star has served as CND director since 1988. Keating, Krumholz, and Star teach courses in Neighborhood Planning and Development as part of the curriculum of the College of Urban Affairs at Cleveland State University.

It is our hope that this volume, made up of the rich contributions of independent scholars residing in several different cities, will prove useful in helping faculty, their students, and the many people and organizations involved in the revitalization of urban neighborhoods solve the problems of the 1990s and beyond.

Acknowledgments

The editors are indebted to the many individuals who made this book possible. We have been inspired by numerous Cleveland State University students who have taken classes on urban neighborhoods, done internships with neighborhood organizations in greater Cleveland, and gone on to work for neighborhood organizations seeking to preserve and revitalize their neighborhood. Janet Smith, a student in our Ph.D. program, was instrumental in assisting us in compiling profiles of neighborhood leaders and reviewing the literature on urban neighborhoods. Research and editing assistance was provided by students Qian Gao, Jeff Rink, Cathy Murphy, and Chris Ronayne. Jeanie Stearns ably prepared the text. Fred Woodward, director of the University Press of Kansas, and his staff guided the book to its completion. We received helpful comments from an anonymous reviewer for the University Press of Kansas.

Abbreviations

ACORN	Association of Community Organizations for Reform Now
AGENDA	Action for Grassroots Economic and Neighborhood Development Alternatives
APA	American Planning Association
BHA	Boston Housing Authority
BHP	Boston Housing Partnership
BRA	Boston Redevelopment Authority
BUILD	Baltimoreans United in Leadership Development
CBD	central business district
CBHO	Community-based Housing Organization
CDB	Community Development Bank
CDBG	Community Development Block Grant
CDC	Community Development Corporation
CHAS	Comprehensive Housing Affordability Strategy
CHDO	Community Housing Development Organization
CHN	Cleveland Housing Network
CMHA	California Mutual Housing Association
CND	Center for Neighborhood Development; Coalition of Neighborhood Developers (in L.A.)
CRA	Community Reinvestment Act; Community Revelopment Agency (in L.A.)
CUED	Center for Urban Economic Development
CUPR	Center for Urban Policy Research
CWED	Chicago Workshop on Economic Development
CWT	Chicago Works Together
DSNI	Dudley Street Neighborhood Initiative
EBALDC	East Bay Asian Local Development Corporation
EBHO	East Bay Housing Organizations
EDC	Economic Development Corporation
ESIC	Enterprise Social Investment Foundation
EZ	Enterprise Zones; Empowerment Zones
FANNIE MAE	Federal National Mortgage Association
FHA	Federal Housing Administration
FIRREA	Financial Institution Reform, Recovery, and Enforcement Act

FREDDIE MAC	Federal Home Loan Mortgage Corporation
GBREB	Greater Boston Real Estate Board
HADC	Hough Area Development Corporation
HAP	Housing Assistance Plan
HAPP	Hough Area Partners in Progress
HMDA	Home Mortgage Disclosure Act
HOME	Home Ownership Made Easy
HOPE	Housing Our People Economically
HPRO	Housing Preservation and Replacement Ordinance
HUD	Housing and Urban Development
IAF	Industrial Areas Foundation
IBA	Inquilinos Boricuas en Accion
KHP	Knoxville Housing Partnership
LACTC	Los Angeles County Transportation Commission
LHOC	Lincoln Heights Organizing Committee
LIHAC	Low-Income Housing Advocacy Coalitions
LISC	Local Initiative Support Corporation
LITC	Low-Income Tax Credit
LTSC	Little Tokyo Service Center
MBA	Mortgage Bankers of America
MCC	Multicultural Collaborative
MCDA	Minneapolis Community Development Agency
MCLR	Midwest Center for Labor Research
MHA	Mutual Housing Association
NCC	New Community Corporation
NCCED	National Congress for Community Economic Development
NDD	Neighborhood Development Demonstration
NEF	National Equity Fund
NHC	Neighborhood Housing Coalition
NHS	Neighborhood Housing Services
NIMBY	not in my backyard
NOMPC	North of Market Planning Council
NPA	National People's Action
NRC	Neighborhood Reinvestment Corporation
NRP	Neighborhood Revitalization Program
NSHD	Neighborhood Self-Help Demonstration
OCCUR	Oakland Citizen's Committee for Urban Renewal
OHO	Oakland Housing Organization
OIC	Opportunities Industrial Center
ONE	Organization of the Northeast
PAC	Project Advisory Committee
PFC	People for Change
PMD	Planned Manufacturing District
PNI	Partnership for Neighborhood Improvement
PPL	Project for Pride in Living
PUSH	People United to Save Humanity
PZAC	Planning/Zoning Advisory Committee
RLA	Rebuild Los Angeles
RTC	Resolution Trust Corporation
SCCRC	Southern California Civil Rights Coalition
SCOC	Southern California Organizing Committee
SON/SOC	Save Our Neighborhoods/Save Our Cities

SRO	single room occupancy
TELACU	The East Los Angeles Community Union
TIF	Tax-Increment Financing
TOOR	Tenants and Owners in Opposition to Revelopment
UDAG	Urban Development Action Grants
ULI	Urban Land Institute
UNO	United Neighborhoods Coalition
WLCAC	Watts Labor Community Action Committee

Introduction: Neighborhoods in Urban America

W. Dennis Keating

Neighborhoods in urban America have long and interesting histories. Historic ethnic neighborhoods (like New York City's Lower East Side) have been studied and their histories and life documented in numerous anthropological and sociological historical studies. These "urban villages" grew in the heyday of the rise of the industrial city in the mid to late nineteenth century. These neighborhoods, though many have changed in demographics, population, and function, remain as places to which city dwellers are attached. They serve as informal personal support networks, destinations for new immigrants (both from within and without the city and the United States), and home.

Howard Hallman, in *Neighborhoods: Their Place in Urban Life* (1984), recounts his first neighborhood experience as a college volunteer in a settlement house in New York City's Lower East Side. Hallman identified the "many faces of neighborhood": a personal arena, a social community, a physical place, a political economy, and an entity within larger surroundings (the city and the metropolitan region). The roles of urban neighborhoods today have often changed. Americans lead more mobile and private lives, reducing the time they spend in their neighborhood and with their neighbors and lessening their involvement in neighborhood activities.

With the decline of central cities in the late twentieth century, most of their neighborhoods have suffered too. They have often lost population, jobs, and a sense of community as public services have been reduced and community institutions (churches, schools, and civic organizations) have declined, disappeared, or moved to the suburbs.

Nevertheless, urban neighborhoods retain an important place in civic life. Although many of them have indeed experienced decline and serious distress, others have experienced a renaissance. Urban neighborhood revitalization has often been inspired by individual leaders and neighborhood organizations. They have led efforts to improve neighborhoods and also to defend them, for example, against demolition for urban renewal and freeways or gentrification-based displacement. Neighborhood resident's efforts have included clean-ups, street fairs, crime watches, and neighborhood service centers. In some cities, there is significant neighborhood participation in the preparation of municipal budgets. For example, Berry, Portney, and Thomson (1993) describe neighborhood associations and their role in citizen participation in five cities that have been supportive of neighborhood participation in civic affairs: Birmingham, Dayton, Portland (Oregon), St. Paul, and San Antonio.

In the face of external threats, neighborhood groups have engaged in protest politics as well in lobbying and litigation. In some cities, neighborhood groups have become involved in city politics, supporting mayoral and city council candidates. In the past few decades, community development corporations (CDCs) have risen to the fore in cities across the country, forming citywide, statewide, and national networks and receiving help not only from government but also from private intermediaries. The CDCs were often the offspring of grassroots neighborhood protest groups, which also saw the need to engage in neighborhood redevelopment activities and "spun off" CDCs. Although self-help has been a theme for CDCs, governmental support has been critical to their formation and growth (CDCs are described in detail in Part Three).

Federal governmental assistance for neighborhood revitalization has been critical, at least since World War II. Only the federal government commanded the resources sufficient to address the overwhelming problems faced by cities and their impoverished neighborhoods, heightened during the Great Depression and later in the aftermath of World War II. For the past several decades, it has been the federal government that has played a critical role in determining the fate of urban neighborhoods, both positively and negatively. Of course, the private sector, which largely determines the course of the housing and employment markets and the direction of capital investment, continues to play a critical role. And certainly municipal governments play an important role in providing public services to urban neighborhoods and their residents.

What is the future of urban neighborhoods in America's central cities as we look toward the end of the twentieth century and the beginning of the twenty-first century? After reviewing the neighborhood's evolution, the authors of this book assess the current status of urban neighborhoods and attempts at revitalization. Most indicators are not very positive (Kasarda 1993). Central cities have a negative image. Most Americans do not want to live in central cities since they typically associate them with crime, poverty, congestion, and decay.

Beginning with urban renewal in the 1950s, redevelopment of the central business district has been the focus of urban policy and local governments (Frieden and Sagalyn 1989; Fainstein et al. 1983). In the 1990s, downtown development has emphasized festival marketplaces, office and retail development, convention centers, sports arenas, and waterfront-related tourist attractions. Logan and Molotch (1987) have labeled this approach the "urban growth machine."

Other observers (e.g., Stone and Sanders 1987) have analyzed this pattern as resulting from the coalition between business and government that favors business and economic development, termed "urban regimes."

As resources are directed to downtown redevelopment, neighborhoods have often been neglected. Trickle-down economics has not worked to benefit the poor residents of distressed neighborhoods, who have not usually benefited directly in the form of jobs through downtown redevelopment (except those people in the lowest-paid jobs in the service sector who park cars, clean office buildings, and work in downtown restaurants and hotels). Much touted public/private partnerships have not usually been extended to neighborhoods (Squires 1989) except in those cities in which the political leadership has sought to reverse this pattern. Such exceptions as mayors Harold Washington in Chicago (1983–1987) and Ray Flynn in Boston (1983–1993) are chronicled in Chapters 5 and 6.

Progressive changes in urban policy favoring neighborhoods have largely resulted from political action by community organizations at the local, state, and national levels. Their efforts have brought about passage of such national legislation as the Community Reinvestment Act (CRA), requiring lenders to invest in inner-city neighborhoods, described in Chapter 14 by Gregory Squires. The most visible accomplishments of the neighborhood movement have resulted from neighborhood organizing, analyzed in Chapter 3 by Robert Fisher. Certainly, its most visible consequence has been the emergence of thousands of community development corporations across the United States. Their origins can be traced to the neighborhood settlement-house movement of the late nineteenth century that spawned the social work profession. The accomplishments of CDCs and the dilemmas they face are mentioned in subsequent chapters, particularly in those by Rachel Bratt, Edward Goetz, Jacqueline Leavitt, June Thomas, and Avis Vidal.

Some notable neighborhood leaders prominent in the neighborhood movement are profiled in this book. They typify thousands of other local heroes who have contributed to urban neighborhood revitalization across the United States.

The revitalization of urban neighborhoods, aided by public and private support, requires planning. Neighborhood planning has a long history in the United States (Rohe and Gates 1985). It has been linked with urban renewal clearance, historic preservation, and housing conservation, and, more recently, with CDC–sponsored redevelopment. Federal support for neighborhood planning has been associated with the ill-fated Model Cities program (Haar 1975; Frieden and Kaplan 1977; Wood 1990) and subsequently with the Community Development Block Grant (CDBG) program, through which cities provided neighborhood planning assistance. New York City has institutionalized perhaps the strongest role for resident neighborhood planning in urban development. Fifty-nine appointed community boards play a major part in the city's land use and budgetary decisions, although they cannot veto development permits that they oppose (Marcuse 1990). In Chapters 5 and 6 Peter Dreier and Robert Giloth discuss reforms in Boston and in Chicago that enhanced neighborhood participation in planning in those cities.

Susan Fainstein and Clifford Hirst in Chapter 7 describe the conflicts that have arisen in Minneapolis in its ambitious twenty-year neighborhood revitalization program.

The Minneapolis experience, featuring inter- and intraneighborhood disputes over representation and conflicts with governmental bodies and bureaucrats over funding allocations, is reminiscent of such previous citizen participation experiments as the federal Anti-Poverty and Model Cities programs in the 1960s. Both required resident participation in decisionmaking. Both ran into considerable opposition by local elected officials fearful of sharing or even losing their power over the use of federal funding. Both have inspired debates over the feasibility of citizen empowerment (Moynihan 1969).

The collective experience of more than three decades has demonstrated that, although citizen participation is likely to be limited and hardly a panacea for urban problems, nevertheless, the residents of urban neighborhoods must be actively engaged to make urban policies and programs work effectively and serve the interests of the urban neighborhoods for which they are intended. Community councils, block clubs, CDCs, and resident advisory committees have been vehicles for neighborhood participation. However, earlier visions of neighborhood autonomy, even governance, have proven to be illusory (Kotler 1969). The experience of CDCs has shown that the partnership of representative neighborhood organizations and city government, with support from private corporations, philanthropic intermediaries, and state and federal government, can provide a basis for successful neighborhood revitalization efforts, even in the poorest of neighborhoods.

A more daunting problem centers on the emergence of a sector of the population that has been termed an urban underclass, the poorest urban residents alienated from mainstream society, especially African and Hispanic Americans living in ghettos (Mingione 1993). In the aftermath of the 1960s riots, the Kerner Commission on Civil Disorders (1968) warned against only "gilding the ghetto." The commission, fearing the spatial, racial, and social segregation of poor minorities in ever-worsening ghetto neighborhoods, advocated an "integration" choice, dispersing poor minorities throughout metropolitan areas. This call was renewed by Henry Cisneros (1993), President Clinton's secretary of Housing and Urban Development (HUD).

Attempts to promote the commission's policy in the early 1970s were rejected because of the political opposition of suburbanites and the Nixon administration (Keating 1994). Urban sociologists such as William Julius Wilson (1987) and Douglas Massey and Nancy Denton (1993) have warned of the consequences of growing concentrations of intergenerational minority poor in our central cities. Urban planners such as William Goldsmith and Edward Blakely (1992) have described the emergence of "dual cities" in which the working and middle classes enjoy a normal urban life while the neglected poor live a marginal existence, reflecting growing inequality of income and opportunity.

The underclass phenomenon and welfare reform proposals have led to a renewed debate over whether public policy should be aimed at poor neighborhoods or in expanding choices for the poor to allow them to leave those same neighborhoods. In the 1990s, the debate has taken place in the context of a majority of Americans living in metropolitan urban areas outside the central city and under growing political and budgetary pressure to reduce the federal role in addressing urban problems.

CDCs located in inner cities are committed to helping the residents of the neighborhoods they represent. Yet, their impact on social problems is limited by their nongovernmental status and their modest resources. In several cities, large-scale demonstrations involving public/private partnerships are under way to empower the poor, e.g., the Atlanta Project initiated in that city in 1991 by former president Jimmy Carter and the Community Building in Partnership project in Baltimore's Sandtown-Winchester neighborhood launched in 1993 by the Enterprise Foundation (McDougall 1992). Both projects aim to attack all aspects of poverty in the targeted areas.

In early 1995 the Clinton administration unveiled its Urban Empowerment and Enterprise Zone program. Reminiscent of the Model Cities program of the late 1960s, selected areas of cities chosen in a national competition will receive supplemental federal funding and, in some cases, special tax incentives to attack poverty, unemployment, and related social problems in poor neighborhoods. Significant federal assistance over ten years was committed to Atlanta, Baltimore, Chicago, Cleveland, Detroit, Los Angeles, New York, and Philadelphia-Camden. Yet the promised federal aid paled in comparison to the level of funding suggested by Goldsmith and Blakely (1992) and, for example, the Eisenhower Foundation, which in a 1993 report on cities proposed annual federal expenditures of $30 billion to reconstruct inner-city neighborhoods and to address the social problems of their disadvantaged residents.

Such federal expenditures for urban aid seem most unlikely following the conservative victory in the November 1994 congressional elections and the subsequent cutbacks in the federal budget. Calls for the elimination of HUD, among several cabinet-level departments, led Henry Cisneros to propose its "reinvention" by decentralizing and privatizing many of its programs to promote greater efficiency and cost savings. Even if the political climate were more favorable to cities, critics have argued that the federal government's past policies for solvinge urban problems have been unsuccessful. Journalist Nicholas Lemann (1994), though appreciative of the efforts of CDCs such as Newark's New Community Corporation in providing affordable housing, has argued that the federal government is incapable of effectively redirecting adequate resources into ghettos to create jobs and to promote economic development. The Clinton Empowerment Zone program seeks to do exactly this over a ten-year period, although with very limited federal financial support.

The alternative is to assist the poor to leave ghetto neighborhoods (Downs 1994). However, suburban resistance to the poor, especially to minorities, in housing and public schools has made this alternative politically unpalatable. Some scholars (e.g., Rusk 1993) have argued for the jurisdictional consolidation of central cities and their suburbs in order to address the disparity between the income and quality of life of central-city dwellers and suburbanites. Yet, there is little sentiment among suburbanites (and many central-city mayors) for such a policy if it means an outward migration of poor central-city residents.

HUD initiated an experiment ("Moving to Opportunity," based upon a previous similar experiment in metropolitan Chicago) in 1992 in five cities that allowed central-city public housing tenants to use housing vouchers to move to better neighborhoods and housing, both in the central city and the suburbs. The program generated considerable controversy in Baltimore, which jeopardized the future funding of the experiment as well as any widespread federal implementation of such a dispersal policy.

What are the answers to the revitalization of urban neighborhoods? The authors in this book point to a combination of neighborhood organizing, neighborhood-based community development, citizen participation and political involvement, and the commitment of government and the private sector to support neighborhood planning and development. Examples abound of efforts that point the way toward a better future for our cities and neighborhoods. Without such efforts, conditions in our cities and neglected urban neighborhoods are likely to grow worse, a prospect that is not pleasant to contemplate.

Part One

The Growth and Evolution of Urban Neighborhoods

With the beginning of mass European migration in the mid-nineteenth century to American cities, led by the Germans and Irish, urban neighborhoods grew in size and significance. This trend was heightened during the period following the Civil War through World War I when America's industrial cities emerged, their population swollen by millions of mostly poor European immigrants seeking jobs and freedom.

Historian Edward Miggins traces this phenomenon, tracking its evolution over several decades. In Chapter 1 he discusses not only the European migration to American cities but also the great migration north of African Americans from the rural South to the promised land of northern cities, which began at the end of the nineteenth century. As his primary example, Miggins uses Cleveland, Ohio, which at the peak of its growth as an industrial city ranked sixth in population in the United States. Cleveland, like other industrial cities in America's Rustbelt, declined drastically in population and employment after the 1950s. Miggins describes this process and points out the conflicts between ethnic and racial groups, both in Cleveland and in other similar cities. He also discusses the contemporary arrival of new immigrant groups.

Change is the hallmark of American society, as its cities and urban neighborhoods demonstrate. W. Dennis Keating and Janet Smith review theories of neighborhood change in Chapter 2. These theories, primarily grounded in economic and social factors, attempt to explain the growth, decline, and revitalization of urban neighborhoods. These patterns are also affected by changes in cities and surrounding metropolitan areas as well as by national policy. Keating and Smith then review examples of neighborhood transition in many cities. The cases they explore involve redevelopment, gentrification, racial segregation and integration, new immigrants, and the rebirth of depopulated, distressed neighborhoods. These instances provide hope for the future of urban neighborhoods, including those with serious problems.

To resolve intergroup conflicts and to combat urban problems, urban neighborhoods have organized. Sociologist Robert Fisher in Chapter 3 traces the history of neighborhood organizing, distinguishing among three different approaches: (1) social work, (2) political activism, and (3) neighborhood maintenance. He analyzes the need for neighborhood organizing in the 1990s amid the social, economic, and political changes that have characterized American cities toward the end of the twentieth century.

The decline, redevelopment, and revitalization of central-city neighborhoods in the United States have been strongly influenced by federal policy. In Chapter 4 W. Dennis Keating and Janet Smith trace the evolution of federal policy toward cities and their neighborhoods, beginning with Roosevelt's New Deal in the Great Depression of the 1930s through the early part of the Clinton administration, which began in January 1993. Federal policy has both helped and hurt urban neighborhoods as federal support, both direct and indirect, has waxed and waned. It peaked during the urban crisis of the 1960s, but since 1980 federal urban aid, especially low-income housing assistance provided by HUD, has declined significantly. The goals and impact, both positive and negative, of federal urban aid programs are discussed in many of the subsequent chapters.

1

America's Urban Mosaic: Immigrant and Minority Neighborhoods in Cleveland, Ohio

Edward M. Miggins

In 1951, Oscar Handlin declared in the first edition of *The Uprooted: The Epic Story That Made the American People* that once he "thought to write a history of immigrants in America," he "discovered that the immigrants were American history (Rembart 1991, 208)." He announced in the second edition two decades later that immigration was a "dimly remote memory" and a "fading phenomena." Handlin underestimated how and why America would remain a nation of immigrants at the close of the twentieth century. The Immigration and Naturalization Service recorded 880,000 legal immigrants in 1993. In addition, an estimated 1.5 to 2.5 million illegal immigrants enter each year. Of that number, 300,000 are estimated to remain as permanent settlers.

Approximately 9 million foreign-born persons settled in the United States between 1980 and 1990—a number higher than in any previous decade of American history. Mainly from Hispanic and Asian homelands, this group constituted 45 percent of America's total of 20 million foreign-born people, or 8 percent of the nation's population. That was, however, less than the 15 percent recorded in the 1910 census, which marked the end of another decade of massive immigration in which more than 8 million foreign newcomers, mainly from southern and eastern Europe, arrived in America.

The 1990 census also revealed that 86 percent of America's ethnic and racial minority groups live in metropolitan areas and account for more than half of the population in the nation's largest cities, with the exception of San Diego and Philadelphia (Martin et al. 1994, 23). Los Angeles followed only Mexico City in having the largest number of Mexicans in the world. With its rising Asian population, it replaced New York City as the nation's major port of entry for new immigrants. Miami had become a major city for Caribbean people after the exodus of 900,000 Cubans following Castro's victory in 1959.

THE URBAN VILLAGE

Foreign immigrants have chosen cities as their first home throughout American history because of the availability of transportation, and jobs and the existence of ethnic neighborhoods with a network of schools, fraternal or self-help organizations, nationality stores, churches, and relatives from the Old Country. The neighborhoods provided them with the resources to survive an often hostile environment and to take the first steps in cultural assimilation in their new homeland. Migration and urbanization did not inevitably lead to the destruction of their social and moral order.

Social historians have investigated the growth of urban neighborhoods as a city's nationality groups have isolated themselves by social and cultural patterns that they either brought to the city or developed by living in it. Herbert Gans (1962, 17–41) has defined these communities as "urban villages" that maintain values and traditions found in an ethnic group's homeland. Residents in ethnic neighborhoods are focused on primary or peer groups and are isolated from most city facilities outside the workplace. Different nationality groups can be found in the same neighborhood, but they isolate themselves through a variety of social devices.

Neighborhoods are human communities that fulfill our needs as social beings by allowing people with common interests to interact with one another in the same physical area. Based on a mix of geographical, cultural, and socioeconomic features, unique neighborhoods are still a part of the social mosaic of modern cities. They represent distinctive places as well as ways of life: "Local areas that have physical boundaries, social networks, concentrated use of area facilities, and special emotional and symbolic connections for their inhabitants are considered neighborhoods" (Keller 1968, 156–57). Urban neighborhoods are constantly changing as a result of the nation's "demographics of diversity" (O'Hare 1992).

The constant arrival of immigrant and migrant groups into American cities during the nineteenth and twentieth centuries was a major reason for the birth, decline, and revitalization of urban neighborhoods. The Chicago School of Sociology described this process as "invasion and succession" as newer groups pushed out older groups from the downtown residential sections to the outlying areas of cities. Between 1820 and 1920, 33 million immigrants arrived in America, the overwhelming majority coming to find a better livelihood. They were also reacting to such "push" factors in their homelands as poverty, overpopulation, persecution, and economic distress. An expanding nation during the antebellum era needed workers for an economy of farming, personal service, commerce, and industry.

As immigrants poured into the coastal and hinterland cities of America, native-born people joined them in the quest for greater economic opportunity. America's cities became the magnet drawing the most adventurous immigrant and migrant groups. Between 1790 and 1830, the Atlantic ports maintained regional hegemony as the population of America increased to approximately 12.9 million people. New York, Boston, Philadelphia, and Baltimore were the leading cities. By 1830, New York had the largest population, with 200,000 residents. Until 1850, those parts of the Old Northwest adjacent to the Ohio and Mississippi valleys grew the most rapidly. By 1870, the cities in the Great Lakes region equaled the growth of cities to the south that had benefited from river and canal traffic, such as Cincinnati with a population of 125,000 and St. Louis with 75,000 residents (Ward 1971, 34). New transportation networks from the Great Lakes to the Mississippi and Northeast regions transformed the economy of a centrally located city like Cleveland, Ohio, which will be used as a prototypical city for immigrants.

THE WALKING CITY

Changes in Cleveland's population reflected the dynamics of national patterns of immigration from foreign countries and migration from other areas of the United States. The starting of the Ohio Canal by Irish and German workers in 1828 doubled the city's population between 1830 and 1832, the year of its completion to Portsmouth on the Ohio River, which connected to the Mississippi River. Cleveland served as a central depot to transport goods on Lake Erie to Buffalo and along the Erie Canal to and from the Northeast. In the pre–Civil War era, Cleveland's merchants acted as middlemen in exporting agricultural products and importing manufactured goods from the East.

Cleveland became a population center for diverse groups as a result of its commercial success. In 1830 the city's population was overwhelmingly native-born; a decade later, more than 25 percent was foreign-born. Cleveland's Irish and German immigrants settled mainly on the near west side of the Cuyahoga River. The impoverished Irish were segregated in such infamous neighborhoods as the Angle and Whiskey Island, but they could easily walk to stores, churches, parochial schools, social clubs, and their jobs along the docks and railways in the Flats. The more skilled workers of the Irish community lived to the west of Twenty-fifth Street and commingled with the German community in Ohio City. As in other American cities before 1850, most of Cleveland's residents walked to work. Their homes were close to the wharves, warehouses, shops, businesses, and factories located next to water transport. The city's elite lived in prestigious homes in important locales.

The poor and rich, native and foreign-born, and black and white residents lived in close proximity during the commercial era of Cleveland. In 1851, the construction of the city's first railway (the Cleveland, Cincinnati, and Columbus) accelerated its social and economic transformation. Rail shipments exceeded 10,000 tons during the first year and tripled by the end of the decade. Farmers could market their goods at twice prerail prices. Cleveland could also take advantage of its strategic location between the iron-ore fields around Lake Superior and the coal fields of West Virginia, southern Ohio, and Pennsylvania. The consumption of raw materials and production of manufactured products were made possible by the railway system (Wheeler 1987, xxv–xxvi; C. Miller and Wheeler 1990).

Ohio City and Cleveland merged into one entity in 1854. The city's African-American community of 800 residents was dispersed around Public Square before the Civil War. Cleveland became known as Freedom City because of its assistance to fugitive slaves. Only after the city's population expanded with industrial growth and additional transportation systems did nationality, race, and social class distinctions increasingly segment the city's people into separate neighborhoods and institutions.

THE INDUSTRIAL ERA

The Civil War acted as a major catalyst to the demographic and economic growth of Cleveland. The 1860 census revealed that of the city's 43,000 residents, 40 percent were foreign-born. Between 1860 and the conclusion of the Civil War, the population jumped 50 percent. In 1870, Germans (15,855), Irish (11,964), and Czechs (3,252) were the largest of the immigrant groups in the city's population of 92,829 people (Rose 1950). By the end of the next decade, the immigrant population, mainly from western and northern Europe, constituted 59,409 of the city's 160,146 residents.

Serving as a major supplier to the Union army and the nation's burgeoning railway system, Cleveland's economy expanded during the decade of the Civil War as the number of manufacturing jobs grew from approximately 4,000 to 9,145. By 1867 fourteen steel-rolling mills were located in the city. At the end of the decade, 18 percent of the work force was employed either in basic metal processes or in the production of such items as nuts, bolts, nails, spikes, castings, stoves, and wire. Specialized agriculture outside Cleveland supported the meat processing, tobacco, and malt-liquor industries. By 1865 the city had thirty oil refineries. Under the leadership of John D. Rockefeller's Standard Oil Company, Cleveland became a major center for the petrochemical business until the 1890s. Cleveland's American Shipbuilding Company owned every shipyard in the Great Lakes region outside of Toledo, Ohio. The city's export products stimulated shipping and related industries and encouraged the arrival of new immigrants and migrants to find employment in the growing job market.

In the post–Civil War era, Cleveland and other industrial cities throughout America increasingly employed foreign newcomers from southern and eastern Europe as the solution to their labor shortage. These groups were described as the "new immigrants" because they came later than the previous groups who were primarily from western Europe. The newcomers came mostly from non–English speaking areas peopled by illiterate peasants in eastern, central, and southern Europe. In 1890, 19 percent of the city's foreign-born population of 97,095 people had immigrated from these European regions; by 1900, the foreign stock had increased to 196,170 residents (Galford 1958, 12). Fifty-seven percent represented the new immigrants.

Cleveland's neighborhoods became more stratified with the introduction of the electric trolley car in 1884 and the automobile at the turn of the century. More affluent residents could move to suburban neighborhoods and travel greater distances to work in the downtown area with the new transportation system. They could escape the overcrowding, pollution, crime, and commercialization in older residential areas, as the city's elite demonstrated when they abandoned Millionaire's Row on Euclid Avenue in the 1890s. They also distanced themselves from the growing population of Cleveland's new immigrants and African-American migrants from the American South.

THE NEW IMMIGRANTS

Foreign newcomers escaped from economic and social distress in their homelands by booking passage on inexpensive steamship lines that advertised the attractions of American society. The new immigrants arrived during a period of unrestricted immigration, except for the Chinese, who were excluded by Congress in 1882. Americans were concerned that the new immigrants might be radicals or that they might bring disease or become dependent on public welfare, fears that led to the construction of Ellis Island in New York Harbor in 1892. Public inspectors and medical officials thus could check out and possibly detain or deport unwelcome newcomers before they reached the shores of America.

Approximately 23 million immigrants entered the United States between 1880 and 1920. They became quite urbanized. In 1911 the Dillingham Commission reported that 78.6 percent of the country's immigrants born in eastern and southern Europe lived in urban areas. By 1910 three-fourths of America's urban population was either foreign-born or native-born of foreign parents. Many newcomers were advised of opportunities in specific areas of America by kin or by people who previously had migrated from their community. In 1885 a Slovenian immigrant in Cleveland explained: "First some bold spirits come to spy out the land; when they found it good they so reported to others, and others followed them. Then the families began to be sent for and homes took the places of boarding houses" (W. Miller, Norman, and Peery 1991). This process often started a chain migration from European villages and towns to American cities. Many new immigrants returned home during hard times or shuttled back and forth across the Atlantic to take advantage of wage differentials. A significant number were "birds of passage" who saw America as a temporary destination to earn money, returning with it to their homelands to help their families. It has been estimated that between 1900 and

1914, 33 to 40 percent of the newcomers returned to Europe. Because of bloody persecutions and intolerance in their homeland, Russian Jews had the lowest rate of return.

The new immigrants arrived during a period of economic expansion and job opportunities for unskilled labor in America's factories. The railway also allowed heavy industries to locate in the outskirts of cities near transit connections. The immigrants concentrated in the industrial cities of the Northeast and the Great Lakes region and settled in urban enclaves like Chicago's West Side or Boston's North End. New York City's Lower East Side—a cauldron of Italian, Jewish, Asian, Irish, and other groups—had the highest concentration of residents in the world by the beginning of the twentieth century. Nationality neighborhoods supported cultural, educational, and religious institutions, working-class and self-help organizations, businesses, politicians, and reforms that responded to their needs.

THE URBAN MOSAIC

Cleveland was a major point of arrival for the new immigrants. Between 1900 and 1910, the city's population from northern and western Europe declined by 2,346 to 69,852 while the population from eastern and southern Europe increased from 43,281 to 115,870 (Galford 1958, 14). Its social and spatial landscape resembled an urban mosaic of first-generation nationality groups that replaced older residents in the cheapest housing located next to the Flats and other commercial and industrial areas of the city. Responding to the changing needs of its neighborhoods and nationality groups, the city gave birth to a variety of new institutions and reforms.

Civic leaders debated the best ways to maintain efficiency and order, assimilate foreign newcomers, and meet the need for more housing, schools, welfare programs, and municipal services. The transitions in Cleveland's civic life reveal not only the response of local leaders and institutions to changing human needs but also the impact of nationality groups in building a new home for themselves in urban America.

Between 1880 and 1920 Cleveland's total number of workers rose from 57,000 to 347,000. In the manufacturing sector, employment expanded from 21,000 to 190,000 workers (Hoffman 1980; Weiner and Beal 1988). Cleveland also grew from the twelfth largest city (160,000 residents) to the sixth largest (nearly 800,000) during this period. Local reporters called the Haymarket neighborhood to the southwest of Public Square, sloping to the river, Baghdad on the Cuyahoga because of the multiplicity of foreign languages spoken by its residents. Local religious leaders saw Babel as the metaphor for the threatening diversity of nationality groups and Babylon as an appropriate description for the city's growing materialism during the industrial era. But the creative dynamics and spirit behind the evolution of communities of new immigrants defied such hasty generalizations.

THE ECONOMIC BASE

Primarily, foreign newcomers were attracted to the burgeoning job market of Cleveland's factories. Automation allowed unskilled, rural, and non–English-speaking immigrants to find work. In some cases, they either competed with or replaced older groups of immigrants. In 1882 the Cleveland Rolling Mills transported recent Polish immigrants from New York City to replace striking members of the AFL's Amalgamated Iron, Tin and Steel Workers Union who were protesting a pay cut. The introduction of Bessemer machinery had allowed the owners to replace skilled with unskilled workers. But the union, mainly composed of groups of older immigrants from Ireland, Wales, and England, was biased against new immigrants. By recruiting only craft workers and excluding the unskilled employees, it prevented the formation of a coalition between new and old workers. However, the same Polish workers struck against lower wages three years later, and after their march to Public Square and other disturbances, the company restored the pay cut (H. Leonard 1979)

In other instances, an entrepreneur from a European homeland would start a business in Cleveland and recruit his compatriots as employees. Such was the case with Theodore Kundtz, who employed more than 2,000 workers, mainly from his former village in Hungary, to supply cabinets for the White Sewing Machine Company on Cleveland's west side. And 1880 Joseph Carabelli, an Italian stonemason from Northern Italy, opened a monumental-works business next to the Lakeview Cemetery, which served as a burial site for the elite members of the city's Anglo-Saxon community (Miggins et al. 1988). Carabelli attracted stonemasons from his province in Italy to settle on the city's east side in the Murray Hill neighborhood, Little Italy, next to the cemetery.

Such middlemen were often employers or businessmen who acted as magnets for the settlement of new immigrants in a particular area. David and Morris Black escaped the failure of the Hungarian Revolution of 1848 and started a successful clothing business in Cleveland. They employed and helped many of their Jewish compatriots settle in the downtown area. John Weizer, also from Hungary, started a grocery store and real estate business that sold over 2,000 lots to immigrants from his homeland in the Buckeye-Woodland neighborhood—the largest Hungarian settlement in the city.

Michael Kinola, who arrived from Poland in 1880, first started as an English-speaking foreman in the Cleveland Rolling Mills but soon became a store owner, interpreter, and travel agent for Polish immigrants in the Fleet Broadway neighborhood, or Warszawa, that was anchored by St. Stanislaus Church, founded in 1881. Under the dynamic leadership of Fr. Francis Kolaszewcki, the parish built a soaring Gothic cathedral in the midst of humble working-class homes. Fr. Kolaszewcki organized a Polish-Catholic church that provided social service and welfare programs, fraternal organizations that sold insurance to their members, and a parochial school that, like religious services, taught in the Polish language. By the advent of World War I, more than 200,000 people were attending nationality churches in Cleveland (Gartland 1973).

Immigrant neighborhoods were also noted for their rapid transition, as older groups left with the "invasion and succession" of newer ones. In the Tremont neighborhood located on Cleveland's southwest side, Slavic groups replaced older groups of New Englanders and Irish and German residents by the turn of the century. As a result of increased employment in the industrial Flats area below the neighborhood and the completion of the Abbey Road Bridge as part of the Central Viaduct that linked the east and west sides of the city in 1878, Polish, Ukrainian, Russian, Greek, and Syrian groups soon arrived.

THE HELPING HAND

With the financial support of Czar Nicholas of Russia, St. Theodosius Russian Orthodox Cathedral with its landmark onion domes was built in 1911. Streets were named after Russian saints as the church's families moved into adjacent small lots. Twenty-five churches representing twenty nationality enclaves were located in the Tremont area by World War I. The Pilgrim Congregational Church, founded by New Englanders in 1859, became an institutional church after its members left but supported religious, social welfare and educational programs for Tremont's residents (McTighe 1988, 237–38).

Older groups also attempted to assimilate members of their religious faith who arrived at a later date. German Jews who had organized Reform Judaism felt anxious about the Zionism, socialism, and Orthodox Judaism of Jewish newcomers from southern and eastern Europe. In 1887 a visitor to a Russian Orthodox service in Cleveland remarked that "the entire surroundings bore the air of scenes in the ghetto during the Middle Ages" (McTighe 1988, 252). In 1899 the Council of Jewish Women organized the Council Educational Alliance, which provided clubs, classes, lectures, a playground, a free synagogue, and Hebrew instruction to assimilate Jewish immigrants in the overcrowded, lower Central-Woodland neighborhood.

The alliance's program imitated the work of George Bellamy, a graduate of Hiram College and a follower of the social gospel movement, who had established Hiram House as the city's first social settlement in the same area in 1896. Like Jacob Riis, the photographer and investigator of New York's Lower East Side, Bellamy blamed overcrowding for most of the neighborhood's ills. In 1901 the settlement's survey of housing—the first of its kind in the city—demonstrated that slum housing in Central-Woodland originated with poor maintenance and the subdivision of single-family homes into multiple dwellings by landlords to maximize their profits. Because the area lacked a housing inspection program by City Hall, garbage, manure, and sheds occupied the little available space. The survey also found that the neighborhood's boys spent almost four times as much time in the streets with "the baser element of humanity" as they spent in the schools (Seventeenth Annual Report, Hiram House 1913). Cleveland's settlement movement pioneered vocational-technical instruction, kindergarten and home economics programs, Americanization classes and adult education. But Hiram House could not arrest the deterioration and growing poverty of the Central-Woodland neighborhood. Bellamy saw less-educated immigrants and migrants from the American South move into the area and concluded that diet and recreation, rather than progressive reform of social conditions, would better improve people. Still, Hiram House's social services, based on the contributions of wealthy, civic-minded individuals to help poor people, became the basis of many of the city's charitable organizations (Miggins 1988, 145–47).

Overwhelmed by rising costs and fearing duplication of services, the Cleveland Chamber of Commerce led a campaign during World War I to establish the nation's first Community Chest as a welfare federation to coordinate the funding and operation of local charities. The social settlement movement also helped reform the Cleveland Public Schools to meet the educational and social welfare needs of immigrant, impoverished, or working-class children. In 1901 special language, or "steamer," classes for foreign students were opened. In 1907 a medical dispensary—the first of its kind in America's schools—was established in Little Italy's Murray Hill School. Among Cleveland's 9,619 high school students in 1918, 4,715 were enrolled in commercial-technical high schools (Miggins 1986, 154).

BEYOND THE MELTING POT

Both the social settlement and the public school movements championed the philosophy of the melting pot, which assumed that America's foreign newcomers would become part of a common culture. Nationality neighborhoods and identities were expected to disappear through assimilation. In 1918 the Federated Churches of Cleveland estimated that the city had 139,273 foreign-born Slavs (46,296 Czechs, 49,000 Poles, 19,000 Slovenes, 18,977 Slovaks, and 6,000 Croatians). Its report did not include smaller but no less significant groups. It also estimated that 23,000 Italians, 30,000 Russian Jews, and 31,628 Hungarians lived in the city (Miggins et al. 1988, 106).

The neighborhoods of Cleveland consisted of separate enclaves of different nationality groups that shared a common language, religious denomination, and often a local affiliation with their homeland. For example, more than 50 percent of Cleveland's Italian immigrants came from ten small villages in southern Italy. They organized hometown societies, which provided mutual support services and celebrated patron saints brought from Italy (J. Barton 1975, 60).

Moreover, immigration prompted other groups from the same homeland to develop regional affiliations or national identities. In 1906 the mutual benefit clubs of the Rumanian community, first started by Michael Baraza in 1902, organized the Union of Rumanian Societies in America; self-made businessmen dominated the organization. The Slovak community maintained religious affiliations to define membership in their nationality group, organizing the Slovak Catholic Federation in 1911. Nationality or hometown organizations, ethnic neighborhoods, and celebrations of cultures of the Old World allowed newcomers to survive nativist hostility and adapted disparate groups to an urban environment.

Americans' fears concerning the loyalties of the huddled masses, whom Emma Lazarus describes in her poem at the base of the Statue of Liberty, meanwhile became more prevalent than the hope for a melting pot. The xenophobic crusade for "100 percent Americanism" during World War I and the postwar's red scare resulted in an attack on hyphenated Americans for their allegiance to nationality cultures. Cleveland's Americanization Council, headed by Raymond Moley, a political science professor from Western Reserve University, organized a coalition of schools, businesses, social settlements, and libraries to promote patriotism and citizenship during and after World War I (Miggins et al. 1988, 130). The war stopped the flow of European immigrants to America, and the labor shortage in wartime industries and other businesses in the North was a major factor in the Great Migration of African Americans.

THE GREAT MIGRATION

In 1924 the postwar campaign against the new immigrants as an inferior class and as the cause of America's political and urban problems resulted in quota laws that severely restricted their arrival in America. Asian immigrants were totally banned. The closing of America's Golden Door provided the opportunity for more black southerners to migrate to the North and for immigrants from countries in the Western Hemisphere to come to America. By 1900 there were already a dozen cities with more than 40,000 black residents. By 1910 Washington, D.C., had the largest number, but a decade later New York City ranked first. Pushed by the violence of the KKK and lynchings that took the lives of approximately 2,500 of their people in the last quarter of the nineteenth century, the enduring poverty of sharecropping, tenant farming, poor crop years, and the racist segregation of the Jim Crow era in the South, African Americans increasingly saw the North as the Promised Land. As in the case of Irish immigration to America, women often were the first to arrive because of the availability of jobs for female domestic servants.

Cleveland's African-American population increased from 8,448 to 34,451 people between 1910 and 1920, and by 1930 it doubled to more than 70,000 residents. In 1884 the introduction of the electrified trolley car allowed more affluent residents to move to such suburban areas as Glenville, Collinwood, and Hough on the city's east side and to outlying areas on the west side. Cleveland's central neighborhoods thus became more stratified by race and the social-class backgrounds of their residents.

By 1910 eight of the city's wards on the east side contained 70 percent of the African-American population. The majority settled in an area known as the Roaring Third because of lax police enforcement. Other enclaves existed in the city, but the lower Central-Woodland area became the nucleus of a segregated, impoverished black neighborhood. Unlike immigrant neighborhoods, Cleveland's African-American community became larger but more segregated because of racial hostility in the housing and job markets. Like immigrant groups, however, Cleveland's African-American community established a variety of businesses, churches, and self-help organizations to meet the needs of its people.

THE SEARCH FOR EQUALITY

Incorporated in 1896, the Home for Aged Colored People served the needs of the elderly members of Cleveland's African-American community. In 1905 Jane Edna Hunter established an organization that became known as the Phillis Wheatley Association to provide lodging and training for women migrants from the South. In 1915 Cleveland's African-American community supported the proposal of Russell and Rowena Jeliffe, graduates of Oberlin College and the University of Chicago, to open Playhouse Settlement on Central Avenue. Like George Bellamy, the Jeliffes were influenced by Jane Addams's Hull House in Chicago and concentrated on using the arts and drama in an interracial program, later known as Karamu House, to discover the common humanity of neighborhood residents.

In 1917 Cleveland's Welfare Federation helped organize the Negro Welfare Association as an affiliate of the National Urban League to improve educational, housing, and employment opportunities for black residents. Between 1915 and 1930 the number of African-American churches increased from 17 to 140 to accommodate the needs of the rapidly expanding community. Two-thirds were Baptist, but social-class backgrounds sorted blacks into different denominations. In 1922 the Catholic Diocese of Cleveland founded Our Lady of Blessed Sacrament for black congregants. Many of the recent migrants attended the more emotional storefront churches of the Holiness and Spiritualist sects.

Older members of Cleveland's African-American community, such as Harry Smith, editor of the *Cleveland Gazette*, believed in campaigning for civil rights and integration into American society. A newer group of leaders saw the segregation of blacks in the Central-Woodland neighborhood as an opportunity for economic and political power. J. Walter Wills, a follower of the self-help philosophy of Booker T. Washington, founded a black funeral home and the Black Businessman's League in 1905. In 1909 Thomas Fleming capitalized on the concentration of blacks in his Eleventh Ward and was elected as the first African American to the city council, thereafter working closely with the Republican party.

The temporary improvement of the economic status of black workers during World War I was reversed with the return of America's soldiers. The number of African Americans employed in manufacturing decreased, and employment as a domestic servant or as an unskilled laborer became the fate of most black workers. Unions of skilled, white workers refused to open their doors. In 1920, 76.9 percent of black workers were in occupations at or below the semiskilled level. Only 49.2 percent of foreign-born white workers and 23.5 percent of native-born whites were employed in that category of lowest-paid jobs (McKinney 1945). As African Americans moved into the neighborhood between East Fifty-fifth and Seventy-ninth streets in the 1920s, the lower Central-Woodland area became poorer and more racially segregated.

Cleveland's older and more affluent white groups migrated to the suburbs. The suburban population expanded from 76,762 to 146,654 (91 percent) between 1900 and 1910 and accelerated to 301,026 by the end of the next decade. Zoning laws and racist real estate practices prevented minority and low-income people from also settling there. The city's foreign-born population decreased from 230,946 to 179,183 between 1930 and 1940. By 1930 twelve census tracts on the city's east side were between 60 and 90 percent black (Kusmer 1976, 157–63). The Great Depression had the most negative impact on the city's minority population, despite the provision of public works programs of the New Deal and the establishment of the CIO, which recruited unskilled workers, minorities, and women into its ranks. Although the NAACP aggressively filed lawsuits against racial discrimination in Cleveland, two major race riots occurred in the city's neighborhoods as a result of worsening conditions after World War II.

THE POSTWAR ERA

World War II and the postwar era of economic expansion served as another catalyst to the Great Migration as the city's African-American population expanded from 85,000 to 205,800 people between 1940 and 1960. By 1980 it constituted 44 percent of the city's population (573,882), a situation that caused overcrowding in the neighborhoods open to black households. White residents fled the city as highways, housing developments, GI loans, and Federal Housing Administration (FHA) insurance made possible their relocation to suburban areas. By 1980 Cleveland contained only 38 percent of the population (1,498,400) of Cuyahoga County.

In 1963 a report estimated that 277,600 of Cleveland's African-American population of 287,000 lived in the eastern third of the central city, an area covering fifteen square miles (Cleveland Urban League n.d.). More affluent members of this community moved to the Glenville, Mount Pleasant, Kinsmen, and Lee-Seville areas. The old Central-Woodland neighborhood was left to the most recent migrants from the American South. The Central Area Council and Cleveland's Community Relations Department, established in 1945, attempted to resolve interracial conflicts, housing and law enforcement problems, poverty, and blight in the Central-Woodland area.

The neighborhood's poorest families lived in houses without running water, toilets, electricity, or heat. The Cleveland Metropolitan Housing Authority, established as one of the nation's first public housing programs in the 1930s, practiced racial discrimination in assigning families. The public schools did the same as white students were allowed to transfer from black to white schools. School districts were redrawn or new schools built to perpetuate racial boundaries.

THE DECLINE OF THE CENTRAL CITY

The city's tax revenues for municipal services and schools fell drastically as houses, factories, and stores were abandoned in the central city. Cleveland's Department of Urban Renewal demolished more housing than that of any other city and created a vast wasteland on the city's east side. The uprooted families were steered according to race into Hough, Glenville, and other areas that had been incorporated into the city before the annexation movement of suburban areas stopped, pre–World War I.

Once the home of middle- to upper-class families at the turn of the century, the Hough neighborhood was transformed between 1950 and 1960 (Leahy and Snow 1984, 101–8). It changed from housing working- to middle-class families with a 5 percent minority population to being a 74 percent black residential area during that period. In spring 1965 the U.S. Civil Rights Commission found deplorable conditions. Slum landlords were overcharging African-American residents as they subdivided single-family homes; building-code violations and neglect became the norm; the neighborhood lacked playground space for an expanding population, of which 50 percent was under twenty-five years old. Lax police enforcement allowed vice and crime to proliferate. Police activity was often brutal and racist. The schools platooned black children into half-day sessions rather than bus them to empty classrooms in white neighborhoods.

In 1964 African Americans protested such negative conditions before the Cleveland Board of Education. Angry whites then marched into black neighborhoods, overturning cars and beating black citizens (Wye 1986, 133). The Congress of Racial Equality (CORE) attempted to unite all black action groups to support self-determination. Still, the school board continued to build schools in locations unacceptable to black families. Cleveland's NAACP filed a federal lawsuit to stop this policy, to improve the educational program, and to desegregate the schools through a busing program.

In 1966 the Hough area erupted into four days of rioting and interracial conflict, and 1,700 National Guardsmen arrived to stop the looting, arson, and violence.

Carl Stokes was elected as Cleveland's first black mayor in 1967, but a gun battle between local police and black nationalists resulted in the Glenville Shootout a year later. In 1975 a Brookings Institution study ranked Cleveland second among fifty-eight big cities having the worst social and economic problems. In 1978 it became the first major city since the Great Depression to declare bankruptcy for its loans from local banks. Mayor Dennis Kucinich, who fought downtown interests in favor of neighborhoods but ended up alienating almost everyone, blamed the default on the business community's retaliation for his refusal to sell the Municipal Light Plant to a private utility. The default, however, was also reflective of the social and economic decline of America's central cities since World War II.

In 1989 it was reported that the city was losing 3,500 households per year. The population of Cleveland declined from 914,808 to 505,00 residents between 1950 and 1990. The second worst racially segregated city in the nation, it was left with a high level of poverty, social decay, crime, drug abuse, single-parent families, and racial isolation. By 1990, 40 percent of Cleveland's households were at or below the poverty line. Almost 50 percent of its schoolchildren failed to graduate from high school in an era that primarily employed people in service and technical jobs. As industries and businesses continued to shut down or move elsewhere and the federal government reduced aid to cities in the 1980s, Cleveland had the worst rate of unemployment for blacks and the second worst rate for all adult workers in the nation—a detriment to newcomers.

Benefiting from America's new immigration law in 1965, which eliminated the old quota laws but favored people with technical and professional backgrounds or families already in America, immigrants with skills have been able to settle in Cleveland's suburban areas. Unlike New York City, Los Angeles, and Miami, Cleveland was not a major center for incoming groups of refugees and new immigrants from Asia and Latin America. Still, the new immigrants have not stopped the flight of more affluent people from older white and minority groups to the suburbs. African Americans were resegregated into such eastern suburbs as Warrensville, Shaker Heights, Cleveland Heights, and East Cleveland. By 1990 the latter had more than a 90 percent minority population with severe social and economic problems.

THE NEIGHBORHOOD MOVEMENT

Neighborhood groups established block clubs or community action groups to improve conditions in Cleveland's central city, pointing to the rising cost of energy and suburban homes as one of the reasons to restore or build new housing there. Cleveland's Famicos Foundation helped to build and rehabilitate more than 200 houses and constructed Lexington Village for moderate-income families in the Hough neighborhood. The Near West Side Development Corporation has done the same for its area. The Lee Harvard Community Association has used the philosophy of the social-settlement movement to provide a variety of programs to meet the needs of local residents. The Buckeye-Woodland Congress fought against redlining by local banks in its neighborhood of minority families.

Organized in 1975 by Patrick Henry, the director of Cleveland's Community Development Program, Neighborhood Housing Services, supported by local banks, charitable foundations, and a Community Development Block Grant, helped Hispanic, Asian, and Appalachian groups that had moved into the city's near west side to improve their neighborhood. Bank One agreed to a joint venture with Cleveland City Hall to invest $67 million in the 1990s in local neighborhoods. Ten Catholic and Protestant churches on the city's west side organized Project Afford to build moderately priced homes in their area. Cleveland mayor Michael White has followed in the footsteps of Carl Stokes and has pursued strategies to redevelop the downtown area and also its neighborhoods with a $90 million empowerment grant from the federal government in 1995 to help reverse the decline of Hough and three other neighborhoods on the city's east side (Miggins 1984, 133).

Cleveland's immigrant and minority groups, who built the city's infrastructure; worked in its factories and commercial businesses; constructed nationality churches, neighborhoods, schools, and self-help organizations; fought discrimination; and endured poverty, should inspire the present generation to see the current situation as an opportunity to witness to the human need for community and self-determination.Encouraged by his own work with the Marshall Plan to rebuild Europe after the devastation of World War II, Paul Porter, in *The Recovery of American Cities*, best expresses the point: "If we miss the beckoning chance to restore our cities to health, it will be because of ourselves—something in our present view of things or in our spirit that sets us widely apart from the generations of Americans who have come before us (1976, 191)."

2

Neighborhoods in Transition

W. Dennis Keating and Janet Smith

Urban neighborhoods in the United States are dynamic, not static. Americans are mobile, with high rates of turnover, especially among tenants (Du 1990). Americans move voluntarily for many reasons, typically because of such factors as change in employment, marital status, family size, and housing tenure. Urban neighborhoods change and residents move for other reasons also, such as redevelopment (for example, urban renewal and freeways); racial change; deterioration of services, conditions, and property values; and crime and gentrification (neighborhood upgrading). In this chapter theories and examples of neighborhood transition are reviewed.

THEORIES OF NEIGHBORHOOD CHANGE

Attention to neighborhood change reflects the broader interest of trying to understand the push and pull factors shaping the entire urban area. Neighborhoods are more than places to live; they are interactive components of a larger urban system, each affecting the other over time and in space. As regions expand, it is important to understand the dynamic nature of neighborhood change, especially as older city neighborhoods experience decline while suburbs continue to grow (Downs 1981).

Theories of neighborhood change identify conditions that alter the status quo of urban neighborhoods. Particular attention has been given to the physical, institutional, and social factors that cause neighborhoods to become unstable or to decline (Gale 1989). Physical causes of decline include technological, architectural, and locational features that make a home or neighborhood obsolete. Essentially, age threatens the viability of any neighborhood because it affects decisions to invest in property as well as decisions to move. Institutional factors, such as zoning, code enforcement, rent control, property assessment, and lending practices shape housing-market operation and can precipitate negative as well as positive neighborhood change. Social characteristics associated with neighborhood decline include change in the racial or ethnic composition, income level, familial status, and age of household members. Employing these factors to explain neighborhood change is controversial since it implies a direct relationship between physical deterioration and the type of people residing in a neighborhood. The difficulty is disentangling the cause and effects of social characteristics in the process change.

All theories of neighborhood change explain some aspect of urban growth and development. It is recognized that even stable neighborhoods are not static and that household turnover does not necessarily change a neighborhood's character (Downs 1981). Early theories of neighborhood change attempted to make sense of change as a "natural" process. Contemporary theories consider both internal and external factors that can affect stability. A review of several theories that attempt to explain neighborhood change follows.

Invasion and Succession

The earliest theories of neighborhood change are usually credited to the Chicago School of Sociology, which introduced a human ecologist approach to understanding urban growth. In this scheme, the city is divided into concentric zones radiating from the central business district. Each zone is identified by dominant household and housing characteristics, with higher-income groups living in lower-density housing farthest from the center. As new inhabitants enter the city seeking employment, the inner zone pushes into the next outer ring (invasion), eventually taking over the physical space of that zone (succession). This process is presumed to be ongoing as long as migration and economic growth continue, maintaining areas for different income groups.

Developed in the 1920s when cities were rapidly growing, human ecology provides a logical, economic order for urban growth patterns resulting from the waves of immigrants to American cities. Neighborhood change is expected when there is a rapid infusion of people. These conditions also limit the explanatory value of the ecological model because it assumes neighborhood change is a "natural" process. Missing from the explanation are the social and political forces that often keep residents segregated by race, ethnicity, and class.

Filtering

Filtering theories also impose a linear framework to explain housing transition. Filtering generally refers to the process in which older housing units become available to lower-income groups as higher-income groups move to newer units on the urban periphery. In this explanation, the metropolitan area is assumed to operate as a single housing market, with a fixed hierarchy of housing units available to different income groups competing for the best housing value (Baer and Williamson 1988).

Although the idea of filtering was introduced more than 100 years ago, Homer

Hoyt first applied the concept in the 1930s to explain urban neighborhood change caused by obsolescence (Leven et al. 1976). Hoyt observed that increasing income levels encouraged residents to seek better housing. This freed housing for lower-income groups to move into aging stock in older city neighborhoods. In the 1940s Ratcliff altered this notion to consider the welfare effects of filtering, noting that while housing units "filter down," households "filter up" as they improve their housing conditions. This distinction allows filtering to appear ambiguous, describing both a process and an outcome.

As a theory to explain the relationship between the aging housing stock and neighborhood change, it helps make sense of physical deterioration observed in cities; as housing filters down, investment decreases and neighborhoods eventually decline. However, its simplicity relies on many assumptions about housing-market dynamics that do not always hold. In particular, the welfare aspect of filtering is not reliable if expectations of the free market are not met (Baer and Williamson 1988). The filtering process stops when discrimination, fluctuations in the overall economy, or spatial mismatch of supply and demand prevent housing markets from operating perfectly.

Racial Tipping Point

Although the notion of invasion and succession describe change in terms of social characteristics (ethnicity, race, class), the concept of tipping presumes race is the primary cause of neighborhood change. Racial tipping attempts to explain why racially changing neighborhoods, particularly ones that had been predominantly white, eventually resegregate. The tipping point hypothesis states that whites will move out of a neighborhood when a certain proportion of blacks move in, allowing the neighborhood eventually, and often rapidly, to become all black (Goering 1978). The tipping point is the threshold (percentage of nonwhite residents) at which whites are no longer comfortable moving into the neighborhood and may consider leaving. Several empirical studies have attempted to determine this threshold, placing it anywhere from 5 percent to 50 percent nonwhite. Although there may not be a single tipping point, many efforts to prevent racially mixed neighborhoods from resegregating focus on a threshold of 30 percent nonwhite.

The tipping point theory presumes that racially mixed neighborhoods are inherently unstable, a view often contested by proponents of racial integration (Goering 1978). Further, the theory links racial change to housing values, which may initially inflate with entry of blacks but then decrease as the neighborhood becomes predominantly nonwhite (Downs 1981). This phenomena has been labeled "ghetto expansion" because the process occurred in successive neighborhoods beginning with those closest to areas that were already predominantly black. It has been difficult to dispute the tipping phenomena, especially when external forces like blockbusting encourage white flight and rapid racial change. Despite fair housing laws and evidence of sustained, racially mixed neighborhoods (for example see Lee and Wood 1991; Denton and Massey 1991), racial tipping remains a concern.

Neighborhood Dynamics and Revitalization

Although much attention has been given to factors that can render a neighborhood unstable and cause it to decline, recent evidence of older city neighborhoods turning around challenges the inevitable decline predicted by ecological and filtering theories. It has also drawn attention to negative as well as positive effects of neighborhood revitalization. In broad terms, revitalization is presumed to be a positive outcome for declining or aging neighborhoods; however, not everyone always benefits from improvements.

Several contemporary theories attempt to make sense of the dynamics that allow declining neighborhoods to revitalize, identifying the stages and agents of change. The process that now might be considered a classic model of neighborhood change, the five-stage continuum in Figure 2.1, describes conditions in relation to social and physical factors that affect the maintenance of a healthy neighborhood. The classification scheme permits both upward and downward movement across stages.

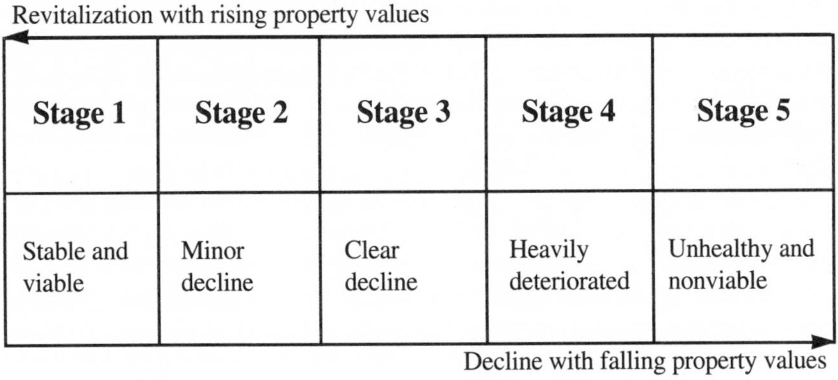

Revitalization with rising property values

Stage 1	Stage 2	Stage 3	Stage 4	Stage 5
Stable and viable	Minor decline	Clear decline	Heavily deteriorated	Unhealthy and nonviable

Decline with falling property values

Figure 2.1. The Neighborhood Change Continuum

A stable and viable neighborhood (stage 1) has rising property values, no visible symptoms of decline such as deteriorating housing stock or abandoned property, and higher rates of ownership. A stage 1 neighborhood can be new but may also be an older neighborhood in a good location with features that attract new households able to maintain the housing quality.

Neighborhoods in stage 2 usually experience minor decline caused by age and functional obsolescence of the housing stock, although prices may be constant or increasing slightly. In this stage, residents are often younger households with little equity and fewer resources to make repairs. The availability and quality of public services are below the level of a stage 1 neighborhood.

A clearly declining neighborhood (stage 3) is distinguished by the widespread (although minor) deterioration of the physical stock and by some abandonment. Decreasing property values encourage some homeowners to leave, opting either to sell property at a potential loss or to become landlords. Unit conversion is also common as property owners try to recoup profits by increasing density.

Heavily deteriorated neighborhoods (stage 4) contain housing units needing major repairs. Property values are lower than the area median, making for little interest by lending institutions or brokers. Household income is relatively low and rental rates are high, which generally reduces the profit margin for landlords and the incentive to maintain or improve property. Public services are likely to be reduced or even nonexistent.

A stage 5 neighborhood is considered both unhealthy and nonviable. Property values are low or even negative if buildings are dilapidated. This is an area to move from rather than to move to (Downs 1981).

Clearly, this model of neighborhood dynamics replicates the linear flow of earlier theories, although it assumes transition is not only downward along the continuum. Improvements can be made to change a stage 3 neighborhood to stage 2 classification. Yet change requires not only effort from residents but also a commitment from public officials and private-sector actors to make upward transition succeed. Unlike the human ecology model and filtering theories, this model identifies institutional factors that affect neighborhood conditions (e.g., quality of public services and the attitudes of real estate and lending institutions). Such factors are especially important in understanding the dynamics of change that can make a neighborhood shift in either direction.

One limit to the five-stage continuum is that it remains linear, positively linking changes in neighborhood quality with the socioeconomic status of residents. The model does not necessarily account for stable lower-income neighborhoods, at least in the long run, since it assumes above-average and increasing housing values. Furthermore, there is a strong relationship between ownership rates and stability. Renters have higher turnover rates, limited involvement in property upkeep, and are more likely to have subsistence level incomes, factors that reduce the chances for stability.

Another method of classification is offered by Rolf Goetze and Kent Colton (1979). Their matrix combines neighborhood market perceptions (strong to weak) with housing conditions (good to poor) to make sense of variations in investment found in similar quality neighborhoods. Neighborhood market perceptions take into account factors affecting the urban context in which a neighborhood is located, considering the effects of metropolitan dynamics, locational features (topography, transportation, spatial integration), citizen expectations of government, and the culture of local government (Goetze and Colton 1979).

By separating market perception as a second dimension, physically deteriorating neighborhoods can still have a strong market standing if there is confidence that they will improve. In this scheme, confidence is indicated by the level of activity in the real estate market. Rising neighborhoods, regardless of the type of housing stock, will have excess demand that is often speculative, creating locational price inflation. The matrix also allows for neighborhoods with good housing stock to have poor market perceptions, which takes into account many older, working-class city neighborhoods that have been maintained but that have below-average housing values.

Gentrification

Gentrification is a pattern of change in the profile of a neighborhood's population, accompanied by an increase in housing values resulting from an influx of higher-income owners into previously lower-income urban neighborhoods. Also termed "neighborhood upgrading" and "reverse filtering," gentrification typically involves higher-income newcomers (often single, white, and professional) replacing lower-income long-term residents (often racial minorities). This change has occurred in those cities where suburban living has not proven attractive to potential gentrifiers, many of whom work and prefer to live downtown, contrary to the desire of most Americans. These so-called urban pioneers have moved into older neighborhoods, restored dilapidated housing, and created market demand for housing and services. In the process, they have often eliminated below-market housing, especially for renters, and converted rental housing into condominiums, thus causing the displacement of many residents unable to afford higher housing costs.

It is also argued that once there have been substantial shifts in the income and lifestyle of such neighborhoods, it is inevitable that middle- and upper-class newcomers will drive out lower-class residents because of incompatibility. In some urban neighborhoods, another factor has been the sexual preferences of the newcomers. Gays have been the leaders in revitalizing such neighborhoods—San Francisco's Castro district, for example, formerly a mostly Irish, working-class neighborhood—which have become gay havens (Castells 1983; De Witt 1994; Godfrey 1988).

Palen and London (1984) offer five alternative explanations of what they term urban "reinvasion": (1) demographical-ecological; (2) sociocultural; (3) political-economic; (4) community networks; and (5) social movements. All of these different analytical approaches are invoked to explain conflict between the newcomers and incumbent residents opposed to such a transformation of their neighborhood. Gentrification combines aspects of the invasion and succession and tipping point models.

PATTERNS OF NEIGHBORHOOD CHANGE

Neighborhood change can be very gradual or dramatically fast. Neighborhoods can change in character quite slowly, as for example in the population mix. Members of one ethnic group may gradually be replaced by members of another similar ethnic group. Elderly residents may move to retirement homes, making way for young families. Larger families may be replaced by smaller families, more affluent households by less affluent. These demographic changes might not be readily apparent and register only during the decennial U.S. census or when such a shift has occurred that it has eventually become obvious to both the residents and outsiders.

Large-scale Redevelopment: Urban Renewal and Freeways

In some instances, however, change can be rapid. In the 1950s and 1960s, many inner-city neighborhoods were destroyed by slum clearance to make way for urban renewal, whether they resisted or not (Gans 1962; Greer 1965). These were typically poor and often minority neighborhoods, selected both for their location and the lack of influence of the residents to stop redevelopment. Once displaced, the residents rarely returned and often were not provided with replacement housing, despite legal guarantees.

One well-documented example of a project that became known as "negro removal" was the destruction of much of Cincinnati's West End, its historic black community. Urban renewal, which began in the early 1950s, and, later, freeways displaced thousands of poor black residents. Resistance did not really materialize until the mid-1960s when the West End Community Council mobilized opposition to further displacement, although by 1970 the neighborhood had lost two-thirds of its 1950-level population (Davis 1991). The West End is but one of many examples of the destruction of minority inner-city neighborhoods, which served to provide land for commercial redevelopment, market-rate housing, civic institutions, parking, and urban freeways.

Only in the late 1960s did some organized neighborhoods successfully oppose such clearance policies. In San Francisco's historic South of Market neighborhood, Tenants and Owners in Opposition to Redevelopment (TOOR), representing the almost 4,000 low-income residents of single room occupancy (SRO) hotels (many retired union members) and small businesses, fought a long and notably successful legal and political battle against the massive Yerba Buena redevelopment project, featuring a convention center, office towers, upscale retail, and market-rate housing (Hartman, 1974). Although the project proceeded with redevelopment continuing into the 1990s (Wetmore and Sause 1995), several hundred subsidized housing units were built onsite to provide replacement housing for displaced residents.

Another well-documented example of successful neighborhood resistance to large-scale redevelopment planning is the Cedar-Riverside neighborhood of Minneapolis, adjacent to the University of Minnesota. A late 1960s urban renewal plan was tied to the short-lived federal New Towns program. Developers proposed to clear the neighborhood of its 1970 population of approximately 4,000 (many long-time residents, university students, and an emerging counterculture community) and to build a high-rise residential New Town in Town with a contemplated population of 31,000. Several community organizations formed a coalition whose opposition eventually led to the demise of the New Town proposal in the mid-1970s. Cedar-Riverside then became the focus of community-based development (Stoecker 1994).

A third example of such opposition was community resistance to the Route 2 freeway in Los Angeles. After purchasing hundreds of homes and displacing many of the residents of a largely Hispanic community, California's transportation department canceled the freeway project in 1976. The community then waged a long and eventually successful campaign to force the state to sell the housing back to residents at below-market prices. This action led to the creation of a unique, scatter-site limited-equity cooperative (Heskin 1991).

Such community resistance, coupled with a changed federal policy, effectively ended federally sponsored large-scale slum clearance and freeway projects by the 1970s. However, such neighborhood displacement did not end totally. The most notable exception was the destruction of the Poletown neighborhood in Detroit to make way for a new General Motors plant. Under heavy pressure from GM, the city of Detroit (and neighboring Hamtramck) exercised quick eminent domain and removed 3,800 residents, as well as demolishing churches, schools, hospitals, and businesses, in 1980 and 1981. This dramatic sacrifice of a historic, interracial, working-class neighborhood in an effort to fight deindustrialization was much publicized, as the underdog residents, in alliance with GM critic Ralph Nader, fought unsuccessfully to save the neighborhood (Wylie 1989).

Gentrification-caused Displacement

For the most part since the 1970s, neighborhood change has come more slowly. The extent to which gentrification has led to widespread displacement has been much studied and debated (Nelson 1988; Palen and London, eds, 1984; Schill and Nathan 1983; N. Smith and Williams, eds., 1986). Researchers have disagreed about methodology, including how to count displacees. Concern was greatest in the late 1970s, when, due to community organizing and inflationary pressures in the housing market, many communities adopted rent, eviction, demolition, and condominium-conversion controls in cities like Boston, San Francisco, and Seattle to prevent gentrification-based displacement (Hartman, Keating, and LeGates 1982). Whatever its overall magnitude, gentrification continues in many urban neighborhoods, usually promoted by city governments anxious to have more affluent residents and an expanded tax base.

San Francisco offers several examples of gentrification and opposition to this phenomenon. The Haight-Ashbury neighborhood adjacent to Golden Gate Park became renowned as a counterculture haven after the "summer of love" in 1967. By then a declining low-income neighborhood, it became a focus of city efforts in the 1970s to transform it into a more conventional area. The combination of its location, a 1972 downzoning, and an influx of gentrifiers, many of whom were gay, led to a renaissance of Haight-Ashbury into a mostly middle-class neighborhood in the 1980s. Low-income minorities, the elderly, and counterculture residents became vulnerable to displacement. Neighborhood organizing focused on opposition to unpopular commercial development (Godfrey 1988, 172–204).

The Tenderloin neighborhood, a poor downtown neighborhood with many residents, including immigrants, living in residential hotels, became a target of gentrification in the late 1970s. In 1980 the North of Market Planning Council (NOMPC) formed to organize against displacement. To prevent the conversion of inexpensive residential hotels into tourist hotels and the construction of more tourist hotels, NOMPC successfully lobbied the city in 1980 to enact regulations to prevent residential hotel conversions permanently (unless replacement housing was provided by developers). To prevent the transformation of a low-rise neighborhood into a high-rise area, NOMPC began a campaign in 1981 that culminated in a 1985 downzoning ordinance. The council also led efforts to rehabilitate substandard housing in the Tenderloin while keeping it affordable to lower-income residents, thus circumventing gentrification-caused displacement (Robinson 1995).

The Racial Factor

Rapid neighborhood change has also occurred when massive racial change has taken place, typically turning a predominantly white neighborhood into a virtually all-minority neighborhood. Unscrupulous real estate practices, such as racial steering and blockbusting designed to induce panic selling by white homeowners, outlawed since 1968, have had the tragic effect of replacing segregated white neighborhoods with resegregated black neighborhoods (Keating 1994; Massey and Denton 1993). This change has led to violent conflicts between white, working-class residents of neighborhoods faced with racial transition in cities such as Boston (South Boston), Chicago (Marquette Park), Philadelphia (South Philadelphia), and New York (Bensonhurst and Howard Beach). In addition to perpetuating racial segregation, the resultant decline in public services and real estate values in many neighborhoods in which lower-income minorities replaced working-class whites has bolstered the idea of the inevitable resegregation of neighborhoods once a racial tipping point unacceptable to a white majority, fearful of neighborhood decline associated with an influx of minorities, has been reached.

In her study of racially mixed urban neighborhoods in five cities (Akron, Hartford, Indianapolis, Milwaukee, and Rochester), sociologist Juliet Saltman (1990) has demonstrated that long-term stability can occur if the neighborhood is well organized and if racial transition is orderly and accepted by the white residents. However, as she notes, such efforts have not always succeeded, as in Hartford's Blue Hills neighborhood, for example.

In Chicago, the nation's most segregated city, examples abound—such as Hyde

Park–Kenwood, adjacent to the University of Chicago (Rossi and Dentler 1961)— of neighborhood efforts to maintain all or predominantly white neighborhoods. A notable effort to promote and maintain racial diversity in Chicago's South Shore neighborhood in the late 1960s failed; most whites eventually left as black immigration transformed the neighborhood, despite the efforts of the interracial South Shore Commission (Molotch 1972). After considerable decline, this neighborhood has received national attention because of the role of the South Shore Bank in promoting community development and revitalization, including the rehabilitation of thousands of apartment units (Taub 1988; Lewis 1993).

Despite antidiscrimination in housing legislation and the continuing efforts of fair-housing organizations, racial segregation still prevails in a majority of urban neighborhoods in U.S. cities. Sociologists Massey and Denton have argued that intense racial isolation constitutes "hypersegregation." As of 1980, they cited sixteen cities in which racial minorities were extremely segregated: Atlanta, Baltimore, Buffalo, Chicago, Cleveland, Dallas, Detroit, Gary, Indianapolis, Kansas City, Los Angeles, Milwaukee, New York, Newark, Philadelphia, and St. Louis (Massey and Denton 1993, 75–77).

INVASION AND SUCCESSION REVISITED: THE NEW IMMIGRANTS

In the mid- through late nineteenth century, U.S. cities experienced the great migration from Europe that resulted in their tremendous growth and the emergence of urban ethnic villages. The Asian and Latin migration and later the northern migration of southern blacks led to the formation of urban ghettos of racial and ethnic minorities. With the end of mass migration after World War I and the suburbanization of America after World War II, most U.S. central cities saw drastic declines in population. Old ethnic neighborhoods lost their identification and most of their residents.

Beginning in the 1960s and continuing in the 1990s, many cities have experienced a new surge of immigration, both legal and illegal. Many urban neighborhoods in older cities have undergone a rebirth, and some cities have seen their population increase, almost entirely because of these new immigrants. They have come from Asia, the Caribbean and Latin America, and eastern Europe, migrating for the same reasons as their nineteenth-century predecessors—to escape from war, political and religious persecution, and economic problems. Three cities can serve to illustrate some of the implications of this new wave of immigrants.

Philadelphia. In the mid-1980s approximately 7,000 immigrants were arriving annually in Philadelphia. The city has long been a destination for Puerto Ricans. More recently, Asians (e.g., Koreans) began to arrive. In some ethnic neighborhoods, Asian and Hispanic residents have been welcome, but in others conflicts have arisen. Like their predecessors, most of the newcomers have accommodated themselves to American culture while changing the composition and cultural climates of their new urban neighborhoods (Goode and Schneider 1994).

New York. In 1980 New York City had 1.6 million foreign-born residents. Within the decade, approximately 85,000 new immigrants arrived annually. The largest group came from the Caribbean Basin, followed by Asians, Europeans, and Middle Easterners. Although many of these immigrants gravitated to traditional racial and ethnic ghettos (e.g., Chinatown, Black, and Spanish Harlem), others have transformed old ethnic neighborhoods (Foner, ed., 1987).

One example is Sunset Park in Brooklyn. Located next to the Brooklyn waterfront, it was a classic polyglot working-class immigrant neighborhood settled in the late nineteenth century by Irish, Italians, Poles, and Scandinavians. After World War II, construction of an expressway and the decline of the Brooklyn Army Terminal, as well as suburbanization, reduced Sunset Park's population from a prewar high of 104,000 in 1940 to 87,000 in 1970. In 1950 only 2 percent of the neighborhood's population was Puerto Rican. In the ensuing decades, Puerto Ricans replaced the departing European ethnic residents who were leaving and transformed Sunset Park into a predominantly Hispanic neighborhood. In the 1980s, in addition to Puerto Ricans, Caribbean blacks and Asians (primarily Chinese) arrived, continuing this old neighborhood's transformation into a bustling, multiracial, and ethnic neighborhood (Winnick 1990).

Miami. Miami has experienced one of the most dramatic transformations of any U.S. city due to immigration from the Caribbean Basin. The post-Castro revolution exodus of anticommunist Cuban exiles since 1959 coupled with the Mariel boatlift in 1980 have made Miami and its Little Havana neighborhood the premier location in the United States for Cuban Americans. The Cubans have been joined by Nicaraguan refugees fleeing the revolution and counterrevolution of the 1980s and more recently by Haitians escaping the poverty and repression of their country prior to U.S. intervention there in 1994.

In 1950, of the population of 495,000 in metropolitan Dade County (including Miami), only 20,000 were Hispanic and 65,000 were black. By 1990 the population had quadrupled to 1,937,000, of whom about one-half (953,000) were Hispanic, 369,000 black, and only 586,000 non-Hispanic white. As the Hispanic population (especially Cuban American) grew in numbers and economic and political influence (including the election of mayors and representatives in Congress), black resentment grew. Conflict between these competing groups contributed to riots in Liberty City and Overtown, Miami's black ghetto neighborhoods, in the 1980s (Didion 1987; Grenier and Stepick, eds., 1992; Portes and Stepick 1993).

FROM DECLINE TO REBIRTH

In many cities throughout the country, neighborhoods have deteriorated to the point of apparent hopelessness, from riot-torn neighborhoods that have never recovered to concentrations of distressed high-rise public housing (for example, the Robert Taylor Homes in Chicago). Nevertheless, there are examples of neighborhoods striving to revitalize themselves without undergoing massive clearance or gentrification, which would displace poor residents.

Boston: Dudley Street. Roxbury is a deteriorated neighborhood of Boston, with a 1990 population of almost 60,000, predominantly minority and one-third poor. Roxbury's decline has been caused variously by urban renewal, racial blockbusting, disinvestment and housing abandonment, arson, and unemployment resulting from deindustrialization. The Dudley neighborhood within Roxbury is almost entirely populated by minorities.

Concerned about the prospect of further displacement of residents if a New Town proposed by the Boston Redevelopment Authority was approved, the Dudley Street Neighborhood Initiative (DSNI) was formed in 1985 to empower neighborhood residents and to promote residential control over redevelopment. Beginning with a campaign to reclaim city-owned abandoned land and to build low-income housing, DSNI pioneered in a unique experiment of neighborhood-based development. After a long battle, the Boston Redevelopment Authority granted DSNI the power of eminent domain (usually reserved to the government) as a tool for urban revitalization through foreclosure of city-owned buildings and lots. DSNI broke ground for its first housing in 1993 and has ambitious plans for commercial redevelopment (Medoff and Sklar 1994).

New York: South Bronx. New York City's South Bronx has long symbolized the urban wasteland in American cities. Two presidents—Jimmy Carter and Ronald Reagan—have journeyed to Charlotte Street in the South Bronx to bemoan its decay and to promise to rebuild it. Yet after a massive depopulation fueled by redlining, deindustrialization, poverty, and crime, few people had hope for a true rebirth of the South Bronx. Its terrible image was portrayed in the 1981 movie *Fort Apache, the Bronx.*

Since then, however, a combination of city, state, and federal programs and the emergence of community development corporations, such as the Mid-Bronx Desperados, the South Bronx Community Organization, and the Banana Kelly Improvement Association, have led to a remarkable change in many parts of the area. Since the mid-1980s, thousands of abandoned apartment units have been rehabilitated and several thousand new housing units have been built or are planned (OMG 1994; Purdy 1994). Though the South Bronx has a long road to recovery, there are hopeful signs. Still, the improvements have not occurred without conflict between community organizations and the city over how best to redevelop the area (Rooney 1995).

Cleveland: Hough. Cleveland's Hough neighborhood was once one of the city's most prestigious addresses, but housing deterioration began in the Great Depression. During the 1950s and 1960s, the combination of suburbanization and the influx of blacks displaced by urban renewal in downtown Cleveland transformed Hough into a black ghetto. In 1950 only 14 percent of Hough's

66,000 residents were black. Population peaked at an estimated 82,000 in the mid-1950s and dropped to 71,000 in 1960, by which time 75 percent of Hough's population was black.

Disaster struck in July 1966 when a week-long riot claimed four lives and destroyed parts of the neighborhood. The Hough Area Development Corporation (HADC), formed in 1967 to rebuild Hough, dissolved in failure in 1984. Housing Our People Economically (HOPE) also failed, but the Famicos Foundation, founded by a Roman Catholic sister and aided by chemical engineer Bob Wolf, assisted many poor households in obtaining rehabilitated housing. Hough's population plummeted to 20,000 by 1990, 98 percent of whom were black and 70 percent of whom lived in poverty. Large areas of the neighborhood remained wasteland.

Efforts to rebuild Hough were renewed with the creation of Hough Area Partners in Progress (HAPP) in 1981. The first sign of revitalization was a heavily subsidized 277-unit rental project (Lexington Village) built in 1987, with a second phase completed a few years later. By the early 1990s HAPP was promoting large, single-family houses ($90,000–$250,000) built on vacant city-owned lots with mortgage subsidies and tax abatements. This housing is intended to bring (black) middle-income professionals back into the neighborhood. Although this venture has created fear of possible future gentrification, it has not yet occurred. Meanwhile, most of the population continues to be poor, living in substandard housing. Hough is one of four neighborhoods within Cleveland's empowerment zone that received federal funding in 1995.

MIXED-INCOME NEIGHBORHOODS

Mixed-income neighborhoods are a rarity in U.S. metropolitan areas. Residential neighborhoods are characterized by their exclusionary status (based on income, social status, race, and ethnicity). Wealthy, middle-income, and working-class neighborhoods typically have resisted any attempt to introduce lower-income housing, especially public housing for the poor, fearing a decline in property values and the status of the neighborhood. In gentrifying neighborhoods, developers have often sought to replace poor renters with well-to-do single-family and condominium owners.

The Whittier neighborhood in Minneapolis illustrates this tension. Whittier was the city's first neighborhood to prepare a plan as part of the city's twenty-year Neighborhood Revitalization Program (NRP). Located near downtown, most of its population of 13,000 were renters, with 22 percent below the poverty line in 1990. In 1978 the Whittier Alliance was organized to promote revitalization. The plan included developing several hundred units of low-income rental housing. However, when the alliance's 1992 NRP plan proposed to continue the building of low-income rental housing, a controversy erupted. Led by home-owners and landlords, an opposition slate took control of the alliance board and shifted its housing strategy to promote home ownership (Goetz and Sidney 1994).

This perceived conflict between the interests of property owners and the poor has led to many such confrontations in neighborhoods undergoing transition. Achieving a balance between homeowners and renters, especially when their dif-ferences are exacerbated by a great disparity in income, has proven extremely dif-ficult in most urban neighborhoods.

NEIGHBORHOOD ORGANIZING AMID TRANSITION

Whatever the issue—for example, racial transition, new foreign immigrants, gen-trification, deindustrialization—the key to neighborhood stability amid change is neighborhood organization. Neighborhood organizing has been centered on block clubs, churches, and community development corporations. Ironically, it can be seen as both positive and negative.

Several examples of successful neighborhood organizing have previously been examined: NOMPC (Robinson 1995) and TOOR (Hartman 1974) in San Francisco, the Cedar-Riverside Community Union in Minneapolis (Stoecker 1994), the Dudley Street Initiative in Boston (Medoff and Sklar 1994), and the Route 2 Community Housing Corporation in Los Angeles (Heskin 1991). Juliet Saltman (1990) documents several examples of neighborhood organizations that successfully promoted long-term stable interracial neighborhoods, such as the Sherman Park Community Association in Milwaukee. On the other hand, failed efforts at neighborhood preservation amid change have also been mentioned: the Poletown Neighborhood Council in Detroit (Wylie 1989), the Hartford Hill Civic Association in Hartford (Saltman 1990), the South Shore Commission in Chicago (Molotch 1972), and the West End Community Council in Cincinnati (Davis 1991).

Neighborhood organizing, whether resisting change or adapting to it, can be idiosyncratic or, more typically, part of a broader trend. Castells (1983) has argued for the existence of urban social movements, a variation of the grassroots commu-nity organizing that has appeared episodically in the United States. Whether there is a class-based interest for neighborhood organizing has been long debated (Castells 1983; Davis 1991; Henig 1982; Stoecker 1994). Whether and when suc-cessful grassroots neighborhood-based opposition to growth politics and redevel-opment is possible is also a much-discussed topic.

The lesson to be found in the history of U.S. urban neighborhoods is the recur-ring theme of change. Change can be positive or negative, short-term or long-term. Change, generally emanating from economic, political, and social forces outside the affected neighborhoods, may be determined by the influence of the residents of these neighborhoods. Yet their influence depends upon how successfully such neighborhoods are organized, how high the stakes are, and how strong the agents of change are. The rise and fall of large-scale urban renewal and urban freeways in American cities provide the most dramatic examples of the strengths and weaknesses of neighborhoods in coping with change.

3

Neighborhood Organizing: The Importance of Historical Context

Robert Fisher

Neighborhood organizing has a history as old as the neighborhood concept it-self. It is certainly not a product simply of sixties' dissent. Community-based resis-tances—around geographic communities such as a neighborhood or communities of cultural identity such as the black or women's community—have become the dominant form of social action since the 1960s, replacing more class- and labor-based organizing (see Epstein 1990; Fisher and Kling, eds., 1993). This ever-increasing significance helps explain the widespread contemporary interest in community-based organizing and the importance of these chapters. But it tends to obscure the rich and fundamental history prior to the 1960s that undergirds current neighborhood-based activity, and it narrows the debates about neighborhood orga-nizing to contemporary limits. To illustrate the point, we begin here with a discus-sion of the varied types of neighborhood organizing that have persisted since the late nineteenth century and the lessons to be learned from them. A discussion of neighborhood organizing in the 1980s follows, demonstrating how the political economy of the larger historical context heavily affects the nature and potential of neighborhood organizing.

Since the 1880s, there have been three main types of neighborhood organizing (See Table 3.1). The social work approach is best characterized by the social settle-ment movement, which began in the United States in 1886, and by contemporary social service delivery at the neighborhood level, such as neighborhood centers or health clinics. The political activist approach is best reflected in the work of oppo-sitional efforts, which sees power as the fundamental issue. These efforts date back to the ward-based political machines of the nineteenth century but as social efforts

*This chapter is based on material from Robert Fisher, *Let The People Decide: Neighbor-hood Organizing in America*, 2d. ed., rev. (Boston: Twayne, 1994), and Fisher, "Commu-nity Organizing in the Conservative '80s and Beyond," *Social Policy* 25 (Fall 1994): 11–21. Grateful acknowledgment is made for permission to reuse these materials.

Table 3.1. History of Neighborhood Organizing: Three Dominant Approaches

	Social Work	Political Activist	Neighborhood Maintenance
Concept of community	social organism	political unit power base	neighborhood residence
Problem condition	social disorganization social conflict	powerlessness exploitation neighborhood destruction	threats to property values or neighborhood homogeneity insufficient services
Organized group	working and lower class	working and lower class	upper and middle class
Role of organizer	professional social worker enabler and advocate coordinator and planner	political activist mobilizer educator	elected spokesperson civic leader interest-group broker
Role of neighborhood residents	partners with professional recipients of benefits	fellow activists indigenous leaders mass support	dues-paying members
Strategy	consensual gradualist work with power structure	conflict mediation challenge power structure	consensual peer pressure political lobbying legal action
Goals	group formation social integration service delivery	obtain, maintain, or restructure power develop alternative institutions	improve property value maintain neighborhood deliver services
Examples	social settlements community centers Cincinnati Social Unit Plan Community Chests United Community Defense Services Community Action Program United Way	unemployed councils tenant organizations Alinsky programs Student Non-Violent Coordinating Committee (SNCC) Students for a Democratic Society (SDS) Association of Community Organizations for Reform Now	neighborhood preservation associations neighborhood civic clubs property owners' associations

are best reflected in the work of the Communist party in the 1930s, the efforts of Saul Alinsky and followers since the late 1930s, New Left neighborhood organizing in the 1960s, and a host of current neighborhood-based groupings since then, perhaps most notably in African-American and gay male communities. The neighborhood maintenance approach also originated in the late nineteenth century, when more middle-class residents sought to defend their neighborhood against change and perceived threats. The ongoing history since the 1920s of neighborhood protective associations, whose primary concern is maintaining or improving property values, is the classic example (Fisher 1994; Davis 1992).

LESSONS FROM THE PAST

Simply stated, a number of key lessons from the past of neighborhood organizing should inform the study of contemporary efforts.

First, neighborhood organizing has a long and important history. It is not simply a product of the past generation, not a transitory phenomenon. It is a means of democratic participation, a means of extrapolitical activity, a way to build community, obtain resources, and achieve collective goals. Neighborhood organization has been an integral, ongoing, and significant basis of civil life in the United States for more than a century. People continually choose in astounding numbers not to participate in the electoral process, underscoring both the inability of politicians to galvanize the electorate and the alienation of citizens from the political process, but this lack of participation is not true in neighborhood organizations. Of course more people vote than work in citizen-action efforts because of voting's relative effortlessness and institutional support. But Americans have always turned readily to organizations at the grassroots level to build community, meet individual and collective needs, and participate in public life. This is as true today as it was one hundred years ago.

Second, neighborhood organizing cuts across the political spectrum. Although all neighborhood organizing is a public activity, bringing people together to discuss and determine their collective welfare is not inherently reactionary, conservative, liberal, or radical. Nor is it inherently inclusive and democratic, or parochial and authoritarian. It is above all a political method, an approach used by varied segments of the population to achieve specific goals, serve certain interests, and advance clear or ill-defined political perspectives. Organizations can be creative efforts open to innovation and supportive of progressive struggles as well as defensive responses to external pressures. The form an organization takes depends on a number of factors, especially the ideology and goals of its leadership, constituency organized, and local context.

Third, neighborhood organizing efforts develop in a larger context that transcends local borders and determines the dominant form of neighborhood organizing in any era. Conditions at the local level directly spawn and nurture neighborhood organizing projects. The organizers, residents, local conditions, and many other factors at the grassroots level combine to forge consistently unique neighborhood organizing experiences. Yet even though neighborhood organizing projects do have a significant origin, nature, and existence of their own at the local level, they are also the products of national and even international political and economic developments. To no small degree, the larger political-economic context determines the general tenor, goals, and strategies, even the likelihood of success, of local efforts.

Examples abound. It was the liberal reform political economy of the Progressive Era, the period from approximately 1900 through 1917, that brought about a positive response to the social settlement idea and that legitimated the first era of neighborhood organizing. Although other types of neighborhood organizing existed in this period, it was the social work approach, best exemplified in the social settlements and the Cincinnati Social Unit Plan, that dominated the era.

In the depression era of the 1930s the social work approach had much less salience and support. As capitalism collapsed, as one reform solution after another failed to halt the economic depression, the political activist type of neighborhood organizing, most notably the radical efforts of the Communist party in many cities and the urban populist work of Saul Alinsky in the Back of the Yards neighborhood in Chicago, epitomized grassroots activity. The hotly debated and precarious political economy of the era legitimated citizen action and political ferment at this basic level.

In the post–World War II era the conservative cold war economy stifled the political activist approach of the depression era and nurtured the neighborhood maintenance type of neighborhood organizing. Of course, homeowners' and property associations had been strong in the United States since the 1920s. Protecting property values was especially important in the United States, where homes were economic investments and where the lack of government protection and support for maintaining communities put the onus of neighborhood maintenance and development on property owners. The conservative eras of the 1920s and 1950s, however, tied this necessity for neighborhood associations to a reactionary politics. Segregationist goals became quite typical of neighborhood associations, interconnecting the protection of property values with a politics of neighborhood exclusion.

Of course, the relationship between the national political economy and neighborhood organizing is not a one-way street where the dominant form of neighborhood organizing is determined by the national political economy of an era.[1] The historical process is much more complex, more of a dialectical interaction between the national political economy and grassroots resistances and initiatives. In the 1960s and the first part of the 1970s, when the political activist type of neighborhood organizing came to dominate again, the national political economy both produced the change and was the product of it. It was the grassroots resistance of the southern civil rights movement, the student New Left, and the rebellion in black urban slums that pushed the national political economy left, that expanded the political discourse to legitimate grassroots resistance, that demanded the passage of social policy to address the needs of the poor and people of color. The shift in political economy at the national level, expanded by LBJ's Great Society and War on Poverty programs, developed in response to these challenges. These policies legitimated further the political activist approach, so much so that a heyday of political activist neighborhood organizing continued well into and through the 1970s, causing some commentators to herald a "backyard revolution" in the making. It is this interpenetration between the national political economy and community organizing that comes across so vividly in the history of neighborhood efforts.[2]

NEIGHBORHOOD ORGANIZING IN THE 1980S: CONTEXTUALIZING PRACTICE

The importance of the national, even global, political economy in shaping the nature of neighborhood organizing is especially evident in the 1980s, in the increasing importance of CDCs and the widespread adoption by most neighborhood organizations of more moderate strategies.

In the 1980s the United States made a clear turn to right-wing politics at the national level. The twelve years of Reagan/Bush policy from 1981 to 1993 promoted a neoconservative agenda grounded in right-wing programs, policies, and political discourse. Responding to the heightened demands of an emerging global economy and the challenged status of U.S. corporations in it, neoconservatives sought to cut social costs. They went after labor unions, government programs, and claimant movements; they shifted even the limited political dialogue about human needs completely to corporate needs; they delegitimized the public sector and public life and urged people into increasingly private spheres and private conceptions of the good life.

In the neoconservative 1980s, the impact of national context on local organizing was enormous. Although a wide variety of efforts continued, promoting democratic resistance and left insurgency, it was the neoconservative political economy that largely determined the directions of most community organizing during the decade, shifting them into community economic development and moderate strategies.

Community Economic Development

In general during the 1980s concern with broader social issues and social action receded. In the economic crisis of the past few decades, economic survival became the paramount issue for most individuals, organizations, businesses, and cities. As economic support for social services and for solving social problems declined due to opposition at the federal level and shrinking tax bases at the local level and as political discourse in the nation revolved around free market solutions to most problems, neighborhood organizing efforts moved into the business of economic development (Pierce and Steinbach 1990, 15–16).

This trend is nowhere more evident than in the rapid growth and spread of community development corporations in the 1980s. These corporations first sprang up in the 1960s, when they were tied to the civil rights and antipoverty movements of the period, and were funded by a few foundations and Great Society programs. This first wave included about 100 organizations, but among them were such well-funded, significant efforts as the Woodlawn Organization and the Bedford-Stuyvesant Restoration Corporation. For its multitude of important projects the "Bed-Stuy" CDC received about $4 million in federal support annually.

The second wave of community development organizations came in the 1970s, when the number of development projects increased tenfold. These were smaller efforts that began in opposition to urban renewal, redlining, factory closings, or the lack of tenant rights. For the groups involved in community economic development, most funds came from foundations, primarily the Ford Foundation, and federal sources, such as the Community Services Administration and the Office of Neighborhood Development. The idea of community economic development caught on in the Carter administration, and by the late 1970s, CDCs, with all their virtues and drawbacks, were central components of the limited but significant federally assisted neighborhood development movement.

Beginning around 1980, however, CDCs found government support drastically cut. The new, third wave of CDCs that developed in the privatization campaigns of the Reagan years were forced into becoming much more businesslike than their predecessors. They had to exhibit "business talent and development skills once thought to be the exclusive province of the for-profit sector," as one report put it (Pierce and Steinbach 1987, 30). The Community Services Administration and the Office of Neighborhood Development were dismantled by the Reagan administration. Other sources of federal funds were dramatically cut back. The bottom line for CDCs, as with seemingly every other federally funded program in the decade, was economic success. The primary goal, as Benjamin Marquez argues in an astute analysis of the CDCs' role, was to "correct the market's failure to provide jobs and services to the community." And for the CDCs in minority neighborhoods, the task was to help build a nonwhite middle class by establishing highly specific and measurable development projects in which neighborhood people could work for their own economic betterment (Marquez 1993). The new CDCs became less like community organization and more like small businesses and investment projects, evaluated on their economic success. Most of the corporations avoided political controversy, were dominated by professionals with a technical orientation, had narrow membership bases, and rejected social action activity.

Though market demands forced most CDCs to become so oriented to economic success that they were unable to sustain their work for community empowerment, they did not always give up on these goals by choice; they were forced into it. The absence of public support, new and rigid interpretations of IRS restrictions on political activity of nonprofit groups, the necessity of seeking funds from and joining in partnerships with private-sector leaders, and the orientation of the CDC approach to economic investment and development decisions distanced CDCs away from politics and an analysis of power. "This lack of fiscal and political support," Marquez concludes, "has forced CDCs to accommodate themselves to rather than redirect the course of the free market."

Economic development has become a central issue for progressive organizing efforts that formerly spurned or discounted the strategy. Many older, prominent community organizing efforts now participate in community economic development, from Association of Community Organizations for Reform Now (ACORN) to National People's Action (NPA) and Industrial Areas Foundation (IAF). To their credit, participants in these political activist projects see community economic development as part of a much larger program of community work that also includes organizing, empowerment, advocacy, and social action. Still, community economic development has become virtually synonymous with neighborhood organizing, as if organizing and empowerment were rooted in economic development issues, as if neighborhood struggles were always the same as community economic development, as if working in partnership with local banks and putting in "sweat equity" were the answers to urban poverty and housing shortages.

It has not quite worked out that way. "If the primary success story of the last twenty-five years has been the development of a legitimate, skilled nonprofit development sector with the proven capacity to create and preserve housing, jobs and businesses," as Bill Traynor of the Community Training and Assistance Center in Boston sums up the problem, then "the major failure has been the proliferation and dominance of a narrowly focused—technical—production-related model of community development which is estranged from strong neighborhood control or direction and which does not impact the range of issues which affect poor neighborhoods (Traynor 1993, 4).

Moderate Strategies

Most activists promoting community economic development would probably defend their consensual approach as appropriate for the Reagan-Bush years. To have a chance at community development, efforts must be in tune with capitalist economic development and have a working relationship with the powers that be in the public and private sectors. Given the shift in the national political economy, organizers think they must now be more in tune with community economic development.

Neo-Alinsky organizer Shel Trapp sees a natural progression in his work. First, organizations defend the neighborhood; then they take an "offensive" stance. "That's when you start to link development with organizing," he argues (Trapp 1990, 49). Robert Rivera, an IAF organizer, puts it similarly: "There are two types of organizing. One that is for, the other is against. Now you have to be for something. It's a different style of organizing (Rivera 1991).

But at play in the 1980s was more than a life cycle of organizing. Community economic development and building community partnerships with local economic and political elites became the dominant form of neighborhood organizing because of the demands and constraints of organizing in a neoconservative political economy. Organizers were willing to rewrite history (good organizing has always been for things) in an effort to distance themselves from the radicalism of the past, maintain current support, and legitimate their efforts in a context hostile to social action.

The changes that took place in community development corporations are emblematic of the way organizing responded to the conservative context of the 1980s, but moderate strategies during that period were by no means limited to CDCs. Most neopopulist, political activist neighborhood organizing efforts during the 1980s and early 1990s adopted more moderate strategies and a more moderated version of oppositional politics. Battle lines shifted. "To a surprising extent," claim M. W. Newman and Lillian Williams in a *Chicago Sun Times* article, "the grass roots no longer 'fight the power.' They fight for a share of the power. Sometimes they win a sizable share. . . . [Sometimes they] team up with the established elite that they once derided and that once spurned them" (1990, 12). Even National People's Action, criticized by some organizers as too confrontational, opposed being "out in the streets making symbolic statements, when you can be in the boardroom negotiating specific agreements that win for neighborhoods" (Trapp 1992, 2).

Consider the evolution of the Industrial Areas Foundation, the direct descendant of Alinsky-style organizing, over the past decade. It currently has twenty-eight organizing projects in New York, New Jersey, Maryland, Tennessee, Arizona, California, and Texas, but it is in Texas, where the IAF network includes ten organizing efforts, that it is the strongest. Throughout the state, in San Antonio, Houston, El Paso, Austin, Fort Worth, and in the Rio Grande Valley, IAF organizers and active members struggle for utility reform, improved public education, government accountability, health care for the indigent, and basic public services, including water and sewers for the "colonias." Most visibly they organize get-out-the-vote efforts to promote bond packages to help IAF neighborhoods, hold "accountability sessions" to keep politicians publicly in line with IAF objectives, encourage voter registration, and work to improve schools by halting the drop-out rate, stopping drug use and violence, and getting parents more involved. More quietly, in the day-in and day-out practice of community organizing, they serve as "schools of public life," empowering neighborhood residents by giving them "an opportunity to do something about things that [they] have been frustrated by all their lives" (Ernesto Cortes quoted in Boyte 1989, 191).

The IAF organizations perform remarkably well, as many commentators have noted. Peter Applebome in the *New York Times* proposed that the IAF Network is "in ways large and small . . . changing politics in Texas" (1988). And Mary Beth Rogers, who was chief of staff to former Texas governor Ann Richards, concludes in her study of the Texas IAF that these "are virtually the only organizations in America that are enticing working poor people to participate in politics" (1990, 2).

Although still following much of the Alinsky style of organizing, in the 1980s IAF made some significant changes in its organizing method to meet the needs of new constituents and adapt to the demands of a new conservative context. The major change in IAF organizing is a shift from a radical politics to a strategy of moderation. Where CDCs look for consensus, IAF groups focus on the importance of "standing for the whole."

Of course, many people in power still see IAF as a radical protest group, and even during Alinsky's lifetime some IAF projects, such as the Woodlawn Organization, shifted from "conflict to coexistence." In the 1980s, however, this position developed into an organizing credo. Now IAF seeks to organize "community sustainers" and "core moderates," especially women in mainline religious congregations and civic organizations. The foundation wants the civic volunteers who already work tirelessly for the PTA or a church group—the folks, IAF says, who already protect the community and stand for the whole.

The strategy of moderation pushes IAF organizers to distance themselves from radicals and social movements. Alinsky took pride in being a radical, but in the current IAF radicals are seen as alienated outsiders. "IAF now almost makes a fetish of its commitment to moderates," notes organizer-trainer Mike Miller in an article in *Christianity and Crisis*. "Will the next book be *Reveille for Moderates?*" (M. Miller 1992).

"Standing for the whole" seeks to legitimize grassroots organizing in the eyes of both the powerless and the powerful, both of whom IAF assumes, as do CDC proponents, to be fundamentally moderate in outlook. To stand for the whole means to create a working relationship between those people with and without power in order to promote the interests of its members. In the 1980s confronting government officials became—according to IAF—less and less productive. Even when local government officials were sympathetic to the issues, they felt they did not have the resources to address them. So "standing for the whole" now includes developing working relationships with business and government leaders in order to further the goals of both IAF constituents and the larger community (Ceasar, ed., 1990, 13).

The strategy of moderation, the commitment to moderates, the grounding of IAF efforts in mainstream religious institutions, and a definition of power that emphasizes building relationships leads, however, to a politics that limits the parameters of IAF's work and excludes alliances with other movement activists and organizations, as Mike Miller and others persuasively argue. It encourages IAF to work alone with its constituency and mainstream allies and to avoid confronting the harsh realities of power that oppress their constituents.

The moderate strategy, for all its short-term gains, is fraught with traps. Most important, the emphasis on moderation and negotiation and the interest-group style of politics changes the role of the organizer. "Standing for the whole" moves IAF away from Alinsky's idea of the organizer being in the background, working his or her way out of a job, focusing on primarily developing community residents to lead the organization. The more IAF gets involved in negotiating with government officials and corporate executives, the more the organizers have come center stage to be the brokers and spokespersons for the organization. And the more the organizer becomes the broker, the more potential, as in all interest group organizing, to be both co-opted and, worse, ignored. Moderate strategy ultimately bargains away the tactic of radical protest. The American Medical Association and other powerful interest groups can afford to be moderate; poor and working people must always fight for power.

NEIGHBORHOOD ORGANIZING IN THE 1990S

The responses of grassroots efforts to shifts in the national political economy always produce strategies that both replicate and challenge existing power relations. Despite its obvious limitations, a focus on community economic development has built a broad base of real technical expertise and created innovative projects that in a limited way help meet the dire need for housing in poor neighborhoods. The politics of moderation gives up on more radical change, but it helps build the capacity for governance, gets advocates to the bargaining table, and wins modest victories.

Given the dramatic tensions and shifts occurring worldwide, both in the global economy and in national political struggles, we can expect in the near future to see the political economy encourage more of the same: continued proliferation and preference for grassroots efforts, continued focus on community economic development as global competition remains heated and as nation-states and corporate-elites persist in avoiding domestic social needs, and continued diverse strategies with most funding and support going to moderate approaches that are willing to work with business and government leaders.

Current events will probably continue to overwhelm such neighborhood efforts. It is much more difficult to be optimistic now about the prospects of neighborhood organizing than it was just fifteen years ago. It is no paradox that neoconservatives call for neighborhood-based solutions and "empowerment" of citizens; they know well that these strategies are less expensive answers to problems that require costly national and global solutions and neighborhood-based initiatives. Without the existence of a social movement able to push the national political discourse left, win funding for social programs and redistributional policies, and struggle for state power, we can expect, at best, incremental change from the top and important but modest victories at the grassroots. Whatever the context ahead, neighborhood organizing, even with its limits, will remain essential: as schools of democracy and progressive citizenship; as seeds of larger resistance efforts; as demonstrations of the persistence of public life in an increasingly private world; as the vehicles of struggle in which we win victories, develop skills, forge identity, and legitimate opposition; and as potential grassroots components of the next major social justice movement.

To play such roles, however, neighborhood organizing must both build on and go beyond the contemporary context. It must benefit from the new skills and strategies learned in the 1980s and challenge the neoconservative political economy that heavily shaped organizing in the past decade. Although the history of neighborhood organizing makes clear that national context is fundamental, it also instructs us that conflict—ideological and direct action challenges—is essential to push the context, policies, and programs toward meeting basic human needs and implementing more democratic processes.

NOTES

1. There are other caveats to offer related to the typology of neighborhood organizing and the relationship between national and neighborhood efforts. For example, each type of neighborhood organizing is evident in all eras. It is not as though one ends and the other begins. For the past century there have been continuous efforts at building service delivery organization, radical opposition, and neighborhood protection associations. It is just that each period tends to produce a dominant form most appropriate to it. Moreover, there is a good deal of overlapping of the types. Political activist organizations also deliver services; service organizations seek to maintain neighborhoods; neighborhood maintenance often entails being quite political and activist. Nevertheless, the essential points of this chapter remain that neighborhood organizing has a long history, its history reveals a highly varied politics, and the national political economy is critical to shaping a dominant form of neighborhood organizing in varied historical eras.

2. A debate currently rages in urban politics between political process and structural theorists, not to mention poststructuralists. For a discussion of the theoretical debate see Logan and Swanstrom, eds., 1990, and Fisher and Kling, eds., 1993. I do not minimize the importance of the organizer and local context in the organizing process; I would, however, argue that changes in organizing strategy that seem natural and internally initiated (decisions made by organizers and activists or influenced by local factors) are usually products of or at least are heavily influenced by larger contextual changes (decisions made within a limited set of externally structured choices).

4

Past Federal Policy for Urban Neighborhoods

W. Dennis Keating and Janet Smith

As America became more urban than rural, neighborhoods and the cities in which they were located had little support from the federal government. Similarly, state government paid little attention to neighborhoods or urban problems, despite having legal power to create and regulate cities. Indeed, before the Great Depression, neighborhoods were entirely the responsibility of cities and local philanthropy. There was no public welfare system to care for the poor, leaving local government to provide limited services financed entirely by property taxes.

The sustained hardship created by the depression finally did call the federal government's attention to cities, as high rates of unemployment and homelessness made it impossible for mayors to help their citizens. In 1932 Franklin Delano Roosevelt introduced the New Deal, which included emergency relief, banking and real estate financing reforms, public works projects, welfare, Social Security, and public housing. Though FDR did not provide direct assistance to cities as sought at the time by the newly formed U.S. Conference of Mayors, many of these programs did improve urban conditions. Furthermore, it was the first time in U.S. history that city mayors had access to federal aid and hopes of federal assistance in rebuilding (Gelfand 1975).

The New Deal era also marks the beginning of a continuing struggle between political and ideological positions regarding the federal government's involvement in improving urban conditions associated with poverty. Over the years, the result of the struggle has been a hodgepodge of federal programs that typically do not distinguish neighborhoods from cities as specific targets for intervention, with most policy as short-lived as the administration that introduced it.

Historically, the apparent ambivalence toward a national urban agenda has been drawn along party lines. Republicans have favored distributive programs that stimulate economic growth through private-sector activity, and liberal Democrats have promoted intervention in the market and redistributive programs. More recently, this distinction has been blurred as economic restructuring, fiscal federalism, and conservative politics cast doubt on the benefits of any type of federal commitment to cities or assistance for distressed neighborhoods. Although there is appreciation for the revitalization work done by nonprofit community development corporations, federal support for these efforts continues to be vulnerable and expendable.

The various directions national urban policy has taken and its impact on urban neighborhoods over time are briefly highlighted in this chapter.

NATIONAL URBAN POLICY SINCE THE DEPRESSION

Since the 1930s, and particularly after World War II, national urban policy has been inconsistent and even conflicting with regard to goals and outcomes. This tension is evidenced in the efforts physically to rebuild America's aging cities, beginning with the Housing Act of 1949. The apparent decay of older cities prompted the federal government to get involved in redeveloping deteriorated areas and outmoded structures. The intent was to facilitate complete transformation of slums into more productive economic uses. Under the urban redevelopment scheme, public funds were used to clear areas, which often were close to downtown, in order to spur private redevelopment. In reality, this method to improve urban conditions, which was continued under the Urban Renewal program, was effective in removing blight. However, it also contributed to the destruction of cohesive neighborhoods, often displacing low-income minority residents. And, because the government did not provide an ample supply of replacement public housing, most residents were forced to move into similar substandard and overcrowded neighborhoods (Fox 1986; Greer 1965).

Even as efforts were made to redevelop urban centers, other federal policy was actually exacerbating declining neighborhood conditions. Most notable are those programs that allowed the exodus of middle-class residents to the suburbs, including housing financing through the Federal Housing Administration and Veterans Administration (VA) and the development of the freeway system (Fox 1986; Jackson 1985). The FHA provided extensive financing for homes in new suburban communities while redlining housing assistance in older city neighborhoods. New highways simply made it easier for a growing population of suburbanites to commute to their central-city jobs.

EXPANSION OF URBAN AID PROGRAMS

The 1960s saw a dramatic expansion of national urban policy that moved beyond the physical improvement of cities to focus on their poor residents. Programs were added to tackle the chronic problem of poverty, especially among minorities. The transition began with the election of John F. Kennedy, whose Democratic liberal ideas included the promise to launch a war on poverty and to create a federal cabi-

net-level department to deal with the problems of urban America. Political opposition from conservative Democrats prevented Kennedy from achieving this goal
before his assassination. Lyndon Johnson was able to fulfill some of his predecessor's promises, however, through his efforts to create the Great Society.

In 1965 the U.S. Department of Housing and Urban Development was created.
Previously, urban-oriented programs had been administered through several departments, with little or no effort made to coordinate them. A cabinet-level position would
allow a cohesive approach and would elevate urban policymaking to a degree that it
could receive regular attention. Johnson appointed Robert Weaver as the first secretary of HUD and the first black to be a member of the cabinet (Gelfand 1975).

The War on Poverty, which Johnson launched upon taking office, was an
attempt to eliminate poverty by empowering the poor and placing more control in
the neighborhoods and cities where they lived. A multitude of new federal programs was introduced. However, underfunding and the resistance of big-city mayors to citizen participation prevented a full grassroots attack on the problem.
Though the War on Poverty was later deemed a failure, many programs such as
Head Start and Legal Services continued, leaving a legacy of models to combat
poverty-related problems.

Johnson's realization of a Great Society was further hampered as urban unrest
grew in response to the Vietnam War, the civil rights movement, and urban
renewal efforts. For five summers, the Johnson administration was beset with
urban riots, beginning in 1964 with Watts in Los Angeles and culminating with
riots nationwide following the assassination of Martin Luther King, Jr., in April
1968. The Kerner Commission on Civil Disorders (1968) found that the causes of
the unrest, mostly in minority neighborhoods, were police brutality, poverty and
unemployment, racial discrimination in housing and employment, and poor housing and public services.

The Johnson administration eschewed the "bricks and mortar" urban renewal
approach for one that offered comprehensive social services to poor neighborhoods. As HUD's first major initiative, the Model Cities program was intended to
be an experiment, concentrating federal assistance in a few neighborhoods to test
the effectiveness of a cohesive and targeted approach. Yet political debate preceding congressional approval eventually resulted in 150 Model Cities sites (Frieden
and Kaplan 1975). The project encountered additional problems with implementation due to inadequate funding and the loss of presidential support when Johnson
announced his decision not to seek another term.

THE NEW FEDERALISM

The election of Richard Nixon in 1968 marks the beginning of the end to large-
scale, from-the-top-down intervention aimed at reducing poverty and improving
urban conditions. In a reaction that is often described as conservative backlash, the

Nixon administration did not necessarily disagree with all previously stated housing and community development goals, but only with the use of liberal Democratic spending programs as a means to achieve them. After Nixon's landslide reelection in 1972, the administration reassessed the cost of fulfilling future HUD obligations for housing and community development projects. In 1973 Nixon ordered a freeze on most HUD programs in order to control looming costs and reported mishandling of funds.

Nixon introduced two major reforms for national urban policy. The first, dubbed "the new federalism," converted several categorical grant programs (including Model Cities and Urban Renewal) into a single block grant. The Community Development Block Grant provided entitlement funds to cities and urban counties with federal oversight to ensure that local government used funds to benefit low- and moderate-income residents. Typical CDBG expenditures often continued programs that had been funded by federal grants, including housing rehabilitation, public works and infrastructure improvements, and social services. The second reform was a program to begin converting federal housing production subsidies that had long been provided to local housing authorities, lenders, and developers into demand subsidies that would provide direct assistance to eligible low-income recipients. This approach also was presumed to help low-income residents disperse throughout the community by expanding housing options to include existing privately owned units. The program also was expected to save the federal government money in the long run as it extracted itself from the business of producing housing.

Both changes reflected the conservative philosophy of supporting the private market over public authorities in meeting housing needs and a belief that programs would be more efficient if the decisionmaking process allowed greater control at the local level (Hays 1985). Although the Watergate scandal forced Nixon to resign in 1974, Gerald Ford continued with these reforms through his short stay in office.

The narrow election of Jimmy Carter in 1976 brought a Democrat into the White House again. The Carter administration was fiscally conservative, however, and often at odds with liberal constituents and representatives. An area of early dispute centered on the method for determining CDBG entitlement communities. At the start, the controversy involved either setting a formula that would continue to benefit older cities in the Northeast and Midwest, as did many past federal programs, or devising a method that would ensure distribution to a broader constituency, including a growing urban population in the Sunbelt. Congressional compromise resulted in a dual formula that could equalize the distribution of new CDBGs. Under Carter, HUD did impose stricter federal oversight of how cities used these funds in order to keep CDBG directed primarily at meeting the needs of low- and moderate-income residents in recipient cities.

The Carter administration introduced two initiatives that had potential to benefit neighborhoods directly: the Neighborhood Self-Help Development (NSHD) program and Urban Development Action Grants (UDAG). The NSHD was a small demonstration program that provided direct assistance to community organizations, allowing them to use funds for organizational development and physical improvements. Although NSHD was considered a success in terms of benefits to urban neighborhoods, its impact was limited by the small budget. In comparison, the UDAG program had a larger allocation. The grants provided federal matching money to leverage privately directed economic development projects in distressed cities. The UDAG-assisted projects did produce housing and commercial and industrial development; however, these effects were overshadowed by the many large-scale downtown development projects that did little to assist distressed neighborhoods.

Carter also created the Office of Neighborhoods, considered a symbolic gesture, in HUD. The assistant secretaryship position was filled by Fr. Geno Baroni, a Roman Catholic priest who previously had worked with neighborhood organizations and the National Commission on Neighborhoods. The commission was the first (and only one) of its kind and made many recommendations to increase federal funding for neighborhood revitalization. Yet most of these proposals were not supported as the administration tried to keep spending down in the late 1970s because of spiraling inflation.

The Carter administration also saw the implementation of two laws aimed at reducing disinvestment in older city neighborhoods, especially those occupied by minorities. The Home Mortgage Disclosure Act (HMDA) was enacted in 1975, mandating all federally insured mortgage lenders to disclose their geographical lending patterns according to the race of borrowers. The Community Reinvestment Act of 1977 required federally regulated lenders to invest in their service areas. Both of these acts grew from a burgeoning grassroots movement. Although the laws were considered to have limited impact, neighborhood leaders learned to use them. Over time, lawsuits and administrative complaints forced many lending institutions to provide needed financing to build new homes and to rehabilitate existing ones in neighborhoods that had long been redlined both by the private sector and the FHA.

THE CONSERVATIVE ATTACK ON HUD

The election of Ronald Reagan in 1980 marked a shift in political power and the beginning of extensive cutbacks in urban programs and outlays. Reagan sought to roll back the prevailing New Deal and Great Society programs while reducing federal taxes and increasing military spending. As for housing and community development, he intended to reduce federal intervention drastically in order to leave this role to the private sector. Among the cabinet-level agencies, HUD suffered the highest proportional budget cuts (Bratt 1989). Immediate changes included the elimination of the Office of Neighborhoods, the NSHD program, and the reduction of CDBG oversight policies introduced by Carter; the elimination of UDAG followed in 1986. As a result, waiting lists for housing-subsidy assistance grew, public housing continued to deteriorate, and the growing number of community development corporations sought alternative sources of funds besides CDBG (Goetz 1993). Moreover, evidence of HUD favoritism toward politically influential developers resulted in the conviction of many high-ranking HUD officials and a general loss of trust in the department.

Two programs beneficial to neighborhoods during the Reagan era were passed by a majority Democratic Congress. First, the Neighborhood Development Demonstration (NDD) program provided matching grants to community groups to expand their development activities by facilitating public/private partnerships. After three rounds of funding, this small effort was considered a modest success, keeping some fledgling organizations going as federal funds were cut back. Second was the Low-Income Tax Credit (LITC), introduced to offset previous tax benefits eliminated under the Tax Reform Act of 1986. With LITC, corporate investors would receive tax credits for their investment in low-income projects, most of which were developed by community development corporations working in distressed neighborhoods. This effort continued a tradition of using tax incentives for private investors to assist in developing below-market units rather than expending funds for public housing.

After Reagan completed his two terms, the Bush administration continued much of the same policy agenda. Even the Affordable Housing Act in 1990 could not make up for the neglect of neighborhoods in the previous decade. New programs to increase home ownership and to help the homeless were funded at levels far below the amount needed to reverse the effects of federal cutbacks for housing and community development, reduced regulation of the private market, a discredited HUD, and a forced reliance on state and local government and the private sector to pick up the slack in urban revitalization funding.

In his effort to defeat Bush in 1992, Bill Clinton expressed concern about urban problems. The Clinton administration increased HUD's budget and introduced new initiatives such as Empowerment Zones (which have been compared to Model Cities). However, the administration's political weakness and federal fiscal constraints, coupled with a decision to downplay any major commitment to cities, have limited its impact. Furthermore, the Republican takeover of Congress in the November 1994 election, followed by the Clinton administration's plan to "reinvent" HUD by reducing its programs and possibly eliminating it as a cabinet-level department, has cast serious doubt on the future of any sort of cohesive national agenda to rebuild cities or neighborhoods.

Federal policy within the past sixty years has waxed and waned, at times beneficial and at other times destructive in its efforts to improve urban neighborhoods. There is no sign of progress being made toward a particular approach to urban neighborhood revitalization, whether it be in favor of programs to intervene directly in the lives of residents or through policies that can offer indirect benefits

Table 4.1 Impact of National Urban Policy on Neighborhoods

Period	Policy	Programs	Neighborhood Impact
1930s	New Deal	banking and real estate reform public works projects welfare assistance Social Security emergency relief public housing	no direct benefits to neighborhoods; temporary assistance helped cities aid poor population
1950s	Slum clearance, rebuilding	urban redevelopment urban renewal	removed some blighted areas at expense of neighborhood residents; short-term benefits to some less blighted areas
1960s	War on poverty	community action programs Head Start Legal Services Model Cities	mixed results: programs short-lived and underfunded; beginning of grassroots activities
1970s	New Federalism	Community Development Block Grants	mixed results: cohesive local approach possible; less targeting over time.
		Neighborhood Self-Help Demonstration	limited benefits due to small scale and funding
		Urban Development Action Grants	direct benefits offset by greater investment in downtown projects
		Home Mortgage Disclosure Act Community Reinvestment Act	positive impact in cities where groups sought funds from lenders to reinvest in city neighborhoods
1980s	Devolution	Neighborhood Development Demonstration Low-Income Tax Credit	sustained some fledgling nonprofit organizations; provided funds to develop low-income housing units
1990s	Reinvention	Affordable Housing Act	insufficient funding to make up for past cutbacks
		Empowerment Zones	anticipate impact to be small and limited to targeted neighborhoods

to poorer urban dwellers through general economic growth (see Table 4.1). The direction of urban policy has been (and continues to be) shaped by politics and reaction to crisis. Within this sixty-year time span, the peak nexus of interest and investment followed the urban riots in the mid-1960s.

Although the future of the federal urban agenda is uncertain, reflecting on the myriad programs and policy approaches taken since the 1930s is important. In particular, some lessons have been learned with regard to distributive versus redistributive tactics used to improve neighborhood conditions and the lives of poor people. On the one hand, redistributive programs, such as those offered in the War on Poverty, are more likely to assist those in need directly than distributive programs such as CDBG. On the other hand, there is a greater likelihood that the latter approach will gain political approval, especially in fiscally conservative periods. There also is ample evidence of the relationship between the degree of federal control over the use of funds and the ability to target those people with the greatest need. Although federal block grants shift the decisionmaking process to the local level, where it is presumed to be more efficient, it also opens up the possibility that funding will be diffused in the community if the intended goal of policy is broadly defined.

As national politics has turned more conservative and the roles of the federal government and agencies such as HUD have been reduced, the residents and organizations in urban neighborhoods have looked for alternative sources to help with revitalization. In contrast to the past, today there are more funding options for neighborhoods (e.g., philanthropy, intermediaries, community reinvestment funds from lenders). However, there are also more people in need and a larger number of groups seeking assistance today, so that any decrease in federal support for neighborhood revitalization will have a potentially negative impact.

Part Two

Neighborhood Decline and Attempts at Revitalization

The period since the end of World War II has not been kind to older American cities or to their neighborhoods. Most older cities continue to lose population, industrial jobs, and economic investment. Their residents, overly burdened with poverty and unemployment, often experience a quality of life which is sharply lower than that enjoyed by other Americans.

Against this backdrop of general decline, two transformations have been taking place. The first is one of economic function, from production and distribution, including manufacturing, to information and research services. Older cities are losing jobs requiring low skills and often gaining jobs requiring higher levels of education and training that are not ordinarily held by most city residents. The second transformation is demographic. Whites have been leaving central cities in large numbers for decades; African Americans have been in these cities for some time and are now being joined by growing numbers of Latinos and Asians. Together, these formerly minority populations now make up majorities in more and more cities. Despite these groups' majority status, however, racial discrimination and segregation in neighborhoods, schools, and workplaces continue to be a major problem, as do sharp economic disparities between various areas of the city and the city and its suburbs.

Local and national leadership generally has responded to these problems in three ways. First, a liberal "growth coalition" (Mollenkopf 1983) made up of politicians, bankers, and businessmen joined together in "public/private parnerships" and attempted to stimulate new investment and thus bring the middle class back to the city, hoping that the benefits of growth would somehow "trickle down" to city residents living in disinvested neighborhoods. This approach was manifested in the Urban Renewal program in the 1950s and 1960s and was prominent through the Urban Development Action Grant program in the Carter administration. To an extent, these downtown-focused efforts have succeeded in reshaping the skylines of many cities, but they have not succeeded in reducing poverty, unemployment, or dependency in the low-income and working-class neighborhoods.

The second approach to urban revitalization was a conservative one: cut funds to urban Democratic constituencies, spend on the military, weaken the federal government and shift powers to the states, cut social spending and subsidize the private sector. Creating Enterprise Zones (EZs) was the major urban policy initiative during the 1980s, and although federal EZ bills were never passed, many states passed their own versions that subsidized business investment and cut regulatory and labor costs. The EZ approach is generally credited with shifting certain business activities to EZ locations at significant public expense, but fundamental problems that plague urban neighborhoods, such as poverty, poor education, and crime, were not attacked. The program served "as a means of redistributing investment and employment, not a means of achieving more of each" (Lemann 1994).

The third approach was the neighborhood-movement alternative, sponsored and supported by "progressive" local governments. Characterized by citizen participation and neighborhood control with an economy of self-help and small enterprises, it focused on rehabilitation rather than on big projects and on helping networks rather than on bureaucratized social services. This approach entailed a shift of federal monies such as CDBG and UDAG from downtown to the neighborhoods, a shift of service delivery systems from public bureaucracies to community-based organizations, and the possibility of new alliances emerging between the urban poor and working class and the new professionals. The neighborhood movement strategy has been adopted by some city governments with considerable success, especially in their assistance to the growth and development of community development corporations.

These corporations originated in the 1960s and grew in the 1980s and 1990s in an attempt to reverse the decline of urban neighborhoods. They are nonprofit neighborhood-based organizations that develop housing and commercial development in neglected communities. Addressing the most serious problems facing urban neighborhoods, including the scarcity of resources, racial and ethnic tensions, and social problems of crime and drug abuse, and with little fanfare or public notice, CDCs around the country have become leading producers of affordable housing. A recent study (National Congress for Community Economic Development [NCCED] 1995) credits CDCs with the production of 125,000 affordable housing units, and in some cities CDCs have also produced commercial enterprises and organized social services.

In Part Two the authors describe the decline of urban neighborhoods in older American cities and the various efforts, successful and unsuccessful, made to reverse that decline, both by progressive city governments and various CDCs.

In Chapter 5 Peter Dreier presents an insider's view of the administration of Mayor Ray Flynn, a liberal Democrat, who promoted balanced growth between downtown and the neighborhoods and supported neighborhood empowerment. Dreier describes the roles cities must play in reducing social and economic problem, as well as the limits of local power, focusing on housing issues.

In Chapter 6 Robert Giloth deals with one of the high points in the political history of American cities, the administration of Harold Washington, Chicago's first black mayor. Washington put together a successful rainbow coalition to defeat the remnants of former mayor Richard Daley's machine but also implemented a redistributive, neighborhood-based economic development agenda. Giloth, who served as deputy commissioner of Economic Development in that administration, discusses Washington's achievements.

In Chapter 7, Susan Fainstein and Clifford Hirst analyze the creation and implementation of Minneapolis's Twenty-Year Neighborhood Revitalization Program, which began in 1991. The authors point to various successes and underlying problems in this ambitious attempt to devolve policymaking to neighborhood organizations.

Jacqueline Leavitt in Chapter 8 examines the neighborhood movement in Los Angeles that began to expand in the 1980s and the role that nonprofit developers played before and after the 1992 civil unrest in South Central. Los Angeles, unlike New York City, does not have a historical legacy of community-based development. A few community-based nonprofits emerged after the 1965 Watts riot, but a lapse of about twenty years occurred before more CDCs appeared. In the 1980s, in response to the ideas of community-oriented providers in housing and social services, Housing L.A. became a focal point for housing activists organizing at the grassroots. Subsequently, the Local Initiative Support Corporation (LISC) began supporting CDCs in the city that were then loosely organized as a coalition. Leavitt comments particularly on the transformation of the Coalition of Neighborhood Developers and the emergence of neighborhood plans.

In the final chapter of Part Two, June Thomas and Reynard Blake, Jr., argue that neighborhood development has little meaning without reference to location, class, and race and that faith-based development is a powerful tool in overcoming economic decline and physical deterioration. Providing examples drawn from distressed African-American communities in Detroit, the authors point to the uses of spiritual and religious motivation in surmounting the most difficult of neighborhood problems. Although they focus on Detroit, they also discuss other examples from such cities as Newark, Baltimore, and New York City.

5

Urban Politics and Progressive Housing Policy: Ray Flynn and Boston's Neighborhood Agenda

Peter Dreier

As the United States faces a deepening housing crisis, what can cities do? This may sound like a daunting question. Cities face overwhelming social and economic problems, especially in their poorer neighborhoods. They simply lack the resources to fill the gap between what poor and working-class people earn and what housing costs to build and operate. Only the federal government—with, in better fiscal times, some help from state government—can solve the crisis of affordable housing.

But cities have a role to play, too. They can develop model programs and policies if they are provided the tools and resources. They can pressure (or forge partnerships with) businesses, suburban governments, and other groups to expand housing opportunities. They can help mobilize support for a more activist federal urban policy and housing program.

We cannot expect a substantial shift in federal housing policy unless the problems of cities—and the urban poor and their neighborhoods—move closer to the top of the nation's agenda. Thus the answer to the question "what can cities do?" depends both on economic realities and political commitment. In this chapter I attempt to answer that question primarily by focusing on a case study of what one city with a progressive government—Boston under Mayor Raymond Flynn—accomplished (and did not accomplish) during the 1980s.

The key dilemma for progressive local politicians is in deciding to what extent city government can intervene in the private economy before business either pulls up stakes or mobilizes politically to oppose elected officials. Since most decisions affecting a city's business climate are made by national (even global) corporations and the federal government, there are limits to what a city government can do to improve the business climate or social conditions. Still, all local government officials are concerned about the business climate because the city's tax base and jobs base depend on whether businesses stay and expand. A major difference among conservative, liberal, and progressive city governments is in the degree of their willingness to test how far government can go before business acts on its threats to leave, cut back, expand elsewhere, or organize political opposition. If progressive elected officials are to challenge business prerogatives, they need to have a strong political constituency that will support them. They also have to know when and how to compromise.

PROGRESSIVE MUNICIPAL POLITICS: HOUSING

Since 1980 the United States has experienced a period of bold housing experimentation. Confronted with a deepening housing crisis and a market-oriented federal government, local housing activists have found new ways to preserve and expand affordable housing (Goetz 1993; Nenno 1986). In 1995 there were thousands of local groups involved in housing activism of some kind. Their success was not primarily a result of discovering new construction methods, new financial techniques, or new planning tools. What is often lacking is the political commitment, particularly from local officials, to restrain or steer housing market forces to benefit poor and working-class people. The recent achievements of America's housing activists are chiefly the result of political activism. They forged new coalitions and partnerships with progressive allies, mobilized voters in electoral campaigns, and made housing an issue in local politics.

In doing so, however, they faced a major dilemma—the dilemma that faces all progressive activists engaged in urban politics: businesses can move, but politicians usually stay in one place. If local public officials tax or regulate the private sector too aggressively, businesses can threaten to pull up stakes and take their jobs and tax base with them. They can also mobilize a sustained political assault (often with the aid of the local media) against an incumbent for being unfair to business. Few politicians want to be labeled with the reputation that because they lost the confidence of the business community, they drove away jobs and undermined the tax base. Thus most public officials accommodate themselves to businesses' priorities.

What about housing policy? The same political forces shape the capacity or willingness of local governments to address the housing conditions of the people not well served by market forces. Housing developers, landlords, and lenders argue that they will not invest in cities that place too many restrictions—rent control, zoning, building-code standards, resale limits, development fees—on housing. The fragmentation of political boundaries gives the housing industry additional muscle. Poor cities compete with more affluent suburbs for middle-class residents and market-rate housing in order to expand their tax base. Landlords threaten to abandon buildings and developers warn that they will not build housing if cities impose rent control or high property tax rates, pointing out that there are always nearby communities that do not have such policies. In both national and local politics, the real estate industry is among the biggest campaign contributors. Because their fate is tied directly to decisions made at city hall, developers, landlords, and their allies (contractors, lawyers, lenders) have a big stake in the outcome of city government races.

These realities led a number of prominent urban experts to argue that local governments have little room for maneuver in adopting progressive policies—including housing strategies—that redistribute wealth, income, and political power. In the most cogent expression of this view, Paul Peterson, in *City Limits* (1981), argues that municipal government policies emerge largely in response to larger economic forces. The market, he asserts, dictates politics and policy. Cities must promote private economic growth; the alternative is decay and stagnation. Progressive redistributive policies hurt cities because they entail increased taxes, reduced services, or both for those residents and businesses that contribute most to the city's tax base and economic well-being. According to Peterson, only the federal government can promote redistributive social welfare policies.

In *Urban Fortunes* (1987), sociologists Harvey Molotch and John Logan portray urban "growth machines" as coalitions of business, developers, labor, the media, and public officials, united in their quest to improve the business climate by attracting new investment. These growth coalitions influence local development policies to intensify land use, increase rents, and generally enhance the profitability of private enterprise. By emphasizing the clearly limited room for political maneuver, this grim perspective could hardly inspire activists to view local politics as an arena for progressive reform.

Just how much room exists, however, is rarely tested. Most elected officials and political movements are unwilling to see how far they can push (Cummings 1988; Fainstein 1986; B. Jones and Bachelor 1986; Judd and Parkinson 1990; Savitch and Thomas, eds., 1991; Squires 1989; Stone and Saunders, eds., 1987). But some groups are bolder than others, particularly when they are emboldened by strong grassroots movements. Indeed, what is missing from these analyses is the potential for political organizing, political skills, and political entrepreneurship in forging an alternative vision and agenda.[1]

In the 1970s and 1980s progressive grassroots movements did gain a foothold in running local governments. In a few cases, their leaders and allies were catapulted to elective office, including mayor and city council. Among America's major urban centers, however, only in Cleveland, San Francisco, Chicago, St. Paul, and Boston did progressive activists achieve electoral success and seek to use local government to promote an agenda of economic and social reform. In every case, housing and community development issues were a key in mobilizing supporters and in forging a governing regime (Clavel and Wiewel, eds., 1991; Clavel 1986; DeLeon 1992; Mier 1993; Krumholz and Forester 1990; Swanstrom 1985).

Only in Boston did the progressive coalition remain in power long enough to carry out its agenda. The Flynn regime demonstrated that, despite major political and economic obstacles, local government can be progressive and humane. The Flynn coalition showed that it is not imperative for big-city mayors to play to racial fears or to embrace the growth-at-all-costs downtown development agenda to be successful politically. In contrast to the other short-term experiments, a progressive regime, led by Mayor Raymond L. Flynn, endured in office for over nine years. First elected in 1983, Flynn was reelected to successive four-year terms in 1987 and 1991. He left office in July 1993 to become ambassador to the Vatican.[2]

Flynn was elected mayor with a populist mandate to "share the prosperity" of Boston's downtown economic boom—particularly in terms of jobs and housing—with the city's poor and working-class residents. He took office in the midst of dramatic federal cutbacks in urban-oriented housing, job training, and economic development programs, which Boston had heavily relied on for over twenty-five years, beginning with the public housing and urban renewal programs.

Housing was clearly the biggest problem facing Boston as Flynn campaigned for mayor and the issue that most galvanized support for his election. It was also the area in which federal cutbacks had been most severe under the Reagan administration and thus put the greatest burden on local government to deal with the consequences of a national housing crisis.

With federal funds declining, the Flynn administration developed policies that looked to the booming local private economy in order to carry out these "redistributive" goals. Some of the policies took the form of so-called public/private partnerships; others involved government regulation (i.e., zoning, rent control) of the private sector. The underlying assumption of these policies is that the benefits of the private economy's growth would not automatically trickle down to Boston's nonaffluent residents; benefits had to be steered in that direction by government action.

At the same time, Flynn's experience reveals that there are real limits to progressive political action at the local level, particularly when the federal government is actively hostile to cities and the poor. An examination of this experience can shed light on how far, and under what circumstances, progressive movements can push the limits of progressive municipal housing policy.

BOSTON: SETTING THE STAGE

The origins of the political coalition that put Flynn into the mayor's office can be traced to Boston's economic and social transformation that began in the 1960s. Boston experienced a steady economic decline from 1950 through the early 1970s. The city's population dropped from a high of 801,000 in 1950 to 563,000 in 1980. As manufacturing and blue-collar employment fell, the city's tax base declined and public services dwindled along with it.

The people concerned with reversing Boston's decline advocated a transformation of the central city and its downtown area into a commercial center to attract business, civic institutions, and middle-class residents. This process, which began in the late 1950s, laid the groundwork for the city's economic revitalization, but it did not achieve visible success until the late 1970s. Boston's revitalization was driven by three primary forces: the restructuring of the global economy, increased federal social spending on health care and education, and an aggressive, federally financed urban renewal program.

Boston's economic transformation also entailed major changes in the city's built environment, social dynamics, and political life—changes that would not have occurred without the formation of a powerful coalition of downtown business leaders, developers, and politicians capable of mobilizing and coordinating the public and private resources necessary to rebuild the city's central business district and adjacent residential areas. The growth coalition ultimately revolved around two newly created institutions: the Coordinating Committee (also known as the Vault), which consisted of the top business leaders, and the Boston Redevelopment Authority (BRA), a superagency that combined the city's zoning, planning, and development functions.

Initiated by mayors John Hynes (1950–1959) and John Collins (1960–1967), BRA director Edward Logue, and the Vault, the growth coalition embarked on an ambitious renewal plan that encompassed more than one-quarter of the city's land area and helped trigger a sustained era of new private investment in the city (Dreier 1983; Kennedy 1992; Mollenkopf 1983; Boston Urban Study Group, 1984). Between 1960 and 1985, more than 20 million square feet of office space was added to Boston, almost doubling the total supply of space. Employment in finance, insurance, and real estate more than doubled, to 85,100, between 1950 and 1985, and employment in a broad range of other services (mainly health, education, and business services) grew threefold, to 225,900 (Boston Redevelopment Authority 1995; Brown 1987; Ganz 1985).

The other side of Boston's revival involved the displacement of thousands of minority and working-class residents from the downtown and nearby neighborhoods. The most dramatic example was the complete razing of the West End, an ethnic mosaic captured in Herbert Gans's *The Urban Villagers* (1962), and the replacement of the city's honky-tonk district into Government Center, a commercial and public-sector complex. The federal bulldozer of urban renewal in the 1950s and 1960s was supplanted by the economic bulldozer of market speculation and gentrification, symbolized by the restoration of Fanueil Hall and Quincy Market in 1975 as the first of the many successful downtown festival marketplaces in major cities.

In addition to increased housing demand by new professional workers, the entry of tens of thousands of Latin American and Asian immigrants into Boston during the 1970s and 1980s exacerbated the competition for housing. By the early 1980s Boston's housing prices and rents were among the highest in the country.

These new factors greatly accelerated the process of change in Boston's neighborhoods. The downtown economy was booming, symbolized by shiny new skyscrapers, but most Boston residents felt left out. Even many middle-class homeowners (who benefited financially from rising housing values) began to worry that Boston's hot housing market would prevent their own children from settling in their neighborhoods. In less than two decades, Boston was transformed from a depressed, low-rise city of mostly white ethnic neighborhoods to a more vibrant, high-rise city composed increasingly of young professional workers and new Third World immigrants.

NEIGHBORHOOD CHANGE AND HOUSING CRISIS

During the 1970s Boston's population continued its postwar downward slide, from 641,071 in 1970 to 562,994 in 1980. Between 1970 and 1975 the city's unemployment rate rose from 4.9 percent to 12.8 percent. By 1980, it fell to 6.1 percent, but by 1983 it had climbed back up to 7.9 percent. Unemployment among minorities was 50 percent above the citywide rate. In 1980 one-fifth of the city's population lived below the poverty line (Boston Redevelopment authority 1985 and 1993).

Boston was a city of distinct neighborhoods and strong neighborhood identities. Boston's residents felt large-scale changes in the regional and city economy as threats to neighborhood stability. Between 1970 and 1980 twelve of Boston's sixteen neighborhoods lost population; only those adjacent to the downtown grew in numbers. Declining population and rising poverty led to considerable housing abandonment, deterioration, and arson, including arson-for-profit, during the decade. In 1980 almost one-tenth of the city's housing stock was vacant. Surpassed only by New York City, Boston had the next lowest level of homeownership (27 percent) of any major U.S. city. During the 1970s rent levels remained constant while the median value of owner-occupied (noncondominium) units declined by 5 percent in constant dollars. However, three neighborhoods close to downtown experienced inflation in both rents and home prices, foreshadowing the gentrification of the 1980s.

Like most older northern and midwestern cities, Boston was highly segregated. Between 1970 and 1980 whites declined as a proportion of the population from 82 percent to 70 percent, and African Americans increased from 16 to 22 percent. In 1970 Boston's black-white "index of dissimilarity"—the percentage of blacks that would have to move to achieve an "even" residential pattern throughout the city—was 81 percent, and by 1980 it had declined only slightly to 78 percent.[3] In 1980 six of Boston's sixteen neighborhoods (East Boston, Charlestown, South Boston, Bay Back–Beacon Hill, Roslindale, and Hyde Park) were more than 90 percent white. The major concentrations of the African-American population were Roxbury (78 percent black) and Mattapan (81 percent black). Several neighborhoods, including Jamaica Plain, Dorchester, and the South End, were undergoing significant racial transition, including a growing number of Hispanic households (Boston Redevelopment Authority 1985 and 1993; Goetze 1992 and 1995). Boston's public schools were racially segregated.

In the mid-1970s court-ordered busing led to severe racial violence as working-class whites sought to "defend" their turf (Formisano 1991; Lukas 1985; Lupo 1977; Levine and Harmon 1992).

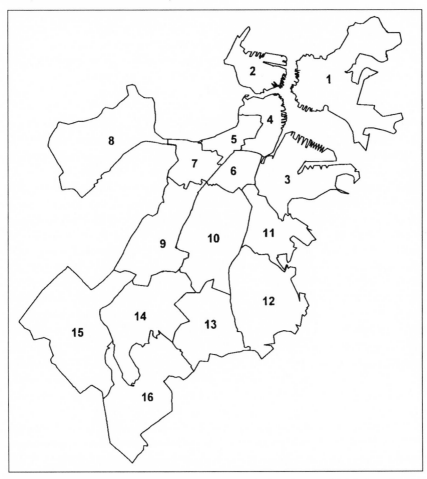

Map 5.1. Boston Neighborhoods and BRA Planning Districts (Source: BRA Research Department)
Legend: Planning District 1, East Boston; 2, Charlestown; 3, South Boston; 4, Central; 5, Back Bay–Beacon Hill; 6, South End; 7, Fenway-Kenmore; 8, Allston-Brighton; 9, Jamaica Plain; 10, Roxbury; 11, North Dorchester; 12, South Dorchester; 13, Mattapan-Franklin; 14, Roslindale; 15, West Roxbury; 16, Hyde Park

Boston's economy began to improve in the early 1980s and accelerated in the mid-1980s, spurred by downtown development, federal military and high-tech spending, and growth in the health care and higher education sectors. The unemployment rate fell from 9.1 percent in 1982 to 5.5 percent in 1984. The city's population began to grow for the first time in the postwar era.

Boston's economic and population growth fueled a strong housing market that displaced many of the city's poor and working-class residents. By 1983 Boston already had experienced several years of sustained real estate appreciation and gentrification. The trend began in the late 1970s in the neighborhoods closest to the downtown, but by the early 1980s it had spread to outlying white and minority working-class areas (Clay 1988; Boston Redevelopment Authority 1985; Goetze 1992).

Boston increasingly was attractive to yuppies and empty nesters who competed with poor and working-class residents for scarce housing. Seventy percent of Boston's residents were tenants, who were particularly vulnerable to displacement from rising housing values. Skyrocketing rents and condominium conversions were pushing elderly and poor people out of their apartments. Escalating housing prices made it almost impossible for young working families to purchase a house.

The city's poor and working-class neighborhoods, especially black and Hispanic areas, were scarred by abandoned buildings and vacant lots, although pockets of these areas were being gentrified. Arson was reaching epidemic proportions. A growing number of homeless people slept in the city's downtown streets, parks, and alleyways.

Building a Progressive Coalition

These social forces—a surge of economic growth and downtown development, the severe fiscal crisis, the emerging housing crisis, and a rapidly changing population—strained the social fabric and fueled a sense of political instability and disenchantment with the administration of Mayor Kevin White. White was elected in 1967 as a neighborhood-oriented, liberal reformer, who supported rent control and "little city halls." By the mid-1970s, however, he had become more conservative, abandoning his neighborhood-oriented policies (Ferman 1985; Lukas 1985). He reversed his support for rent control and endorsed unbridled new downtown development, earning him the backing of the real estate industry. Among voters, he was increasingly viewed as favoring downtown interests over neighborhood interests.

In May 1983 White declared he would not seek reelection. When Ray Flynn announced his candidacy for mayor in front of a public housing project—pledging to be a people's mayor, to share the city's prosperity with the city's have-nots— few people gave the maverick city councillor a chance. In 1970, Flynn had run successfully for the state legislature from South Boston and had generally represented the views of his white working-class constituents. In 1977 Flynn had been elected to a seat on the Boston City Council and had begun a transformation from a parochial neighborhood politician with progressive leanings to a crusader with citywide appeal. He recognized that residents in black, Hispanic, and white poor and working-class neighborhoods faced similar problems.

On the city council, Flynn's tenants' rights bills were usually easily defeated in the face of the city's powerful real estate lobby, the biggest donor to politicians. As councillor, and later as mayor, he often said, "Washington has the oil lobby. We have the greedy Greater Boston Real Estate Board."

In the hotly contested preliminary election to choose two finalists, Flynn and Mel King, a radical black state legislator, were the top two vote-getters against the other downtown-oriented candidates. The voters had made a clear choice for a neighborhood-oriented agenda. In the run-off, Flynn bested King by a 2-to-1 margin (Jennings and King, eds. 1986).

Building a Governing Regime

After the election, Flynn's challenge was to build a governing populist coalition that included working-class whites, the growing minority populations, and progressive activists—to focus on issues that built bridges to connect these groups. Flynn and his activist cadre developed a new approach to government—the permanent organizing campaign. Actively reaching out to include neighborhood residents in city government, Flynn turned the tables on the idea that "you can't fight city hall." More often than not, it was city hall working with neighborhood groups fighting the banks (for redlining), the developers (to require linkage and other concessions to neighborhood preservation), the landlords (for promoting gentrification), the elected school committee (for ignoring the needs of the students), the state government's Beacon Hill establishment (for treating Boston, the state capital, like a Third World colony), and even the federal government (particularly Reagan's HUD) (Dreier 1993b).

HOUSING POLITICS

Like most local governments, Boston had limited powers and resources at its disposal to address the housing crisis—primarily regulatory powers, some discretionary funds, and control of public property. But the ability of the Flynn administration to use even these limited tools was shaped by a number of political and administrative factors. In Boston, as in most cities, the constituencies for housing policies include a number of varied elements with quite different interests. The relative political influence of these groups shapes the room for maneuver within city politics.

Flynn wanted Boston's economic expansion, and the jobs, taxes, and other benefits that went with it, to continue. With the exception of some preservation and environmental groups and some neighborhood organizations in the downtown residential areas, most Boston residents supported the progrowth agenda and could thus be viewed as part of the "growth coalition."[4] Proponents included the business community, labor unions, neighborhood associations (outside the downtown core), and minority group organizations. They differed, however, on the type of growth and on methods to distribute the benefits of growth.

Within the broader business community, the real estate industry, in particular, had the most immediate stake in city policy. It had benefited from the city's downtown building boom and the resulting skyrocketing land and housing values. Landlords, developers, contractors, management firms, brokers, and real estate attorneys exercised considerable political influence. Through the Greater Boston Real Estate Board (GBREB), they opposed measures that threatened to reduce real estate development and profits. The board opposed the general thrust of Flynn's housing platform, and its members donated heavily to his opponents.

Housing activists, another political constituency, favored regulatory and development policies that supported the preservation and production of low- and moderate-income housing. Compared with their counterparts in other cities, Boston's housing activists were numerous and sophisticated. They had fought for tenants' rights, subsidized housing, and antiarson programs. Flynn, as candidate and mayor, was able to win the support of their constituency largely on the basis of his housing policy platform, programs, and recruitment of housing activists into his administration.

Neighborhood associations, as varied as Boston's neighborhoods, represented a third housing constituency. Their geographic turf ranged from blocks with a few hundred residents to large neighborhoods of 20,000 people. These voluntary organizations tended to be dominated by middle-income homeowners and focused on basic municipal services. But housing and development issues forced their way onto association agendas.

The real estate and development boom of the early 1980s added opposition to unbridled private development to their concerns. The neighborhood associations sought a greater voice in reviewing housing developments proposed for their neighborhoods. Some groups simply opposed any new developments, particularly those involving low-income or special-needs housing (for example, homeless shelters or group homes for the mentally ill). In low-income neighborhoods, the blight of abandoned buildings and vacant lots became issues. In the past, neighborhood groups tended to voice their concerns on an ad hoc, project-by-project basis, typically by appearing at public hearings of the Zoning Board of Appeals to support or oppose variances for new developments. Their influence was based primarily on their informal ties to local politicians, many of whom had emerged from these voluntary neighborhood groups.

HOUSING POLICIES

The degree of Flynn's success or failure in overcoming the obstacles posed by the city's housing politics—the various factions of the housing lobby and the city hall bureaucracy as well as the city council, the courts, HUD, the governor and state legislature, and the media—is best measured by examining his administration's housing policies and their implementation. The key issues included tenants' rights, linkage and inclusionary housing, nurturing the nonprofit sector, bank redlining and community reinvestment, and the integration and modernization of public housing.

Tenants' Rights

Since the mid-1960s Boston's major housing battleground has been the regulation of rents, evictions, and condominium conversions. The issue has become the litmus test for identifying political candidates as conservative or liberal. Boston enacted a strong rent control law in 1969 that covered all private rental housing except owner-occupied two- and three-unit buildings. Subsidized and public housing also were exempted. By the mid-1970s political support for strong rent control had eroded. Rent control had become a convenient scapegoat for housing abandonment and high property taxes on homeowners—problems more accurately linked to the city's overall economic problems, the busing controversy, and its fiscal crisis (Appelbaum 1991). In 1975 Mayor White and the city council adopted vacancy decontrol, which permanently removed an apartment from regulation after a tenant left. As a result, by 1983 the number of apartments covered by rent control fell from over 100,000 units to under 25,000 units. In the late 1970s a wave of condominium conversions fueled another round of tenant protest.

A cornerstone of Flynn's platform was an overhaul of the tenant protection laws, a return to full rent control, and either a ban on evictions for condo conversion or a ban on conversion itself. Shortly after Flynn assumed office, his administration introduced comprehensive tenant protection legislation. From the outset, Flynn and his aides recognized that this policy was an uphill, perhaps impossible, fight. With its huge campaign contributions, the real estate industry had enormous influence on the city council.

During Flynn's first two terms, the city substantially strengthened tenants' rights. Rather than the dramatic sweeping change he sought in his first year in office, however, the improvements came incrementally. In October 1984 the city council rejected Flynn's plan but passed a compromise measure to strengthen the city's control over rent increases. In 1986 Flynn and tenant activists successfully persuaded the council to enact a condo conversion/eviction ban, and in summer 1988 they pressured the slightly more progressive city council to give the rent board the authority to regulate condo conversions and lodging houses. With Flynn's support, the city council passed a law to place HUD–subsidized developments under rent control if owners exercised their option to prepay their federally subsidized mortgage. Without such protections, up to 10,000 subsidized units in Boston would have eventually been at risk if owners had taken advantage of Boston's strong housing market and converted to market-rate housing.[5]

Tenants' rights law involved government regulation of private property. Opposition from landlords and the Greater Boston Real Estate Board and support from tenant groups were expected. Although Flynn was unable to enlist the Vault and major employers to support his tenants' rights agenda, he helped shift the balance of political forces by enlisting the support of labor unions, religious leaders, and some neighborhood association leaders who previously had been neutral on the issue (Dreier and Keating 1990).

Linkage and Inclusionary Housing

Boston's strong real estate market and the severe decline of federal housing funds led housing advocates to seek new revenues and techniques to create affordable housing by extracting additional public benefits from private developers. Linkage (requiring large-scale commercial developers to subsidize affordable housing) and inclusionary housing became two hotly contested mechanisms for achieving this goal (Dreier and Ehrlich 1991).

During the 1983 mayoral contest, all but one of the seven major contenders endorsed some kind of linkage. Flynn and King advocated the strongest versions—in terms of the fee, the scale of projects covered, and the proposed uses of fees. In October 1983 a committee appointed by lame-duck Mayor White recommended a linkage policy requiring downtown office and institutional (e.g., hospital) developers to pay $5.00 per square foot over a twelve-year period, with the first 100,000 square feet exempted. In terms of its present value, the formula actually amounted to only $2.40 per square foot. Flynn, Massachusetts Fair Share (an activist community organization), and other housing advocates criticized the recommendations, calling for a full $5.00-per-square-foot formula instead. Once in office, despite the opposition of the city's real estate industry, Flynn increased the fee to $6.00 per square foot to be paid over a seven-year (rather than twelve-year) period, which almost doubled the existing linkage formula.

In 1986 housing activists and the Flynn administration began a push for another policy that sought to take advantage of the city's strong real estate market—inclusionary housing. This policy requires developers of market-rate housing projects to set aside units for low- and moderate-income residents. The effort was triggered by the realization that publicly subsidized housing developments were inadequate to meet lower-income housing needs in Boston's expensive housing market. In July 1986 Flynn submitted an inclusionary housing policy to the BRA calling for private developers to set aside 10 percent of all housing units (in projects with ten or more units) for low- and moderate-income residents.

Opposition to inclusionary housing was broader than opposition to linkage. The latter affected a small number of major developers who were building large downtown office towers and institutions (e.g., hospitals, universities) that needed to expand their facilities. Inclusionary housing, however, would affect a much larger number of more diverse housing developers. Moreover, it was not at all clear that many neighborhood associations, which in the past had opposed many subsidized housing projects, would support a policy that would bring more low-income housing into their neighborhoods.

By the end of 1992 linkage had contributed close to $70 million and over 10,000 affordable housing units. The inclusionary housing policy had added about 400 affordable units that would not otherwise have been created. Flynn had overcome the opposition of GBREB and the fears of neighborhood groups.

Nurturing the Nonprofit Sector

When Flynn took office in 1984, Boston had a fledgling network of nonprofit housing developers; they were a marginal part of the city's civic landscape. During the next nine years, they became the backbone of Boston's affordable housing program and key players in neighborhood politics. From a handful of organizations, Boston's nonprofit housing-development sector grew to more than thirty organizations.

The Flynn administration inherited a sizable inventory of properties that had come into the city's hands through foreclosure and urban renewal takings during the previous decade—most of it in low-income and minority areas. The White administration's policies toward these city-owned properties reflected its development priorities: it auctioned them off to the highest bidder—typically speculators.

The Flynn government reformed the way the city disposed of its properties. It aggressively foreclosed on tax delinquent owners of abandoned buildings or vacant lots in order to assemble parcels for neighborhood development. It ended auctions of city-owned property to the highest bidder. Instead, the properties were sold for affordable housing through a public competition with the involvement of neighborhood organizations in establishing the ground rules. The city sold public property for a nominal amount—typically one dollar—to reduce development costs, losing substantial revenues in order to encourage affordable housing.

Having put most of its eggs in the nonprofit basket, the city government recognized the weaknesses of the CDC sector. The administration understood that it needed to help expand the capacity of the CDCs to undertake large-scale, financially complex projects, or else the sector would repeat the mistakes of the past. The city drew on Boston's foundations and business groups to help support and expand the CDC network. The major vehicle for the effort was the Boston Housing Partnership (BHP).[6]

The BHP was an outgrowth of the joint efforts of several key businesses, foundation executives, community activists, and government officials. The partnership's initial role was to help the CDCs improve their development capacity by taking advantage of economies of scale and by assembling subsidies from several sources to reduce transaction costs.

The BHP was perhaps the most successful public/private community housing partnership in the country. Through it, the CDCs rehabilitated, owned, and managed the developments. The BHP involved at least twenty sources of financing.

The city contributed CDBG and linkage funds to acquire private properties as well as city-owned properties and tax abatements. The state provided tax-exempt mortgage financing and rental subsidies. The federal government provided tax credits for corporate investors and, in many cases, Section 8 rent subsidies for tenants. The city, state, several local foundations, the United Way, and the Local Initiative Support Corporation provided funds for CDC operations and to hire the core staff.

At the end of Flynn's second term in 1991, CDCs had built or rehabilitated more than 5,000 housing units. The BHP projects accounted for less than one-half of this figure, but its role in expanding CDC capacity helped the nonprofit groups to take on additional projects on their own.

In allocating city resources to housing projects sponsored by nonprofit organizations, city officials sought ways to guarantee that the housing would be affordable for the long term. The city instituted resale restrictions on all housing created for sale in order to stop buyers from selling their subsidized homes for windfall profits. As for rental projects, the city encouraged their transformation into limited equity cooperatives, and it also had a preference for mixed-income developments (Collins and White 1994).

The siting of housing projects sponsored by a wide assortment of nonprofit groups was often controversial and frequently met with neighborhood opposition. This experience led Flynn to object to demands from some neighborhood groups that they be given a final veto over the disposition of city property or funds.

In one unprecedented situation, the city government delegated its urban renewal authority to a community-based organization, the Dudley Street Neighborhood Initiative. This group was a foundation-funded coalition of churches, neighborhood associations, and other groups in a severely troubled black and Hispanic part of the Roxbury area. In 1987 DSNI proposed assembling development parcels from the patchwork of privately owned and city-owned vacant lots that scarred the area. Given the complexities involved in purchasing the privately owned sites, the DSNI asked the BRA to delegate its authority to take properties by eminent domain. Mayor Flynn agreed to the idea, despite opposition from the real estate industry that this approach was not only illegal but also an outrageous intrusion on private property rights. The city government worked closely with DSNI to develop a revitalization plan for the neighborhood. It agreed to donate city-owned land to the redevelopment effort and to target housing and commercial development funds for the effort. The city's antiredlining efforts contributed the lenders' willingness to work with DSNI. The group's own internal problems and the slowdown of the real estate market delayed the start of construction on the first projects, but by 1990 several housing developments were under way (Medoff and Sklar 1994).

Redlining and Community Reinvestment

By the middle of Flynn's second term, bank redlining dominated the news—due, in no small part, to the city government's aggressive efforts to focus public attention on the problem. Working with a coalition of community activist groups, including several CDCs, the Flynn regime orchestrated a campaign to expose and reform discriminatory banking practices in Boston.

In 1989 Mayor Flynn asked the BRA to undertake a systematic analysis of lending practices in Boston's neighborhoods. Shortly after his request, the *Boston Globe* published the preliminary results of a study by the Federal Reserve Bank of Boston showing significant disparities on the basis of race and geography in bank mortgage lending in Boston's neighborhoods. The two studies put Boston's banks on the defensive and triggered a year-long series of protests and negotiations involving city hall, community groups, and the banking industry. In the midst of the discussions, and to further prod action, Mayor Flynn enacted a "linked deposit" policy. Under this plan, the city would regularly examine the banks' track records on home mortgages, affordable housing development, hiring practices, neighborhood branches, small business loans, and participation in city-sponsored housing and neighborhood improvement programs. The evaluations would be made public to inform consumers and local organizations about their banks. City funds would be invested only in those banks that had demonstrated their commitment to Boston's neighborhoods. Meanwhile, Congr. Joe Kennedy brought the U.S. House of Representatives Banking Subcommittee to Boston to hold hearings at the Federal Reserve Bank on the redlining issue. Throughout this period, Boston's news media gave thorough coverage to the redlining controversy.

The result of the public controversy was a comprehensive community reinvestment plan, announced in January 1990, to put more than $400 million in private investment into Boston's low-income and working-class neighborhoods. This agreement culminated over a year of public debate and sometimes heated discussion about the role banks were to play in Boston's neighborhoods.

Despite delays in carrying out some of their promises, the banks changed the ways they did business in Boston's low-income and minority neighborhoods. By 1991 the city's analysis of banks lending patterns showed an almost equal distribution of mortgages in black and white neighborhoods. Most of the major banks in Boston were participating in a new mortgage program (called the "soft second" mortgage) that made it possible for low-income working families to purchase homes. By 1992 five new branch banks had already been opened or had broken ground in inner-city neighborhoods. The state's stronger CRA law, passed during the redlining controversy, had netted millions of new dollars for affordable housing (Dreier 1991).

Integration and Modernization of Public Housing

The racial integration of the Boston Housing Authority (BHA) was potentially the most explosive issue facing the Flynn administration. It threatened to pit poor whites against poor blacks—a conflict that the populist Flynn had labored to avoid by focusing on the common economic problems of poor and working-class people regardless of race. But the integration of public housing and all-white neighborhoods could not be addressed without focusing on race. Like Boston's busing controversy, it raised profound questions about the conflict between individual rights and communal solidarity. It posed an enormous challenge to Flynn's efforts to maintain a progressive governing coalition.

Founded in 1935, the BHA was the nation's fourth largest housing authority, with 18,000 apartments and 60,000 tenants in sixty-nine developments. In 1975 Greater Boston Legal Services, on behalf of the tenants, sued the BHA for mismanagement in order to force it to address the extensive violations of the state sanitary code. At the time, about one-quarter of the BHA's units were boarded up, despite a long waiting list. In 1979 Housing Court judge Paul Garrity took the extraordinary step of abolishing the BHA board, placing the housing authority in receivership. Convinced that Flynn would make the restoration of the BHA a priority, Garrity ended the receivership in 1984, and the city regained control of its public housing.

In January 1985 Flynn appointed Doris Bunte, a black state representative, as BHA administrator. Bunte was the first former public housing tenant to run a housing authority. Like its counterparts in other big cities, Boston's public housing projects had been systematically segregated by race. About 44 percent of the BHA's tenants were people of color, but almost all of them lived in all-minority or predominantly minority projects.

During Flynn's first three years as mayor, 1984 to 1987, his administration quietly moved families in to integrate BHA projects in several neighborhoods. The city government wanted to test this strategy in several neighborhoods before attempting to integrate the public housing projects in South Boston, a white working-class enclave that had been the fiercest bulwark of resistance to busing. Flynn was understandably cautious about attempting to integrate South Boston's BHA developments.[7] This stop would be his biggest challenge and, to the media, the biggest test of his leadership. In 1987, a few weeks before he was up for reelection, the mayor announced his intention to desegregate the BHA developments in his own neighborhood; he won every ward in the city except South Boston. Flynn then personally oversaw the planning for the integration of BHA's South Boston developments. On 11 July 1988 two black families moved into the Mary Ellen McCormack development in South Boston without incident, followed by others in this and other BHA projects in the neighborhood.

THE LESSONS AND THE LEGACY

The resources available to local governments to solve housing problems are limited. For a variety of reasons, when federal largesse is withdrawn, most city governments throw up their hands in frustration and await a new change of priorities in Washington—or they resort to promoting growth at all costs while dividing-

and-conquering poor and working-class residents and black and white residents, competing over public services, public-sector jobs, and symbolic rewards.

Mayor Flynn's Boston was an exception to this rule. Perhaps more than any other major American city, Boston under Flynn's leadership sought to address its local housing crisis actively. Using existing tools and resources—and seeking to invent and create new ones—the city has made an aggressive effort to develop a housing policy that seeks both to protect and produce housing for poor and working-class residents. These efforts met political resistance, legal challenge, and bureaucratic inefficiency and confusion, but they nevertheless reflected a strong commitment to serve the needs of Boston's poor and working class.

Boston's efforts to develop a progressive housing approach during the Reagan/Bush austerity years can tell us a great deal about the potential, and the limits, of local housing policy. In evaluating such policy, four criteria offer a comprehensive set of standards: better housing conditions, model programs, empowerment and participation, and leadership and advocacy.

Better Housing Conditions

Are Boston's poor and working-class residents better housed than they would have been had the free, unregulated market been allowed to operate without local government's intervention? Clearly, Flynn's policies improved the housing conditions for Boston's residents. Renters were more secure and paid less than they would have had the tenants' rights law not been strengthened. The supply of affordable housing was expanded, providing greater choice. Public housing residents lived in better conditions.

At the same time, city governments, including Boston's, lack the legal tools and financial resources to stem the forces of the private labor and housing markets that create a wide gap between available incomes and housing prices. Private market forces pushed housing prices in the unregulated sector beyond what most Boston residents could afford. Local governments lack the resources to fill the subsidy gap needed by people not well-served by the private housing market.

The housing conditions for Boston's poor and working-class residents were better than they would have been without the Flynn administration's policies. Generally, however, housing prices increased faster than the incomes of these groups, and developers continued to speculate on private land.

Model Programs

Local government can develop policies and programs that can become models for federal housing programs. It can show that innovative concepts are feasible and can be replicated elsewhere if given adequate support. The Flynn administration's greatest legacy in this regard is its support for the nonprofit (or "social") housing sector. It nurtured a housing delivery system that serves as a model for other cities and for federal housing policy.

Empowerment and Participation

The Flynn administration gave neighborhood organizations and housing activist groups a significant role in the city's housing and development policies. In addition to the unprecedented authority granted Roxbury's Dudley Street Neighborhood Initiative, the city created Neighborhood Councils (NCs) and Planning/Zoning Advisory Committees (PZACs) to serve as a voice for neighborhoods with city hall. These groups worked with city housing agencies in drafting guidelines for development of city-owned land, developed guidelines for megaprojects, and reviewed every proposed development in their neighborhoods. With the exception of low-income and special-needs housing, no project would gain city approval without neighborhood support. They worked intensively with the BRA in revising the city's outdated zoning code for their neighborhoods. Through these efforts, neighborhood groups developed greater expertise and sophistication, a true legacy of Flynn's term.

The most contentious aspect of the NCs and PZACs was Flynn's unwillingness to grant them veto power over development decisions. Flynn argued that such vetoes could potentially conflict with the administration's responsibility to site low-income housing, homeless shelters, and group homes for the mentally ill. In most situations, however, the administration allowed the NCs, PZACs, and other community groups sufficient input in the development review that the veto issue never came to a head.

Leadership and Advocacy

Does the local government accept the need to "live within its limits" during a period of austerity, or does it challenge those limits by advocating for greater resources and progressive policies at the state and federal levels? In Boston, the Flynn administration changed the composition and the rules of the growth coalition. Flynn also used his visibility and popularity as mayor and as president of the U.S. Conference of Mayors to support progressive state and federal housing policies. He became a major part of the state and national housing coalition, lobbying for new policies and greater resources for the poor, including housing.

Flynn became a leading advocate for what became the McKinney Act, the first federal legislation during the Reagan years (originally passed in 1987) to fund services for the homeless. Flynn also initiated the Community Housing Partnership Act, which was filed in February 1988 by Congr. Joseph Kennedy, to provide federal funds to nonprofit housing developers. The act eventually became incorporated into the National Affordable Housing Act of 1990, requiring that at least 15 percent of federal housing development funds be targeted for nonprofit housing organizations.

LIMITS AND OPPORTUNITIES

The Boston case study demonstrates both the potential and limits of progressive housing policy at the local level. Yet the Boston case cannot be replicated in all cities. Clearly, Boston's economic prosperity offered the Flynn regime opportunities that are not available in other cities facing economic hard times. But other mayors in similar situations have chosen other options—promoting the downtown development agenda over neighborhood concerns, eschewing neighborhood involvement in planning, using racial and ethnic divisions for political gain (Mollenkopf 1983).

The Flynn regime was willing to test the city's limits. On a variety of policy questions, it called the bluff of business leaders and firms who warned that business would disinvest if the city pushed its agenda. In pursuing its policies, the Flynn regime relied in part on the technical capacity and negotiating skills of city staff.

Ultimately, however, the decisions were political. Whatever their economic impact or technical feasibility, these policies had to be sold to the public even as business groups warned that they would undermine Boston's economic well-being. As a skillful politician, Flynn promoted a progressive agenda and remained extremely popular, as indicated by his overwhelming reelections in 1987 and 1991. Through his populist appeal and policies, Flynn broadened and redefined the growth coalition. His regime sought to accommodate the development community (if not the landlords), the business community, and the construction trade unions by promoting "managed growth" and "balanced development." Flynn also walked a tightrope between confrontation and compromise with the powerful business and development community while promoting a progressive housing agenda that has helped unite white and minority communities around common interests (Dreier 1993b).

The efforts of Boston and other local progressive regimes play an important role in mobilizing the political will for a renewed national policy. They also demonstrate that with sufficient national resources and clear policies, localities and community organizations can administer housing programs without excessive bureaucratic red tape or corruption.

But no city can solve the housing crisis on its own. Although municipal policies can make a difference, they cannot address the root causes or even most of the symptoms. Unless the federal government is committed to a major housing program, cities will continue to suffer from housing shortages, displacement, racial discrimination, uneven development, and homelessness (Dreier 1993a).

NOTES

1. Not all academic reports share this perspective. Partly in response to the success of local activists, some political scientists and sociologists offered some cautiously optimistic appraisals. Logan and Swanstrom (1990) and Stone (1993) discuss this new thinking.

2. City council president Tom Menino served as interim mayor and was elected to a full four-year term in November 1993.

3. Both figures were slightly below the average for northern cities, according to Massey and Denton (1993).

4. The groups who objected were concerned about "over-building," "Manhattanization,' and the erosion of Boston's historic character. Flynn later addressed these issues, primarily through zoning policies.

5. In 1994 the state's real estate industry put a referendum on the state ballot to preempt municipalities from adopting rent control. In November the state's voters approved the measure by a close margin. Faced with firm opposition from Gov. William Weld to strong tenant protections, Boston, Cambridge, and Brookline filed separate home-rule petitions to permit them to adopt a weak form of rent control; these were rejected by the legislature and governor.

6. In 1992 the BHP merged with another organization to become the Metropolitan Boston Housing Partnership.

7. In 1983, while still on the city council, Flynn voted for a controversial citywide fair housing law that penalized private landlords for discrimination against minorities. At a neighborhood meeting in South Boston following his mayoral victory, the militant anti-integration faction criticized Flynn for his vote.

6

Social Justice and Neighborhood Revitalization in Chicago: The Era of Harold Washington, 1983–1987

Robert Giloth

The mayoral administration of Harold Washington in Chicago (1983–1987) represented a distinct blend of black political empowerment, neighborhood activism and development, and progressive governmental reform.[1] Much of its energy, imagery, and roots was related, in particular, to its connection to the neighborhoods as a source of electoral power, policy ideas, service delivery mechanisms, allies, and audience. In a broader sense, neighborhood became a metaphor for equity, justice, citizen participation, and jobs—the strong electoral and governance themes of the Washington administration (Mier 1993).

Yet it would be misleading to represent neighborhood revitalization under Harold Washington simply as a story of good guys, many of whom came out of the neighborhood movement, taking over the hallways of corrupt government and doing the right thing. Such a narrative would underestimate the complexities and multiple meanings of neighborhood, the deep-seated impact of race on neighborhoods, and the economic changes affecting cities and neighborhoods in the 1980s. It would also be a misreading of the strengths and weaknesses of Community Development Corporations, community organizing, and citywide coalitions in Chicago, the legacy of patronage and the progrowth bias of government performance and capacities, and the sheer difficulty of turning around municipal government in the face of constant and frequently vicious political opposition.

The administration of Harold Washington advocated values of fairness and equity for the people who had been left out, a policy framework that emphasized the role of neighborhoods and their organizations, and a set of government tools that above all increased the capacity of nongovernmental actors to pursue a decent future for Chicago citizens. This approach was brand new for Chicago and remains a goal for most cities. The story of the Washington administration is really about how this approach to neighborhoods fared, whether it was effective, how it worked in conjunction with neighborhoods, whether there was learning, and whether it was sustainable.

In this chapter I first describe the role of neighborhoods in the Harold Washington administration. I then focus on how the administration made its neighborhood commitments into day-to-day organizational practices. Recounting several examples of how the neighborhood agenda failed to come to fruition provides insight into the dilemmas and shortcomings of Washington's neighborhood policies. Finally, I offer reflections on the lessons learned from the experience of neighborhood revitalization under his administration.

THE COMING OF THE WASHINGTON ADMINISTRATION

Although Chicago mythmakers eulogized their city until recently as the "city of neighborhoods," a place where you could always get a job, and an ethnic mosaic, a much different reality existed in the post–World War II life of this Midwest capital. As with many cities between 1950 and 1980, Chicago lost substantial manufacturing, gained a larger African-American and Hispanic population, and experienced a faltering of downtown investment. An almost classic political machine, under Mayor Richard Daley, helped promote a downtown growth agenda while seeking to contain and absorb the chaotic dynamic of a city undergoing multiple social and economic transitions (Squires et al. 1987).

In general, neighborhoods—especially poor neighborhoods of color—were left out and frequently bulldozed as a part of a thirty-year process of restoring downtown and high-income neighborhoods, modernizing transportation, and containing the poor. This set of interventions produced, with the help of feisty and committed grassroots leaders and organizers such as Saul Alinsky and Gail Cincotta, a widespread and diverse community movement by the 1970s, including neighborhood organizations, citywide coalitions, city council advocates, technical assistance centers, and foundation resources. It also contributed to the development of an independent black political movement. The response that emerged in these nodes of opposition was a sense of neighborhoods as being pitted against downtown development schemes, unresponsive bureaucrats, and exclusionary city hall politics. Neighborhood became a watchword for reform (Mier 1993; Gills 1991).

By the early 1980s the demographics were promising for a black/Latino electoral campaign for mayor. The faces of Chicago had changed. This electoral opportunity was made more feasible because of the faltering of Mayor Jane Byrne—particularly in relation to the black community—the on-again, off-again readiness of Congr. Harold Washington to run for mayor, the energy and resources of grassroots black political activists, and a diverse neighborhood movement (Rivlin 1992).

In some respects, the ultimate electoral victory of Harold Washington in April 1983 was a replay of what was happening in many cities. Black mayors were becoming commonplace. The distinction in Chicago, however, was that a progressive, politically savvy, African-American mayor advocated an ambitious agenda that emphasized fairness, equity, and neighborhoods. Much of this agenda grew from a merging of civil rights and neighborhood activism. The economic development platform for Harold Washington, for example, derived largely from the Chicago Workshop on Economic Development (CWED), a diverse coalition of low-income neighborhood organizations and leaders that was formed in opposition to State of Illinois enterprise zone legislation (Mier 1993). Moreover, Washington brought into government enough advocates of and sympathizers with this agenda to enable it to gain credence as a public philosophy and as the framework for transforming government culture and practice.

What was Washington's urban agenda for fairness and neighborhoods? Entitled *Chicago Works Together (CWT): 1984 Development Plan,* it translated the moral and civic directions articulated in the campaign and by neighborhoods into goals, policies, programs, and outcome measures (Mier, Moe, and Sherr 1986). It was produced under the auspices of the Development Subcabinet, a cluster of seven city departments responsible for development activities, in winter and spring 1984. The Department of Economic Development and its commissioner, Robert Mier, took the lead. Together, CWT's five goals represented an activist vision for rebuilding Chicago and its neighborhoods: jobs, balanced growth, neighborhood development, public participation, and a legislative agenda. There were fourteen policies and more than 200 specific projects identified in the plan to accomplish the five development goals.

As Harold Washington and his reform coalition took office in June 1983, they inherited a government infamous for patronage and neighborhood insensitivity and an economy that was losing well-paying manufacturing jobs as it entered a boom period of real estate and downtown development. Chicago neighborhoods were experiencing gentrification or the effects of concentrated poverty and disinvestment. Although armed with a reform platform and accompanied by an energetic and eclectic group of administrators and planners, Washington, unfortunately, was not able to grasp the full reins of power to implement his agenda: he did not have a city council majority or control of important boards and commissions, such as the Board of Education and the Park District, until late in his first term; and he simply did not have enough time before he died in November 1987 to use the tools of government to achieve his social justice and reform vision. At the same time, he discovered that governing transformed the meaning of neighborhood. He was mayor of Chicago: he had to be concerned about everybody's neighborhood.

TOOLS FOR NEIGHBORHOOD JUSTICE

Two early policy and organizational decisions shaped the way the Washington administration would implement its neighborhood agenda. The first decision, or fight in this case, occurred in the early months of Washington's mayoralty. It involved transforming the existing Department of Neighborhoods into an extension of the grassroots electoral campaign capable of bringing the neighborhood agenda and activism into halls of government. Not surprisingly, the council majority—in concerted opposition to any change that might enhance Washington's power—dismantled the department and fired its commissioner (Brehm 1991; Mobery 1987).

Washington officials waged a second less visible and ostensibly less important fight, in their view, against a proposal for neighborhood planning boards, a plank within the neighborhood section of the Washington Papers, the 1983 campaign platform. The new administration opposed this proposal for structural decentralization of power as too resource-intensive, organizationally inflexible, and as liable to be captured by the opposition (Brehm 1991; Moberg 1987).

The challenge for the administration was to implement a neighborhood agenda without government or neighborhood-level structures to coordinate, focus, and advocate neighborhood policies and projects. It meant that the administration's approach to neighborhood revitalization would be strategic, not comprehensive, pursuing opportunities and engaging collaboratively with neighborhoods that typically had the most capacity. Consequently, because the administration would rely upon community organizations and coalitions to advocate and implement policy, it incrementally devised an array of government tools to empower and strengthen its neighborhood partners: (1) financial resources for neighborhood programs, (2) open door/information sharing with neighborhoods, (3) new service delivery and policy roles for neighborhoods, and (4) neighborhood issue advocacy by city government.

Resources

Redirecting financial resources to support and strengthen neighborhood revitalization was one of the mayor's first efforts. Beginning in 1983, $13 million in federal funds—Community Development Block Grant resources, for example—was taken out of city staff and administrative overhead and invested in neighborhood "delegate agencies," nonprofits that performed specific services for the city. In 1983 the Department of Economic Development supported forty-eight delegate agencies; in 1985 it supported 100 local business, industrial, and community organizations (Mier 1993). In this same period, the Department of Human Services shifted $7 million of new and existing resources to support 124 new delegate agencies (J. Walker 1991).

In 1985, in the midst of council wars that pitted the majority old-line political machine against the minority Washington coalition, the mayor managed to pass a $250 million bond issue devoted largely to neighborhood improvements, the first such neighborhood-oriented bond for decades (Hollander 1991). Every ward would receive street, alley, and sewer repairs. Unpaved streets were paved. Industrial districts were made accessible. By the close of Washington's first term, city officials and neighborhood advocates were beginning to talk about examining the entire capital budget through the neighborhood lens.

Financial resources for innovation were also made available to neighborhoods. The Planning Department initiated a Neighborhood Planning Grant program to support a range of "bottom up" physical planning efforts (Hollander 1991). The Department of Housing supported a housing-abandonment-prevention effort that funded thirteen delegate agencies (Moberg 1987). The Research and Development Division of the Department of Economic Development (DED) invested $1.2 million between 1984 and 1987 in business incubators, resource recycling, microenterprise, capital pools, sectoral research, and worker-buyout opportunities. Joint projects with other DED divisions focused on building early warning plant-closing networks, industrial displacement organizing, and city purchasing from youth enterprises (Giloth 1991).

Information

A hallmark of Chicago machine politics was the deliberate withholding of information about the functions and impact of government from the public. This politics of secrecy certainly had a bureaucratic dimension of risk aversion and incompetence, but it also performed an intentional role in maintaining political control, even of the machine's allies. Lack of access to information about government activities undermined the organizing efforts of neighborhood and civic activists. It was difficult to monitor and evaluate the performance of city government, and it was equally onerous to conduct local planning that required basic public facts. Not surprisingly, freedom of information became a central tenet of independent politics in Chicago and of the Washington mayoralty campaign (Kretzmann 1991).

Washington sought to open the windows and doors blocking access to government information in several ways. Promising an executive order for freedom of information (FOI) on his first day of office, it actually took the new administration three months to draft, review, and authorize its own FOI approach.

The new FOI effort, however, was a relatively narrow interpretation of the types of information that neighborhoods needed. It was fine for advocacy and good government oversight, but it was less useful, by itself, for broader planning efforts. In conjunction with the Center for Urban Affairs at Northwestern University, the city therefore undertook an affirmative information experiment, in which neighborhoods could obtain on a regular basis a number of indicators about neighborhood quality of life—such as building violations and vacant land (Kretzmann 1991). After several years of fighting bureaucratic roadblocks, the affirmative approach to information-sharing became a regular feature of the Department of Planning. Similar efforts at affirmative information-sharing involved DED's business files and the city's capital budget.

There was also a sharing of information between city officials and neighborhood advocates that was strategic, informal, and issue-oriented. Such exchange of information represented the breaking down of bureaucratic barriers and the opening up of particulars about who had access to city departments. For example, city officials shared records and data about controversial plant closings and big development projects, such as the planned World's Fair, with neighborhood activists.

Roles

A fundamental theme of the Washington administration's approach to neighborhoods was the development of cooperative partnerships to address specific issues and opportunities. On the one hand, this approach meant that neighborhood activists were suddenly sitting on advisory committees such as the one overseeing CDBG funding or participating as welcomed members on the scores of task forces convened under Washington, focusing on issues such as steel and southeast Chicago, homelessness, and linked development. On the other hand, the emphasis on partnerships meant entirely new roles for neighborhoods in the delivery of services.

Two examples from the Department of Economic Development illustrate the types of new roles for which partnerships with neighborhoods were established. The first example was the consortium contract with the Midwest Center for Labor Research (MCLR) and the Center for Urban Economic Development (CUED) at the University of Illinois to establish an early warning plant-closing network on Chicago's West Side and to fine-tune a set of indicators to help the city develop faster, more effective responses to closings as well as to expansions (Giloth and Rosenblum 1987). The network consisted of neighborhood organizations, churches, labor, and small businesses. The idea was to tap local knowledge about what was going on in large manufacturing plants—the movement of equipment, shift changes, or the relocation of personnel. Soon the effort was paying off: predictions about closings came much earlier, and there was a broader constituency ready to act to prevent and oppose them. Thus the challenge was to find the most effective interventions to prevent plant closings and the methods to promote future investments.

The second example was the contracting out of business visitation services to neighborhood-based industrial councils. For ten years city representatives had made yearly visits to thousands of industries to identify problems and opportunities related to expansion, financing, infrastructure, and labor force. That effort was less than effective for a number of reasons, including the basic, but pervasive, mistrust of the city by the business community. In many cases, the city was not a dogged advocate for business when a problem or an opportunity was identified. Consequently, DED contracted out business visitations to neighborhood industrial councils, first on a pilot basis and then more broadly. In general, more contacts were made, and there was better information and follow-up (Mier 1993).

Issues

The administration of Harold Washington not only provided a policy framework and set of tools for neighborhood revitalization, but it also took the side of neighborhood interests in a number of development controversies. The policy framework made this advocacy possible. The administration supported neighborhood interests in several ways: by strategically staying out of issues; by requiring open public processes; by using the standing of the city to get the public to pay attention; and by taking positions, often unpopular, on neighborhood-related issues. Because the Washington agenda had taken hold in a number of development departments, advocating the neighborhood agenda did not simply emanate from the top. But it is also fair to say that the neighborhood agenda was not unopposed by other elements in the administration who were more risk averse or overtly pro-growth. Two examples serve to give the flavor of neighborhood advocacy under Harold Washington.

The World's Fair. A growth coalition with the assistance of Mayor Jane Byrne had won Chicago the designation for the 1992 universal class World's Fair—the centenary of the Chicago Columbian Exposition of 1893 (Shlay and Giloth 1987). This billion-dollar extravaganza, planned for Chicago's lakefront, promised economic benefits and infrastructure capital improvements. Neighborhood interests, however, soon organized in opposition to the closed planning process for the fair and its most likely negative environmental, small business, residential, and fiscal spillovers. The recent history of fairs, particularly in Knoxville and New Orleans, suggested that uncritical fair boosterism could be disastrous for neighborhoods and the public balance sheet.

When Harold Washington took office in June 1993, he quickly moved to open up the planning process for the fair and to articulate principles for city participation and support of it by establishing a World's Fair Advisory Committee. The principles that were developed (and later embodied in the Intergovernmental Agreement with the State of Illinois and the World's Fair Authority) emphasized that the fair should pay for itself, including many hidden public-service costs, and that the city should not be the financial backstop of last resort. In other words, although the mayor did not directly oppose the fair, he withheld critical mayoral support (Mier 1993).

Ultimately, fair planning died in June 1985 when the Illinois legislature refused to continue funding. There were too many question marks about fair attendance, cost projections, and benefits, and opposition was evident from many directions. The fair had become a bad idea.

Industrial Displacement. Many American cities experienced expanding downtowns and declining manufacturing employment in the 1980s, an outcome of growing service employment and favorable tax treatment for commercial real estate investment. The policy response of many planning departments was to let industrial land, especially that surrounding central business districts, change to office, retail, and residential uses. Indeed, municipal governments frequently encouraged these changes by awarding grants, loans, and incentives for the conversion of industrial land and buildings.

In Chicago, the notion that manufacturing was dead did not sit well with community-based groups concerned about neighborhood economic development. They recognized manufacturing decline but also saw sectors of manufacturing stability and areas of potential growth. Moreover, they understood that the existence of manufacturing jobs was linked to the viability of neighborhoods as residential and commercial places.

A struggle ensued in Chicago, beginning with the administration of Harold Washington, to protect industrial districts surrounding the downtown (Giloth and Betancur 1988; Ducharme 1991). The impetus, creativity, and energy for that campaign came from outside government—from community-based organizations such as the Local Employment and Economic Development (LEED) Council associated with the YMCA and the Forty-third Ward alderman Martin Obermann. Their effort garnered credibility, support, and resources from the Department of Economic Development, at first through research about the impact of industrial displacement and then in specific zoning battles. Planners in charge of zoning were sympathetic but had to be won over and shown that ways of protecting industrial land made sense and that tougher negotiating was not only possible but could yield important public benefits.

Eventually, collaborative advocacy by the city and community and citywide coalition-building won the day. The Chicago City Council passed enabling legislation to protect manufacturing districts in April 1988; subsequently it passed three Planned Manufacturing District (PMD) ordinances for specific industrial areas. City/community cooperation to preserve industrial land made so much sense that the strategy survived three mayoral administrations, beginning with Washington's.

DILEMMAS OF NEIGHBORHOOD AGENDAS

Although the administration of Harold Washington achieved notable progress on the neighborhood agenda during its first term, there was still much to be done as the second term began in 1987. Reforms of schools and public housing, for example, had shown modest progress at best, yet they were at the heart of the city services that neighborhood residents experienced daily. In a broader sense, conceptual and organizational problems with Washington's neighborhood agenda existed. There was a lack of policy coordination concerning neighborhoods, despite the usefulness of subcabinets for sharing information. There were no effective mechanisms to facilitate ongoing community planning and participation: neighborhood forums, CDBG hearings, and inclusion at city hall were not sufficient by themselves. Moreover, a number of department leaders did not endorse the neighborhood agenda or preferred treating it as a one-sided partnership in which they called the shots.

Four examples illustrate the dilemmas of Harold Washington's neighborhood agenda. The first two address internal, organizational challenges: department cultures and missions embrace neighborhoods in different ways, and coordinated action is organizationally and intellectually difficult. The second two examples deal with development controversies involving city government, which produced policy stalemates or negative effects for neighborhoods. Neighborhood-oriented policies may not always meet the test of credibility and support in the larger political-economic arena.

Department of Housing

At the close of Washington's first term, many community activists pointed to the Department of Housing (DOH) as unreformed. DOH did not embrace the neighborhood movement and CDCs, nor was it a policy entrepreneur on behalf of housing or neighborhood revitalization (Brehm 1991; Moberg 1987). Yet this organizational quagmire of patronage and dealmaking, inherited from past administrations, had made progress: housing production numbers were up; there was a better spread of housing investments in low- and moderate-income neighborhoods; and DOH had supported innovative initiatives related to housing abandonment, energy conservation, acquisition of tax delinquent property, and low-income housing trust funds. Many of these investments involved neighborhood organizations.

The basic problem, in addition to the DOH legacy, was that DOH wanted to act like a bank, leveraging dollars and maximizing return to city coffers. More dollars went to low- and moderate-income neighborhoods, but DOH did not advocate a comprehensive neighborhood policy and a set of coordinated interventions to rebuild the fabric of neighborhoods. Consequently, there was little, if any, coordination between DOH, the Department of Inspectional Services, Housing Court, and other public, private, and community agencies.

Coordinated Management Program (CMP)

The CWT plan identified the need to coordinate the services and investments of development departments to achieve the maximum positive neighborhood impact. Limited resources were the rationale for strategic and coordinated programming. The Development Subcabinet convened a working group to implement coordinated government action.

Despite the priority placed on this endeavor, the administration never implemented the Coordinated Management Program. Its failure, however, was not due to a lack of meetings, field trips, and mapping exercises. Indeed, planning for coordination foundered on every possible aspect from defining neighborhoods to identifying investments that should and could be realistically coordinated. In some neighborhoods, for example, the public investments were too few or too diverse to coordinate in any meaningful way.

After choosing a dozen neighborhoods to pilot coordinated investment, the ultimate blow to the effort was the political assessment that pilot projects would be interpreted as targeting, which in turn would be understood by allies as neighborhood triage and by opponents as funneling resources to allies. Further action on coordinated investment postponed until after Washington's reelection.

Linked Development

Soon after taking office in 1983, the organization Save Our Neighborhoods/Save Our Cities (SON/SOC) confronted Washington with a linked development organizing campaign. Representing white moderate and middle-income neighborhoods on the southwest and northwest sides of the city, SON/SOC launched a campaign of economic populism, tinged with racial hostility, at a new black mayor who proclaimed a neighborhood agenda and the need for balanced growth. The group wanted to place a linkage fee on all new development in Chicago's booming downtown and to use these funds for enhancements in all Chicago neighborhoods.

Washington established a task force to study SON/SOC's linkage proposal. Made up of neighborhood advocates, developers, and other civic leaders, the task force began and ended in a deadlock, the majority calling for linkage fees, and the minority arguing for a voluntary linkage program to avoid undermining Chicago's commercial business climate (Hollander 1991; Brehmn 1991; O'Connell 1985). Majority and minority reports were issued in fall 1985, followed by several theatrical hearings that aired all possible opinions on the subject. The Washington administration never acted on the linkage proposal, except for establishing a technical assistance pool, letting it slide until the urgency of the approaching 1987 electoral campaign swept it off the agenda altogether.

The White Sox

The Washington administration spent the last year of its first term predominantly on sports and other megaprojects such as the new library, an ironic focus for an administration with a neighborhood agenda. But a perceived electoral weakness of Washington, exploited by the sports-team owners, was that he could not make the big development project happen. Losing a beloved sports team in an election year would be a political disaster. Washington assigned his dollar-a-day business leader Al Johnson to work with Robert Mier, the acknowledged administration advocate of neighborhoods, to become Chicago's sports czars.

The Chicago White Sox initially threatened to move to the western Chicago suburb of Addison, Illinois, with St. Petersburg, Florida, as a lingering possibility. Comiskey Park, according to the owners and a phantom engineering report, was structurally unsound and unable to be retrofitted to accommodate additional skyboxes and premium seats. The owners wanted a new stadium. Antigrowth forces in Addison defeated the Sox development proposal in a November 1986 referendum.

Back at the drawing boards in Chicago, the Chicago sports czars and the State of Illinois put together a deal that would enable the Sox to build a new stadium south of its current location (Mier 1993; Euchner 1993). The surrounding white ethnic community would be protected from redevelopment and exposure to the wider black community. Unfortunately, the plan required moving a small community of 1,000 residents—85 houses and 420 units of low-rise public housing. The project that started under Washington culminated in a new stadium under Mayor Sawyer and was controlled by a state-dominated Stadium Authority. The owners obtained a new stadium with minimal investment, and a community was displaced, with only some of the residents, mostly homeowners, receiving relocation benefits. A class-action lawsuit on behalf of the public housing residents continues to be negotiated (Mier 1993; Euchner 1993).

HAROLD WASHINGTON AND THE
NEIGHBORHOODS: THE LEGACY

Despite impressive steps forward, the administration of Harold Washington experienced limitations and, at times, missteps in promoting neighborhood revitalization. Certainly factors beyond local control, such as deindustrialization, and urban disinvestment shaped the limitations. But there were also factors related specifically to the Washington administration: spotty appointments, lack of coordinated policies and government action, and failure to engage neighborhood interests consistently. The Washington administration created an uneven and frequently a one-sided collaboration with neighborhoods. By the end of Washington's first term, many friends and allies of the administration spoke openly about their frustration with city hall colleagues.

How to relate outside grassroots reform to inside government reform is a challenge for all progressive cities (Clavel 1986). Many of the most astute Chicago activists at the time, inside and outside government—including Washington—believed that the two had to be integrally related. It was their synergy that would bring about reform. But how to do this and how to learn along the way never became the priority it should have been. The neighborhoods believed that the administration moved too slowly and without a real partnership that respected their definition of process. Washington's administrators thought that neighborhood activists and organizations were frequently unrealistic in their demands, organizationally weak, and deemed unaccountable by a broader, often hostile, public.

Lessons drawn from this clash of neighborhood and government progressives are instructive. First, because neighborhood has many meanings, more time should have been spent sorting out conflicting expectations. Neighborhood is a powerful metaphor for home, family, justice, poverty alleviation, human scale, and political control. It worked well as an electoral campaign theme but less well as a conceptual tool for reforming government. Although the Washington administration often erred in its broad and pluralistic definition of neighborhood leaders, some neighborhood advocates were almost sectarian in their delineation of who was and was not a real neighborhood leader. Thus it is no wonder that a common neighborhood agenda was lacking among neighborhood groups.

Second, structures and processes should have been established by the administration at the outset to guide neighborhood planning, policymaking, and implementation. The Washington administration favored strategic and discretionary action; that approach was pathbreaking and agenda-setting in many respects, but it frequently usurped or ignored the advocacy spirit and practice of grassroots organizations. Given that neighborhood revitalization is complicated and long term, tapping grassroots energy, creativity, and power should have been a priority.

Third, the Washington administration was ineffective in engaging its grassroots base in a mutual learning process about governance. Governing requires a recognition and balancing of many and diverse interests—political, business, civic, and neighborhood. That is the burden and challenge of electoral victory and governance, a particularly difficult burden for progressives elected to office, because other interests in addition to their constituencies make a difference on policymaking. Inevitably, the balancing of interests erodes progressive support.

Fourth, community organizers should have kept organizing despite the protestations of progressives inside government. Governments need focus and accountability; too often the pressure they get is only from their political opposition, the corporate community, and the media. Sustained community organizing makes it possible to develop a practice of problem-solving and collaborative politics between the grassroots and government.

Rising above these progressive debates and irritations, the administration and its neighborhood allies came together in spring 1987 to stave off opposition electoral politics. A few months later neighborhood and government allies were again lumped together in a series of articles by the *Chicago Tribune*, "Chicago on Hold: Politics of Poverty," that railed against the antigrowth policies, campaigns, and collaboration of the neighborhood movement and the administration (McCarron 1988). Later that fall Harold Washington died.

What is so unfortunate in retrospect is that there was so little time to experiment with a reconfiguration of government to promote neighborhood revitalization and social justice. Frustrating question's remain: How would Harold Washington have fared in his second term? Would obstacles to neighborhood development have been overcome? Would the administration have grown more distant from the grassroots? Still, the municipal administration of Harold Washington provides a rich example, full of hope, breakthroughs, and frustrations, that serves as an inspiring guide for future progressive municipal campaigns and their neighborhood allies.

NOTES

1. The mayoral administration of Harold Washington does not fit any simple model of progressive, reform, or machine politics. See, for example, Larry Bennett (1993).

7

Neighborhood Organizations and Community Planning: The Minneapolis Neighborhood Revitalization Program

Susan S. Fainstein and Clifford Hirst

Popular, professional, and scholarly attention to neighborhood planning (NP) in the United States has ebbed and flowed over the years. One sign of revived interest in its potential is the recently established Neighborhood Revitalization Program in Minneapolis, Minnesota. This program constitutes an ambitious experiment in which the urban neighborhood is both subject and object of a locally mandated and funded revitalization endeavor.[1] In this chapter, we provide a brief overview of NP in the United States and then turn our attention to a detailed description and assessment of Minneapolis' attempts at community-based planning. We conclude by highlighting those aspects of the NRP that have general implications for the practice of neighborhood planning and by listing the chief advantages and disadvantages of such planning.

NEIGHBORHOOD PLANNING IN THE UNITED STATES

Neighborhood planning has moved through four stages since the turn of this century, each of which reflects a distinct conceptualization of the neighborhood and its role in urban society (Rohe and Gates 1985). In the first stage (1900–1919) NP efforts arose as part of the social reform movements of the Progressive Era. Participants in the settlement house movement viewed the neighborhood as a social unit and regarded neighborhood organizing as a tool for hastening the assimilation of immigrants. In the second era (1920–1963) concern shifted from assimilation and social reform to an emphasis on the neighborhood as a physical unit, exemplified in Clarence Perry's "neighborhood unit plan." The focus of this strategy was the physical design of new neighborhoods for an automobile age. Its practical effect was the construction of socially and economically homogenous, private residential districts centered on the elementary school. In the third period (1964–1974) city governments, with federal urging, responded to militant community-based protest movements by instituting participatory mechanisms at the neighborhood level. During the fourth period, extending from 1974 to the present, neighborhood-based citizen participation in planning became a routine activity but of varying effectiveness.

As views of the function of neighborhoods changed, so did the relations between neighborhoods and city government. In the first two phases of NP, the neighborhood was viewed as the object rather than the subject of policy; to early planners NP was an endeavor conducted by professionals on behalf of existing or potential residents. Only since the 1960s has NP engaged local residents themselves. The third phase, in which the federal government increasingly required cities to ensure neighborhood participation, developed out of protests against centrally imposed policies such as highway and renewal programs that disrupted urban communities. On one front, intellectuals such as Jane Jacobs and Herbert Gans offered arguments against the idea that old urban neighborhoods were expendable. On another front, urban movements erupted in many cities, often in direct response to publicly sponsored instances of neighborhood destruction. The federal government endeavored to co-opt protest by channeling opposition through participatory bodies. Once established, federal regulation changed over time, evolving from requirements for project advisory committees (PACs) under Urban Renewal to "maximum feasible participation of the poor" under the War on Poverty to neighborhood boards under Model Cities. Federal requirements were frequently paralleled by independent efforts of city governments to decentralize the administration of municipal services.

Although federal funding of and regulatory mandates for neighborhood participation under the urban renewal and poverty programs ceased rather quickly, many neighborhood organizations spawned by these national programs survived their termination. Further, neighborhood-based, participatory planning continued to be supported by the federal government, albeit with fewer resources and less regulation, through the Community Development Block Grant program, initiated in 1974. In this most recent phase, however, although city governments routinely consult neighborhood bodies and use neighborhood organizations to implement programs, neighborhoods have largely stopped acting as a framework for transformative activism.

Current efforts in NP reflect concerns quite distinct from those of the 1960s. Declining federal funding has considerably reduced the stakes involved in publicly sponsored redevelopment. Consequently, the retention and attraction of private investment and the control of its character, as well as the provision of local government services, are the chief objects of NP efforts in the present era. Rather than focusing resources on needy areas and persons to which substantial federal resources were once directed, contemporary NP efforts are instead more broadly distributive, taking as their aim the retention of middle-class, home-owning residents and the stabilization of the residential districts in which they live. Indeed, NP, along with other participatory mechanisms, may be more effective at retaining middle-class residents within the city than they are at promoting the interests of the people at the bottom of the social hierarchy.

At present, in the absence of detailed federal requirements for participatory mechanisms, NP practice varies considerably across cities, from nearly nonexistent to institutionalized. As of 1984 over fifty cities in the United States employed NP programs that involved continuous, citywide neighborhood participation in municipal planning and service delivery (Rohe and Gates 1985, Appendix B). The total population of the municipalities using such programs at that time was nearly 30 million persons. More recent data reinforce the continued salience of NP: in 1990, 60 percent of all U.S. cities with populations over 100,000 practiced some form of NP, with 70 percent of these cities using officially recognized neighborhood councils (Scavo 1993). Although CDBG has stimulated the formation of many neighborhood planning programs, it has not determined their character. Many cities that have neighborhood planning programs give neighborhood groups roles in municipal decisionmaking that go well beyond federal CDBG requirements. The areas such groups address are diverse, but in addition to the traditional concerns of land-use planning, land-use regulation, and capital budgeting, the groups often are involved in social services provision, crime-prevention initiatives, and community-building activities. At a minimum they provide a formal channel of communication between citizens and their local governments. Most neighborhood planning bodies are, however, formally limited to an advisory capacity, with elected officials or their appointees retaining final decisionmaking powers.

There are currently three broad forms of NP in the United States (Rohe and Gates 1985, 4–5). The first form comprises the administration of federally sponsored community development programs by departments of municipal governments. The second involves planning by nonprofit organizations such as community development corporations. The third refers to municipally sanctioned programs that call on neighborhood groups to participate in one or more of the following activities: (1) review of plans or budgets developed by municipal agencies, (2) development of neighborhood plans, and (3) provision of services. The Minneapolis NRP represents the latter two forms of NP.

THE EBB AND FLOW OF NEIGHBORHOOD PLANNING IN MINNEAPOLIS: 1950–1990

The respective roles of public agencies and neighborhood organizations in the redevelopment of Minneapolis have been largely consistent with the pattern observed in other large U.S. cities in the postwar period (Nickel 1995). Redevelopment policymaking in Minneapolis has moved through a period of elite control aimed largely at downtown investment, to a concessionary period in which neighborhood residents' interests were incorporated into the process and substance of local policy, and later into a more entrepreneurial, conserving stage where market forces and private actors were permitted to dominate decisionmaking (Fainstein and Fainstein 1986). More recently, neighborhood interests have enjoyed a resurgence of influence and a claim on local resources. Despite these many changes, two constants are visible in our analysis: throughout the postwar period neighborhood groups in Minneapolis have largely been led by and promoted benefits for the middle class, and their relationships with elected officials have been tense and volatile.

Initially the redevelopment agenda was set by an elite group of businessmen, the Downtown Council, with minimal input from neighborhood residents and civic organizations. By the mid-1960s, though, new federal requirements for citizen involvement led to the formation of a number of neighborhood organizations of varying effectiveness (Henig 1982; Stoecker 1994; Lauria 1980). Then in 1975 Minneapolis established ten planning district advisory councils to recommend expenditures under the CDBG program. The independence of the councils soon provoked a negative reaction among politicians, and in 1982 the city council eliminated their advisory powers, slashed the city redevelopment authority's citizen participation budget to one-fifth of its previous level, and fired or reassigned public staff that had been supporting the planning bodies' activities (Hult 1984a; 1984b). Yet another policy reversal occurred when a political backlash against the dismantling of city-sponsored community participation produced a new city council majority sympathetic to neighborhood interests. The transformed council would ultimately sponsor a new mechanism for citizen participation and neighborhood planning under the rubric of the Minneapolis Neighborhood Revitalization Program.

THE GENESIS OF THE NEIGHBORHOOD
REVITALIZATION PROGRAM

Interest in a locally funded program for citywide neighborhood revitalization emerged in Minneapolis in the late 1980s for a variety of reasons. First, a number of senior civil servants and local elected officials became concerned over emerging social and physical decay in the city's neighborhoods as well as over growing public dissatisfaction with neighborhood quality. Second, after a phenomenal round of retail and commercial development in the central business district (CBD) during the mid-1980s, a number of city officials noted rising vacancy rates and concluded that the downtown simply could not absorb any substantial additional development. Third, the transformation of the downtown led many residents to believe that the city's efforts in rejuvenating the core had come at the expense of the neighborhoods. Finally, a new grouping had emerged on the city council that proclaimed its sympathy with neighborhood interests. This coalition would provide political support for the establishment of a number of task forces and advisory committees to design a program for neighborhood revitalization.

Although informants agree on the chief concerns that spawned the NRP, they differ on which individuals were responsible for its conceptualization. Some locate the source of ideas among redevelopment officials, others identify particular city council members, and a few the mayor's office. Yet others suggest that pressure from investment bankers to refinance many of the city's tax increment bonds provided the ultimate impetus for the program's development.[2] One point of consensus, however, does exist: the vision of the NRP did not emerge directly from neighborhood groups. Although they had a voice in its development and currently play major roles in its implementation, neighborhood organizations were not its chief architects.

THE TWENTY-YEAR REVITALIZATION PLAN

In 1987 the city council appointed a task force of leading citizens and charged it with identifying potential new funding sources to be used for neighborhood revitalization. The task force suggested a planning process linked to an $84 million-per-year public spending program that would extend over twenty years, modeled after the city's successful twenty-year plan for street improvements. Another blue-ribbon committee was then asked to address issues of implementing the program, most crucially the question of its financing. The committee's report recommended major reallocations within the regular operating and capital budgets of the five governmental entities with jurisdiction over Minneapolis and, in addition, identified tax-increment financing (TIF) as a major source of support for the NRP.[3] A successor committee of public officials then developed the procedures for operating the twenty-year program, although it left much to be worked out in practice.

THE ROCKY START OF THE NRP

The NRP began in earnest in early 1991. Dedicated funding for the program came from $400 million of tax-increment financing (TIF) money, to be spent at a pace of $20 million a year for twenty years, in accordance with plans developed through neighborhood participation. The program's initial structure and operating procedures were largely the product of recommendations made by the groups already described. These panels contained no scholars, did no research on neighborhood planning models in other cities, and deliberately made no attempt to reproduce the planning structures used elsewhere, even in nearby Saint Paul. Consequently, in its early years the NRP proceeded through trial and error and ran into a number of unanticipated difficulties.

The founding documents and legislation establishing the NRP offered little in the way of a detailed blueprint for its operations. The program's authors decided on an unusual method of organizing participation, whereby a community organization in each neighborhood would be designated as an official representative body, would set up the planning framework, and would be responsible for plan implementation. Where no such organization already existed, it would be called into being. Neighborhood-level staffing depended on the resources that the organization already had available and requests it might make during the course of its planning. Each neighborhood would initiate and develop its own plan, which would prescribe projects within its boundaries for the next five years. The way in which these projects would interact with activities generated by regular city and county agencies was not specified. The framers chose to use the structure of eighty-one neighborhoods, varying in population from 700 to 17,000, that had been delineated decades earlier by the City Planning Department as the basis for plan development. Some of these neighborhoods had established identities, but others were simply lines on a map.[4] Although the creators of the NRP stressed that the plans would address the social as well as the physical aspects of the neighborhoods, the tenor of the program documents—and their interpretation by many participants—favored physical revitalization.

Program Governance

Minneapolis' unique governing structure both stimulated the desire to coordinate public services at the neighborhood level and made such coordination especially difficult. The NRP involved a collaboration of five separate jurisdictions: Hennepin County, the city of Minneapolis, and the boards of the schools, libraries, and parks systems. The latter two entities were part of the city's taxing jurisdiction and thus, despite having independent boards, were constrained by the city's budget process. Hennepin County and the school system, however, were wholly independent jurisdictions that levied their own taxes. Moreover, though the school system was coterminous with the city, the county also encompassed Minneapolis' large suburban diaspora. Since the county delivered most social services within the city, it relieved the city of the tax burden resulting from a concentrated poverty population. At the same time, however, its assumption of this responsibility had the effect of removing decisions concerning social services delivery from city control.

The existence of multiple independent jurisdictions severely limited the potential of the NRP. The city's NRP ordinance indicated that the neighborhood plans would direct the spending of both the NRP's own TIF monies and funds belonging to the five jurisdictions. In fact, the city could not impose any requirements on the county or schools. Even for the agencies within the city's taxing jurisdiction (i.e., regular city agencies, libraries, and parks), the ordinance did not lay out any procedure for revising the normal budgetary process, which was not organized on a geographic basis.

Governance of the NRP itself rested in the hands of a Policy Board, consisting of elected officials, neighborhood representatives, and representatives of major not-for-profit civic organizations. Any financial decisions it made, however, had to be ratified by the city council and by the boards of the other jurisdictions if they were affected by the decision. Thus, for example, the county commissioners had to approve any social service program and the parks board any recreational initiative within a neighborhood plan.

From the start the Policy Board had serious problems in functioning. In part, this resulted from personal antagonisms that developed between some of the neighborhood representatives and elected officials, the weak legitimacy of the neighborhood representatives, who were elected by only a few hundred people, and a tendency of the board to micromanage. But fundamentally the board was rooted in a structure in which nobody commanded authority and where each of the participating jurisdictions was concerned not to relinquish its autonomy to a body it could not control.

None of the founding documents stipulated who would be responsible for ensuring implementation of the neighborhood plans. Day-to-day administration of the program rested with a small office, originally consisting of only a director, two deputies, and two office staff. Although subsequently enlarged, it never had the capacity to operate programs. It was assumed that regular public agencies would take on the implementation chores that fell within their purviews. Thus, for example, the Minneapolis Community Development Agency (MCDA) would administer housing programs; Hennepin County would carry out social service programs; the park board would follow up on recreation proposals. But nothing in the legal framework of the NRP positively bound these agencies to give priority to the neighborhood plans nor even to act on them at all. The NRP office and the MCDA took on much of the burden of contracting and monitoring associated with plan implementation, but the other demands on the NRP staff and the past performance of the MCDA lawyers in the letting of NRP contracts suggested that it would be impossible for this arrangement to continue once many plans were completed. Much of the responsibility for keeping track of projects and pressing for their conclusion seemingly rested with the neighborhood organizations.

All of Minneapolis' neighborhoods were eligible to participate in the NRP and receive some of the TIF funds, regardless of economic and social situation. Nevertheless, it was recognized from the beginning that some neighborhoods would have greater needs than others, and there was a tacit understanding that poorer neighborhoods would receive more funds.

For the first two years of the NRP, because limited staff resources precluded the eighty-one neighborhoods from simultaneously preparing plans, neighborhoods entered the program through a lottery. By the end of 1992 about half the city's neighborhoods had begun planning activities. Then, after a year's hiatus in 1993 when no new neighborhoods were selected due to program overload, the remaining interested neighborhoods were admitted to the program on a limited basis in an initiative called First Step.[5]

The Neighborhood Level

The first neighborhoods to enter the NRP received little direction concerning spending levels, the content of their plans, or procedures for translating wish lists into sets of priorities. Before embarking on planning activities, the designated neighborhood organizations had to work out a "participation agreement" with the NRP office, essentially a contract in which they stipulated how they would include all the diverse elements of their community in the process. The participation agreements provided for the establishment of an NRP steering committee that would extend beyond the board of the neighborhood organization and listed the devices, including meetings, surveys, and outreach activities, whereby the steering committee would elicit popular opinion. Just achieving this agreement on how to proceed turned out to take considerable time. Once the participation agreement was established, the steering committee attempted to collate opinions and formulate a comprehensive neighborhood plan, which would eventually be formally ratified at a general neighborhood meeting. Despite considerable effort at including minorities and renters in the process, they were substantially underrepresented.

The steering committees received assistance from NRP staff members and from city planners, but the quality of the help varied. Staff feared seeming intrusive, and participants were wary of direction from government officials. Neighborhoods often lacked knowledge of what types of programs could address their concerns or became bogged down at the stage of translating a series of ideas into a plan. Consequently, a planning process that was originally estimated to take about eight months took a minimum of a year and a half. Three years after the program's inception, only six neighborhoods had completed their plans, although fourteen were close to finishing. In the words of one neighborhood participant:

> In general, the [neighborhood planning] process is slow and bureaucratic. Some of this, however, is to get input from a diversity of sources, many of whom are not interested in getting involved.

Difficulties

A variety of factors, some resulting from the program's structure, some from inexperience, and some from the inherent dilemmas of community participation in planning, caused the NRP serious problems. During 1993 negative publicity began to overwhelm the NRP as a series of difficulties snowballed and as the mayoral election focused public attention on the program. Just when the city was facing a budget crisis, it was revealed that the NRP was failing to draw down the money that had been allocated to it. Thus, at the end of 1993 it had an unexpended balance of more than $60 million.

Politicians condemned the program's inefficiency and identified a painless way to address the city's financial shortfall in the NRP's unspent funds. Meanwhile, neighborhood participants complained about burn-out and decried the lack of program effects. In those neighborhoods that did finally manage to enact plans, implementation was bogged down in the process of gaining final approval from the responsible agencies or in the legal formalities surrounding competitive bidding and the contracting process. The participating jurisdictions, with minor exceptions, failed to modify their normal practices to accommodate the neighborhood plans and, therefore, had reallocated hardly any of their own funds to conform with neighborhood desires. Leveraging from private and philanthropic institutions was similarly disappointing. Most Policy Board members castigated their meetings as wastes of time, and the political representatives often did not bother to attend.

Although many neighborhoods managed to move through the planning process without acrimony, in several there were serious conflicts over uses of NRP funds that further delegitimized the program. One activist from a particularly contentious neighborhood accurately observed:

> The NRP has increased controversies in the neighborhood because money or the prospect of money always brings people out to fight over it. Frankly, I think it's been a turn-off to others in the neighborhood because we are asked to take one side or the other.

In a number of neighborhoods middle-class homeowners, long-term residents, and whites dominated the planning process, emphasizing beautification schemes and homeownership subsidies while neglecting programs to assist renters and low-income people.

To counter the negative momentum, the NRP office sought to speed up the planning process by bringing in the remaining neighborhoods, providing more staff support, and encouraging collaboration among neighborhoods. The NRP director gave neighborhoods an unofficial target figure for their total expenditures, thereby placing realistic constraints on their deliberations. Neighborhood volunteers and paid staff received training. Early Access funds allowed neighborhoods to begin spending NRP money before final plan approval, and First Step, begun in 1994, introduced a method through which neighborhoods newly entering the NRP process could proceed by setting out their initial priorities and getting funding before having developed a comprehensive plan.

These reforms began to achieve results, as levels of citizen participation moved higher, projects started to materialize, and participants in some neighborhoods expressed considerable satisfaction with the NRP. The NRP office's ability to improve the program, however, was limited by its lack of leverage over the participating jurisdictions. Although it could expedite the spending of NRP monies, it could do nothing to make other public agencies modify their budget procedures or respond to neighborhood demands. Moreover, it could only stand haplessly aside as rivalries began to crop up between NRP steering committees and city council members who felt that they were the genuine representatives of their neighborhoods.

LESSONS OF THE NRP

The NRP is in certain respects an idiosyncratic program, the workings of which reflect the peculiarities of Minneapolis rather than the flaws and advantages of neighborhood planning in general. Minneapolis has a particularly weak executive, who has only limited authority over the heads of many city agencies and none over the main social service providers. Its long progressive tradition has bred a mentality among its public agencies that supports a "nonpolitical" formulaic distribution of services, based on statistical indicators of need rather than on the demands of neighborhoods. Only the police and fire departments are geographically based, meaning that most of the city's bureaucratic officials do not have a first-hand familiarity or identification with particular areas of the city.

Nevertheless, the experience of the NRP indicates a number of political and administrative issues endemic to participatory NP. It also shows that participatory programs do mobilize an active citizenry with a strong willingness to take part in such a program if the structure is made available. Another of its achievements—and indeed, one that has proved somewhat surprising to its evaluators—is the extent to which neighborhood participants have overcome parochialism, seeking to work with other areas on common projects and showing concern for the externalities of their plans. So far the NRP has not stimulated competition among neighborhoods but instead has led them to identify common problems and opportunities.

The difficulties of the NRP are not irremediable, nor are there obvious better alternatives. But the selling of the program as a panacea for urban problems, the vagueness of its mandate, the limited amount of funding, the difficulty of fitting a geographically defined program into a highly centralized and functionally segregated public administration, and the lack of specificity concerning how the neighborhood plans would be formulated and implemented meant that some disillusionment with the process was inevitable.

Neighborhood-level Problems and Opportunities

A number, but by no means all, of the participating neighborhoods manifested three patterns typical of community participation. First, the process was largely dominated by predominantly white, middle-income homeowners. Even in those neighborhoods where steering committees made valiant efforts to attract renters, their participation remained low. A neighborhood planner lamented:

Getting renters involved is so difficult. Try and try, and they don't come. To demand that they come is utopian. What should we do? Pay them to come? Really, what can be done?

The interests of homeowners frequently were at odds with the goals of other community-based organizations. In particular, officers of CDCs felt that their affordable housing goals were being undercut by the homeowner orientation of the NRP organizations (Goetz and Sidney 1994). Nevertheless, a number of neighborhoods did provide for affordable housing in their plans, and it is not yet clear that the perceptions of CDC staff are correct.

Second, some of the neighborhood organizations showed themselves vulnerable to actions that undermined their goal of broadly representing a neighborhood. The informality and limited membership of neighborhood organizations allow a small, determined number of people to take over control with little trouble. Or, even if they do not intend to do so, a few dominant individuals can easily overpower the other members, who decide it is not worth it to them to engage in regular confrontations or to endure endless talking. Thus, though small groups do make participation rational in the sense that individual efforts can produce recognizable results (Olson 1968), they also are quite susceptible to manipulation and distortion.

Third, most participants found the planning process wearying and had difficulty in producing a final document. There was considerable reluctance from almost everyone involved with the NRP to spend much of its money on administration. As a result, volunteers had to struggle with tedious procedures for which they were not well equipped, ranging from compiling spreadsheets on proposed expenditures, to researching existing programs, to carrying their proposals to five different governing bodies for plan approval. The lack of long-term neighborhood-level staffing is likely to prove an even greater problem during the implementation period, since the numerous separate projects in each plan will require continuous monitoring, supervision of third-party contractors, and negotiation.

Bureaucratic Resistance

Public officials have historically been resistant to neighborhood government because decentralized personnel tend to act as neighborhood advocates. The history of decentralization efforts, ranging from Model Cities to little city halls, has shown a tendency by municipal officials to retract out-stationed administrators when they begin to threaten their authority (Needleman and Needleman 1974). Yet service coordination and plan implementation are possible only when there is managerial capacity at the neighborhood level (A. Barton et al. 1977).

Genuine decentralization and neighborhood participation generate resistance from bureaucrats for both unjustifiable and appropriate reasons. There is a feeling widely shared among both neighborhood activists and politicians that bureaucrats intensely dislike changing their routines or yielding their exclusive control of information. One planner commented:

> It's hard for the departments to change. They're caught up in deadlines and the budget cycle. They're afraid to risk making their staffs unhappy and losing lines in their budgets.

Undoubtedly reflexive foot-dragging tendencies constitute part of the bureaucratic response to citizen initiatives. But bureaucratic resistance also originates in a normative system that values fairness, impartiality, and efficiency. Agencies that must husband scarce resources are loath to distribute benefits just because communities want them. Thus, for example, the Minneapolis Parks Department opposes building tennis courts in wealthy areas when inner-city neighborhoods lack recreation centers. In general, the professionalism of city officials causes them to doubt the legitimacy of parochial demands. Some objections that we heard from agency personnel sum up their discontent:

> We lose all economies of scale, . . . [and the NRP] also leads to more discrimination.
> The concept of trying to do things uniquely for eighty-one neighborhoods is impossible.
> The money required to meet the wishes [of the neighborhoods] could never be produced. Limits were already there that neighborhoods did not know about.

For the bureaucratic agencies to modify their behavior to accommodate greater neighborhood democracy requires that their political leaders give them clear direction. Statutory authority would be necessary for revised budgeting processes that would take into account territorial units, for assignment of personnel to places rather than functions, and for job descriptions and incentives that would mandate service to neighborhoods. Political leaders, however, though willing to blame bureaucratic obduracy for program failures, are typically reluctant to adopt such measures. A neighborhood participant complained: "It seems the elected officials aren't taking their role [in the program] seriously." Moreover, the historical evidence in Minneapolis suggests that political leaders are quite capable of opposing neighborhood-based structures, even if they once advocated them.

Political Leadership

Ultimately the successful implementation of greater participatory democracy requires a commitment from political leaders. Such a commitment, however, necessarily causes a weakening of their own power. Thus, even those elected officials whose route to office led through neighborhood organizations become sharply aware of the flaws of such groups once they achieve higher office. Because the number of people in a neighborhood who participate actively in organizations is always substantially less than the number who vote in elections, politicians are at least technically accurate in their assertion that they represent more people than the groups ostensibly speaking for the community. Nevertheless, their claim to a public mandate does not really extend to the policies that they promote, which are not subject to referenda and which are not readily analyzed by voters choosing candidates in periodic elections.

There is no simple institutional solution to resolving the tensions between community participation and political leadership. One possible approach is to create a measure of executive power within council members' districts, comparable to the role that borough presidents play in New York City. By establishing a collaboration between elected representatives and civic activists, rivalries would be diminished and the possibility for fruitful development enhanced. The lack of coterminality between communities and council districts, however, is an obstacle to such a strategy. Another approach to overcoming the inherent conflict of interest between elected officials and community bodies is to give council members and the mayor appointment powers over the membership of community boards.

Finally, it is important to note that many of the NRP's difficulties also troubled the city's earlier experiments with various forms of NP in the 1960s, 1970s, and 1980s. The fact that similar issues have resurfaced in the NRP, a program quite different from its predecessors in Minneapolis, suggests that at least some of the current program's difficulties are inherent to community participation in planning rather than unique to the circumstances or personalities involved in the present NRP effort. On a more positive note, this similarity also suggests that, should the NRP conquer at least some of these difficulties, its innovations would be transferable to other places. Whether such innovations will emerge, however, remains an open question.

Outcomes

As of early 1995, it was still too soon to evaluate the impact of the NRP on Minneapolis' neighborhoods. The only clear-cut result so far was the greater involvement of many citizens in planning for their neighborhoods. Thus, a number of neighborhood participants praised the NRP for increasing their feelings of community and efficacy:

> For the first time I feel like a citizen.
> People are committed. . . . We've created a vision.
> The single most important thing about the NRP is the feeling of community it has created in particular places.
> The point is, the neighborhood will control things that they've never controlled before. They will be empowered.

Given the resources at the disposal of neighborhoods, it is extremely unlikely that the program will fulfill the highest hopes of its originators—reversing the decline caused by increases in the number of people in poverty. At best, NP is likely to have marginal effects on economic development, employment, and income. Its greatest potential is in improving the quality of life for residents. Here the promise is real, but its achievement depends on the commitment of public officials, both elected and bureaucratic, to exercise leadership and to adapt to a different, and possibly diminished, role.

ADVANTAGES AND DISADVANTAGES OF NEIGHBORHOOD PLANNING

The continued practice of participatory NP in many cities, despite loosened federal mandates and substantially reduced funding, suggests that it offers some benefits to urban regimes. By accounting for the unique needs and sensibilities of cities' subareas and by offering an alternative forum for civic activity over issues of immediate interest to city residents, NP does offer a corrective to a number of the disabilities of centralized planning: its skew toward downtown development, its tendency toward technocratic domination, and its insensitivity to the particularities of individual neighborhoods. It also can serve to insulate elected officials from neighborhood conflicts as well as providing a ready resource for gauging constituent concerns. The variable deployment of NP across U.S. cities, however, implies that its effects are not always perceived as positive.

Notwithstanding its potential contributions to city governance and neighborhood quality, participatory NP is vulnerable to a number of weaknesses. These may be summarized under the broad categories of parochialism, representation, and scale.

Parochialism

By providing a forum for the articulation of localized grievances, NP can undermine efforts to benefit the city as a whole. In some instances, enhancing neighborhood power has led to racial and income exclusionism (Goering 1979), and not-in-my-backyard (NIMBY) conflicts have often blocked the development of socially necessary facilities.

Representation

Although many of its proponents have advocated neighborhood empowerment as a means to redistribute power to the poor and disenfranchised, considerable evidence points to an inverse relationship between participation and socioeconomic status (Berry, Portney, and Thompson 1993, 81). Thus, many NP efforts have demonstrated disappointing levels of involvement by low-income, renter, and minority individuals. NP's potential to promote social equity is further undermined when such efforts pit one neighborhood against another in competition for public resources, thus dividing the poor from the working class (Fainstein 1990). Indeed, in his review of community planning in New York City, Peter Marcuse (1990) asserts that NP structures have had a "net negative effect" on the redistribution of wealth and power to poor areas. Such evidence reinforces the enduring leftist critique that citizen participation programs, of which participatory NP is but one example, serve to co-opt and fragment political protest (Piven and Cloward 1972, 256–82).

Even when they are not biased toward middle-class interests, neighborhood institutions do not reliably produce effective representation. Neighborhoods are limited in their human resources. Some neighborhoods simply lack the leadership cadre and institutions necessary to articulate the interests of residents. Or, to the vexation of many participants, a few individuals with irritating personalities may dominate a neighborhood organization, eventually driving out other potential contributors.

Scale

The small size of the neighborhood presents planners and community groups with economic, political, and logistical difficulties. First, neighborhoods are not economic units in their own right. The creation of many small programs tailored to individual neighborhood needs necessarily sacrifices the economies of scale characteristic of centrally administered programs. Of even greater consequence, growth and investment in neighborhoods are largely a function of forces beyond the control of any given neighborhood (Teitz 1989). Though neighborhoods may be appropriate units for fostering the face-to-face, continuous relations that are a prerequisite of strong democracy (Barber 1984), they have little power over the forces that impinge upon them from afar (Dahl 1970). In those cases where NP has been most effective, contextual factors are often determinative. Thus, for example, citizens can be most influential when the desire of investors or government to redevelop a neighborhood is so great that they are willing to bargain with neighborhood residents (Fainstein and Fainstein 1985). Such opportunities, however, may be few and fleeting in many neighborhoods.

Despite these liabilities, neighborhood-based planning offers the potential to overcome the disabilities of centralized planning and administration and offers a forum in which democracy might be reborn. The case of Minneapolis suggests that these benefits are quite real and of value to ordinary citizens. It will be important, however, for NP practitioners to develop strategies that build on these strengths while addressing neighborhood planning's core weaknesses—parochialism, representation, and scale—weaknesses that are evident to varying degrees in the experience of Minneapolis.

NOTES

1. The Center for Urban Policy Research (CUPR) of Rutgers University began a three-year evaluation of the NRP in September 1991, funded by a grant from the McKnight Foundation of Minneapolis. This paper is based on data collected for that evaluation, including material from confidential interviews with NRP participants and observers, attendance at NRP-related meetings, and published materials. All unidentified quotations used herein are drawn from the confidential interviews conducted during the years 1991–1994. Two research associates, first Clare Gravon, then Judith Tennebaum, have been based in Minneapolis and contributed much of the research and many of the insights from which this analysis derives. The findings are those of the authors and are not necessarily endorsed by the foundation or other participants in the study. The results of the study are contained in three reports (Fainstein et al. 1992, 1993, and 1995).

2. Bond dealers made over $2 million in fees for the refinancing (Rubenstein 1991).

3. TIF is a fiscal device that works by enabling local governments to use additional property taxes generated by development to finance certain development costs within a designated district. Initially the funding stream comes from the issuance of bonds to be repaid through the anticipated additional tax revenues. Then, the tax revenue generated by any increases in the district's tax base over a period of years (the "tax increment") minus the amount needed for debt service is earmarked to support further development costs within the district's project area. As a consequence, the locality's general fund will forfeit the increases in revenue created by new development within the district. The fundamental premise of TIF, however, is that new development in the district—and the tax increment—would not have occurred "but for" the public investments financed by the TIF scheme

4. A number of the eighty-one neighborhoods have subsequently combined or are planning to combine for purposes of plan development and implementation. The probable final total of neighborhood units, when all have entered the program, will be in the mid-sixties.

5. As of early 1995, four of the city's residential neighborhoods had not chosen to participate in the NRP.

8

Los Angeles Neighborhoods Respond to Civil Unrest: Is Planning an Adequate Tool?

Jacqueline Leavitt

The response to the 1992 civil unrest within organized parts of Los Angeles neighborhoods prompted a turn toward planning. Community development corporations and social service providers formed the Coalition of Neighborhood Developers (CND), which developed cluster plans and issued a composite report, *From the Ground Up: Neighbors Planning Neighborhoods*. Within the L.A. context, this quasi-institutionalizing of citizen participation as a centerpiece raises fundamental, and recurring, questions about the appropriateness of planning as a strategic response to social problems that led to the unrest.

Federally funded urban renewal programs of the 1950s were plans developed "from the top down," with the business elite, ostensibly to renew the inner city. Yet the urban renewal projects resulted in the demolition of more residential units for low-income people than were replaced, acceleration of neighborhood blight, and benefits to real estate interests by providing land write-downs and other subsidies. In the wake of project designations of many minority areas, "Negro removal" became a rallying cry among the displaced and their advocates, and advocacy planning emerged as a means to include the voice of the unrepresented. Skirmishes in urban renewal areas—lying down in front of bulldozers, picketing at the homes of developers and appointed officials, sit-ins at government offices, squatting in targeted buildings—typified the protesters' acts of resistance.

These acts were a preview to the eruptions that led to riot-torn areas in the mid-sixties, which were precipitated by a combination of police brutality, infringement of civil rights, the draft for an unpopular war, poverty, and lack of jobs. The federal response—as Americans were stunned by the assassinations of Pres. John F. Kennedy, his brother Robert, Martin Luther King, Jr., and Malcolm X—emphasized direct service programs to the poor in riot-torn neighborhoods, which resulted in an expansion of public-sector city and county jobs.[1] The Westminster Neighborhood Association, for example, located in Watts, concentrated on housing production and management.[2] Programs such as the War on Poverty promised far more improvements than the funding allocated could deliver. Within the arena of planning, social planning became a subspecialty.

Almost thirty years later, the cutbacks and dwindling number of social and physical programs have been tantamount to public sector abandonment of economically poor neighborhoods. Warning signs existed prior to the congressional elections of 1994 and the full-scale attempt to reverse New Deal–inspired programs. The response to the Los Angeles unrest in spring 1992 became a dress rehearsal for federal officials who turned their backs on residents within the inner city.

AN OVERVIEW OF THE LOS ANGELES CIVIL DISTURBANCE

The eruption in L.A. began on 29 April 1992, after a jury in Simi Valley, in Ventura County, acquitted four policemen of multiple charges in the arrest and beating of Rodney King. Whatever name is applied to the events in late April and early May—riot/rebellion/unrest/civil disturbance/civil unrest—the physical outcome was the same: widespread damage throughout the Los Angeles metropolitan area. When the unrest was over, 58 people were dead, 2,383 sustained injuries, more than 17,000 were arrested, and property damage was estimated at $785 million (Sonershein 1994, 63). In comparison, the Watts rebellion in 1965, which escalated from an incident in which the California Highway Patrol stopped an African-American motorist, left 34 persons dead, over 1,000 injured, 4,000 arrested, and more than $200 million in property destruction. The igniting point was at 116th Street and Avalon Boulevard in the Watts neighborhood, in the most southeastern part of South Los Angeles, and the unrest spread throughout South L.A. In 1992 the intersection of Florence and Normandie Avenues in South Los Angeles became the epicenter when television cameras captured the beating of Reginald G. Denny, a white truck driver. This time, the unrest did not remain contained within South L.A. but spread to the borders of wealthier areas within the city, other parts of Los Angeles County, and beyond.

The unrest in 1992 reflected black-on-white conflicts but also exposed the conflicts within a diverse community, as African Americans and Latinos attacked Asian Americans and each other. Antagonism or fear or both resulted in armed Korean-American merchants fending off looters and African Americans scrawling "black-owned" on boarded-up stores to forestall looting. The media's ignorance of changed demographics within Los Angeles and especially South L.A., their misinterpretation or unawareness of different cultural responses, and the absence of reporters of color on their staffs led to distorted coverage, especially initially.

After the unrest, Mayor Tom Bradley turned to the private sector, established Rebuild L.A. (RLA), and appointed Peter Ueberroth as director. The assumption (or hope) was that Ueberroth's stewardship would lead investors to the inner city and provide the favorable public relations that he had achieved for the privately financed 1984 Olympics.[3] The grassroots leaders of CDCs, as well as other opinion makers who agreed to join RLA's large committee structure, were skeptical.

Municipal agencies were not as highly visible in their response to the unrest. Councilman Mark Ridley-Thomas (whose Eighth District include South Central) set up an ad hoc L.A. Recovery and Revitalization Committee, comprising four department heads, including City Planning, Community Development, Housing, and the Community Redevelopment Agency (CRA), who were joined later by the head of the Los Angeles County Transportation Commission (LACTC), a predecessor to the Metropolitan Transportation Authority (MTA). They agreed that a strategy and development plan that could be implemented within three to five years were needed for targeted areas.

The Washington, D.C.–based Urban Land Institute (ULI) offered advisory service to the city and met first in August 1992 to offer assistance in "establishing a multibank community development corporation . . . for economic development" (ULI Report 1992, 7) and convened a second panel at the request of Gary Squiers, general manager of Los Angeles' Department of Housing.[4] The ULI was asked to focus on the Vermont Avenue corridor south of Wilshire, between Century and Martin Luther King boulevards. Considerable damage to retail businesses had occurred in the more developed parts of Koreatown closer to Wilshire. The focus of the ULI study, further south on Vermont, was the site of existing vacancies and disinvestment, tangible reminders from the mid-sixties that offered relatively fewer looting opportunities, and was emblematic of other underused corridors in South Central.

The City Planning Department, notoriously slow to react, sent to the city council an ordinance to expedite the reconstruction process (Bernstein 1992, 7, 9). Responding to the lobbying of a coalition of community groups, the City Planning Department started discussions on 6 August 1992 that led to tighter zoning regulations for properties where alcoholic beverages were sold and indoor swap meets were held. In another example of using pressure to win planning gains, the CND, in its earliest days, had helped defeat a state legislative proposal to expand the redevelopment project-area boundaries in Watts. Residents in Watts, wary of urban renewal, had been organized since 1990 to stop its expansion. When the proposal to expand the boundaries surfaced, CND demanded more time and more citizen participation and ultimately defeated the proposed expansion.

In other venues, planners, architects, and designers floated ideas for mixed commercial/residential uses, heretofore largely unpopular and unfamiliar in Los Angeles. The Los Angeles chapter of the American Planning Association (APA) received a $10,000 grant from the national association and invited a team of seven people (six outsiders) to meet with local planning directors and their staffs.[5] The purpose of the meeting was to allow the planners to contribute ideas to the rebuilding efforts. Robert Mier, a member of the panel, stated that they were there for the purpose of "assessing planning's role, good or bad, in the civil disturbances" (Mier 1994, 58). He concluded that "many of us questioned whether what was done as planned development in the previous twenty years had helped much, or at all, to temper the conditions that fueled the disturbances."

In Sacramento, in addition to having tried to expand the Watts redevelopment boundaries, the state assembly set up a committee and issued a report in September 1992. The recommendations to end economic isolation, promote economic development, support community self-determination, develop a long-term economic strategy, and address criminal justice, housing, education, and transit concerns as well as improve human relations and media coverage of the city's communities are reminiscent of other studies in periods following unrest.

At the federal level, the immediate response was a walkabout. President George Bush toured the riot sites, accompanied by HUD secretary Jack Kemp. Kemp had developed a following in public housing communities around the country, and resident leaders in Los Angeles public housing, for example, were on a first-name basis with him and many of his aides. But the Bush administration did not favor Kemp's dual-pronged (but not necessarily connected) approach to poverty— selling public housing units to residents and wooing businesses with tax breaks in enterprise zones (De Parle 1993). When the Los Angeles civil unrest occurred, the Bush administration had no other immediate recourse and brought forward Kemp's programs despite White House reservations about costs, impact, and the recycling of a 1960s' message about empowerment. Little came of the effort, and the enterprise bill was vetoed when it arrived on Bush's desk after his defeat. As a presidential campaigner, Bill Clinton endorsed enterprise zones, and his administration, unlike the preceding ones, included a central role for local government.

THE RODNEY KING ZONE

The 1993 federal empowerment/enterprise zone legislation was attributed to the Los Angeles uprising, so much so that followers of government operations referred to the area involved as the Rodney King Zone. The assumption was that L.A. was a shoo-in recipient. The legislation required municipalities to submit proposals for designated areas, or zones, that included a certain population and where benefits were to be concentrated. Within the zones, tax benefits were available to employers who hired local residents and to businesses that invested up to $20,000: tax-free bonds for public investment could be issued for the zones and existing federally funded social services redirected to them. The proposal also needed to include a strategic plan. Only six urban and three rural areas around the country would be tapped; one was to be an urban area with a population of less than 500,000 and a second an urban area embracing two states. At the same time, greater numbers of federally designated enterprise-zone communities would receive more limited tax benefits.

To the chagrin of the newly elected mayor, Richard J. Riordan, Los Angeles did not receive empowerment zone funds.[6] Also newly elected, and aware of the California voting bloc, perhaps remembering of the impetus for the legislation, President Clinton promised a consolation cash prize to establish and operate a Community Development Bank (CDB) modeled after Chicago's South Shore Bank.[7] The CDB would establish underwriting criteria for economic development loans, guarantees, and technical assistance grants.

The Community Development Banking Act was signed into law in September 1994: it authorized $382 million for more than four years, less than half the amount Clinton originally proposed. In July 1995 the Los Angeles City Council approved $450 million ($125 million in Economic Development Initiative grant funds and $325 million in HUD Section 108 Loan Guarantees). Riordan is credited with securing private pledges that had been missing from the original empowerment zone application. Four local banks, First Interstate, Wells Fargo, Bank of America, and Union Bank, promised $210 million and later agreed to a colending strategy. Priority lending would will extend to more areas than the neighborhoods that experienced the 1992 unrest, or the twenty square miles or so identified in L.A.'s original empowerment zone proposal. To be eligible for loans, at least 20 percent of the residents in areas of Los Angeles city or county must fall below the poverty line.

Guidelines for the makeup of the bank's fifteen-member board are under negotiation at this writing. There is a proposal for eight private or corporate directors and for seven public directors. For the former group, incorporators will select one resident of the empowerment zone, one senior executive officer of a financial institution, and two senior executive officers in business. A group of four community college/university presidents will select four persons in the same categories, but a representative with the proper qualifications from an educational institution can be considered in the business category. The seven public directors will include a representative who is a resident of the empowerment zone to be confirmed by the County Board of Supervisors. The mayor of the City of Los Angeles will select and the city council will confirm five representatives, including one resident from the empowerment zone. An Empowerment Zone Committee, selected either by the mayor and city council or by the county board, will designate one public director who is also a resident of the empowerment zone. This proposal means that five of the fifteen incorporators will be from the zone, four of whom will be nominated by the city council. The city has held several public hearings for the CDB and, as of this writing, is finalizing technical details with HUD that require council approval, as well as clarifying issues about the governance structure and conflicts of interest.

While negotiations, meetings, and high level talks about a Community Development Bank were occurring at the macrolevel, the residents of Los Angeles who were more immediately affected by the 1992 civil unrest were going about their lives without neighborhood services, facilities, or jobs. Quality supermarkets are sparse, as are banks, both outnumbered by liquor stores and check-cashing shops. Existing markets charge the highest prices in town for the poorest quality foods. Movie theaters have long since departed. There are no sit-down family-style restaurants. Such circumstances have long been a part of people's existence in South Los Angeles and were not the direct result of the 1992 civil unrest.[8] Indeed, events in 1992 dramatically demonstrated that such conditions existed far beyond the blocks that went up in flames in the 1965 Watts rebellion.

At the neighborhood level, in the aftermath of the 1992 civil unrest, the Coalition of Neighborhood Developers emerged as a major institution. Under its rubric, area clusters were identified and plans were developed. Its report, *From the Ground Up*, received mixed reviews, however. Subsequently, participants from CND member groups were involved in preparing the city's unsuccessful empowerment/ enterprise zone proposal. Privately, rumors about the lack of in-house staff began as soon as the city contracted out the proposal writing, followed by mutterings about divisiveness among the outside consultants. Publicly, the proposal was criticized as too vague and unfocused, as causing "turf battles over which neighborhoods would benefit from the designation," and as lacking "specific, innovative programs" and "support from state government and the private sector" (Schwada and Richter 1994).

Some of the criticisms appear unwarranted at best. The proposal does contain references to specific programs in response to needs that have been reidentified on a regular basis, stretching back at least to the 1960s. Evaluators in Washington, D.C., cited flaws concerning commitments of money and proposed timing in a number of the feasibility plans presented. Problems about specific designations stemmed from misunderstanding: some proposal participants were told by federal representatives that they could be flexible while others focused mainly on the role that community residents in the riot-torn region should play. Corde Carrillo, director of economic development for the County Community Development Commission said, "We felt this should be a grass-roots-generated application and so the city emphasized the kinds of programs that would be involved and the grass-roots infrastructure that would be set in place (Brownstein 1994).

Perhaps if that had been the only point, a fight for designation might have been waged in the public arena, but the sharpest criticism must be directed toward the mayor's office. The application lacked dollar figures and programs demonstrating the kind of partnership with the business and financial community that other cities showed, which Riordan, a successful venture capitalist with strong ties to business, might have facilitated as he did with the more recent Community Development Bank.

The participation of active CND members and their allies in the empowerment/enterprise zone proposal contrasts to the way city hall consulted with finance and business representatives in shaping the Community Development Bank proposal. Politicians and grassroots leaders have expressed suspicion about the privately held CDB negotiations. Concern surfaced over loan criteria. For example, Mark Ridley-Thomas has pointed out that priorities do not exist for "socially beneficial businesses—say supermarkets over liquor stores" (1995, B7). Community participation from CDCs occurred largely through public hearings and some of their suggestions were incorporated, but CND was not an influential player.

THE EMERGENCE OF CND

Los Angeles' proliferation of CDCs loosely formed around the Local Initiatives Support Corporation. A year before the uprising, LISC-LA had provided "more than $4.5 million in start-up grants and loans for new projects" in metropolitan Los Angeles (Local Initiatives Support Corporation, 1992, 6). Anita Landecker, a program vice-president, had started capacity training for new groups, making Los Angeles the first city in the LISC network to move in this direction. Fifteen CDCs completed the 1988–1989 training program. When LISC promoted Landecker, Denise Fairchild became the new director of LISC–LA.[9] The corporation administered a second training program in 1992 funded by the Los Angeles Collaborative for Community Development. This consortium included a mixture of national and local foundations as well as the City of Los Angeles. A third round of training occurred in 1994.

Prior to 1992 this trade association of community development corporations included some of the oldest groups, such as Westminster Neighborhood Association in Watts and Vermont Slauson Economic Development Corporation in South Central Los Angeles. Other nonprofits included Ward Economic Development Corporation (EDC), an offshoot of a prominent AME church, and the Little Tokyo Service Center, which expanded its focus from social service delivery to housing development. Relative newcomers to development frequently had had a longer history in the community. For example, the Dunbar EDC was housed in the landmark Dunbar Hotel built in 1929 to serve African Americans in an era of segregation; EDC rehabilitated it as senior housing.

Thus when Los Angeles fell apart on 29 April 1992, a CDC structure was loosely established. After 1992 the Coalition of Neighborhood Developers became the core of a multicultural and multiethnic organization of CDCs and other community-based agencies in ten clusters of the inner city (see Map 8.1). Over time fifty-six groups participated. Knowledgeable about the needs remaining from the 1965 disturbances and aware of the new scars from 1992 in neighborhoods in which LISC was involved, Fairchild was clear about where mobilization should begin: "The neighborhood is the most potent nexus for bridging the widening social divide . . . and the logical place for working out racial and class differences" (Estrada and Sensiper 1993, 133).

Fairchild inspired the neighborhood groups within CND and solicited funding from members of the collaborative, particularly the California-based Irvine Foundation, which took the lead. In December 1992, the Liberty Hill Foundation launched a Fund for a New L.A. and awarded CND $10,000 for the purpose of building "a broad-based constituency that will represent the needs of low-income communities in the decision-making process" (Liberty Hill Foundation 1992, 3). Local banks contributed. The Los Angeles City Council approved almost $366,000 in June 1993 that helped alleviate a shortfall when a funder substituted in-kind services for a money allocation that had been previously agreed upon.

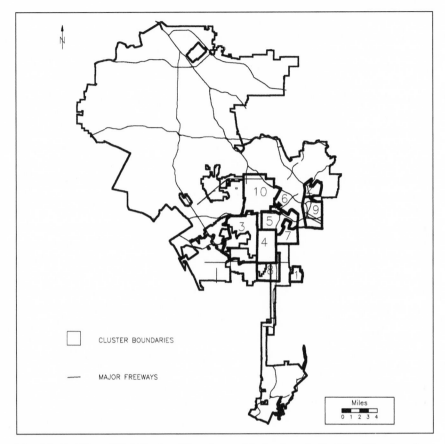

Map 8.1. Coalition of Neighborhood Developers: Cluster Areas in the City of Los Angeles (Source: Coalition of Neighborhood Developers, *From the Ground Up: Neighbors Planning Neighborhoods* [Los Angeles, 1994])

Legend: Cluster Area 1, Watts; 2, Lincoln Heights; 3, Crenshaw; 4, Vermont-Slauson; 5, Adams-Maple; 6, Pico Union; 7, Vernon-Central; 8, Broadway-Manchester; 9, Boyle Heights; 10, Mid-Cities

Each group initially received $50,000, half for community planning and the other half for leadership development. The intent, consistent with LISC and the collaborative philosophy, was to sustain long-term organizations that would train their constituencies. On the basis of a verbal agreement with funders, LISC advanced the money for efforts to start. In 1994 CND hailed its own successes in a press conference. But by mid-1995 the executive director of CND had resigned and Denise Fairchild had left LISC in order to pursue implementation of other projects. After her departure, CND failed to capture an advocate within the agency.

DEFINING CND

James A. Regalado writes that multicultural coalitions are "formed on the basis of a call to meet an identified need or set of needs affecting coalition partners" (1994, 221) and might be initiated by formal government agencies, foundation support, or religious organizations.[10] Other older coalitions in Regalado's review include the Southern California Civil Rights Coalition (SCCRC), the United Neighborhoods Organization (UNO), and the Southern California Organizing Committee (SCOC). UNO has organized extensively on the East Side, and SCOC has been influential in leading the environmental justice movement. Leobarda Estrada and Sylvia Sensiper (1993) refer to "cross-ethnic" efforts that crisscross member organizations and include social service providers, homeowners, and others in the community. Regalado gives scant attention to CND but sets it apart from other types of coalitions because of its composition of "community constituency organizations," an apt characteristic.[11] Those constituency organizations spent considerable time after 1992 in defining themselves as a group and in determining the boundaries for target neighborhoods, calling attention to the fact that

> there are hundreds of neighborhoods in Los Angeles, all of them as diverse as the people who live in them. Many communities suffer from the same problems. But, how a community responds to a particular problem may vary. . . . The CND is aware that planning in the past has encompassed far too large of an area, with boundaries imposed on and not defined by the community. (Hoover/Adams–Maple/Adams Neighborhood 1993, 3)

CND's neighborhood boundary lines evolved as an amalgam of place-based locations governed by organizational strengths, where members had "a long history of social relationships with residents":

> The clusters are well-known community designations. Their boundaries, however, do not conform to traditional city-community planning areas, political, school, or other governmental jurisdictions. Rather, they consider a combination of "natural boundaries" and consolidated service areas of CND members. Most of the clusters include more than one neighborhood with different assets and opportunities. They are held together, however, by a network of community organizations which form the area's economic, physical, and social foundation. (Coalition of Neighborhood Developers 1994, 11)

Ten clusters, "for the most part the older portions" of the city, were mapped (Coalition of Neighborhood Developers 1994, 12): (1) Watts, (2) Lincoln Heights, (3) Crenshaw, (4) Vermont-Slauson, (5) Adams-Maple, (6) Pico Union, (7)Vernon-Central, (8) Broadway-Manchester, (9) Boyle Heights, and (10) Mid-Cities. Within each cluster, a lead group was responsible for coordinating efforts among existing organizations. These ran the gamut from established to new and included groups representative of a citywide or a nationwide organization, groups with either a comprehensive or a single-issue approach, and groups formed to respond to redevelopment proposals.

For example, within Vernon-Central, participating members included Concerned Citizens of South Central Los Angeles, the Dunbar EDC, CANAAN Housing Corporation, Inc., Vernon-Central Neighborhood Housing Services, and the Vermont-Slauson EDC. In the Crenshaw Neighborhood Planning Cluster, the steering committee included representatives from the Rebuild Crenshaw Committee, Crenshaw Neighborhood Development Corporation, Helpers for the Homeless and Hungry, Crenshaw Neighbors, L.A. Neighborhood Housing Services, Inc., and the Corridor Economic Development Corporation. The Watts cluster was made up of two of the oldest organizations that emerged after the 1965 rebellion: the Westminster Neighborhood Association and the Watts Labor Community Action Committee. They were joined by the Drew Economic Development Corporation, Charles Drew University of Medicine and Science, and the newly formed Watts Community Policy and Planning Institute.

CND organized a committee structure that reflected three main goals: (1) the importance of coalition building; (2) long-term continuity of CND itself, and (3) implementation of plans. A nine-member executive committee, with representatives from both old and new organizations, hired an executive director in November 1992, and in August 1993 it became a 501(c)3 nonprofit organization. Members of CND also included a Coalition of Design Professionals and academics, some of whom were hired later to provide technical assistance. Cooperation with government agencies, such as Los Angeles' City Planning Department, permitted greater accessibility to data than might have occurred otherwise and the assistance of the department's staff at the beginning of the process.[12] At the same time, other members of the planning community voiced doubts and questioned whether "the new plans will be as unreal as the plans prepared by public agencies during the 1970s (Winogrod 1993, 11).

CND participants felt a sense of urgency and a limited window of opportunity. The unrest had exposed conditions that were well known to nonprofit neighborhood developers and social service providers. The time seemed ripe for viewing plans as organizing tools to inspire hope and produce visions that would be more meaningful than community plans prepared by the City Planning Department and that could be included in the Citywide General Plan Framework that was to begin in 1993.[13] Throughout Los Angeles, the majority of community plans had not been updated for more than twenty years. The CND meetings involved some participants who were recent graduates of the Urban Planning Program at UCLA; others were committed community activists, a majority apparently influenced by notions of planning shaped by the Community Redevelopment Agency's reports on project-based developments, other official planning documents, or both. One CND participant compared meetings to "growing pains" as members struggled to set forth principles and time schedules. Some participants wanted to jump directly to a format, asking, "What are we going to present?" Gilda Haas, however, a seasoned organizer/planner, argued that it was premature to discuss the uniformity of the product. The distinction was made between process, with its variants, and product, which would have similar variants.

PRINCIPLES OF CND PLANNING

A set of suggested community-planning principles evolved:

1. *Be inclusive and unifying* so that we can bring together different ethnic and interest groups around common policies and goals.
2. *Be comprehensive,* including social, physical, and economic development.
3. *Promote ownership* by the community of both the development process and product.
4. *Promote equity/parity* in the distribution of public resources.
5. *Promote institution building/strengthening* of community support systems (mediating structures), including family, church, neighborhood, and public (e.g., educational institutions).
6. *Promote capacity building* of underutilized human resources, including the transfer of knowledge and skills.
7. *Promote participation* of all underutilized resources and people in the economic process.
8. *Promote self-determination and self-sufficiency* of the community.

A proposed community planning process/schedule was developed but scrapped as participants chose to meet their needs for self-education. The revised timetable acknowledged that neighborhoods were at uneven stages of organizing, planning, and developing projects and that the groups needed to build an internal consensus in order to be able to recognize each other's problems. Sample job descriptions were drafted for a community organizer and a community planner; each organization was responsible for identifying relevant skills. Cluster planning committees or staffs also decided what types of information to collect or whether to collect information. In Watts, the planners "felt that enough information exists about the community's priorities that conducting an entire needs assessment would not only be redundant, it would risk angering and alienating community residents" (Henderson n.d.). The Crenshaw cluster focused on a "Strategic Land Use Plan—what should be built and where . . . land use solutions only, versus systems and service programs which do not have a corresponding built form" (Pride-Wells and Macauley 1993). The Hoover-Adams–Maple-Adams report concludes with plans for continued local organizing to implement ideas for food services and youth programs.

SOME RESULTS OF THE CND EFFORTS

The composite report from CND, *From the Ground Up,* states its purpose as a marketing tool for investors who might commit dollars to implementation. The report provides Geographic Information Systems (GIS) maps that clearly identify the primarily contiguous ten clusters as housing predominantly renters and having a greater percentage of youth and high-school dropouts than elsewhere in the city. Compared to the rest of the city, CND clusters include limited areas where people earn $75,000 and above and pockets where people earn less than $20,000; the vast majority of cluster households earn between $20,000 and $35,000.

All the clusters reveal "massive growth and population shifts, without commensurate investments and growth management strategies." *From the Ground Up* identifies common issues that were either "compelling or widespread": these include the need for new family housing, youth services, and connections to major local and regional businesses and the need to counter the negative perceptions of the inner city. Specific recommendations target the credit barrier to homeownership; the lack of a coordinated and accessible youth program, especially for twelve- to eighteen-year-olds; the need to form a direct community-employer relationship in the clusters where major employers, with more than 250 employees, are already located and to recruit other businesses; and the need for mayoralty sponsorship of a BUY-LOCAL campaign that focuses on CND communities.

Reviewing the reports by each cluster provides a fuller picture of residents' perspectives as well as the variations in report presentations and emphases. But the common element and the one about which expectations both inside and outside CND may have been highest, concerns participation. This was to be the feature that distinguished CND planning from any city-generated plan. Nonetheless, many of the reports expressed the inherent frustration in organizing people from the community to attend a series of meetings that culminate only in a paper document.

Some reports specifically discussed organizing strategies. For example, the Hoover-Adams–Maple-Adams Neighborhood cluster held two community meetings, made more than 150 contacts, and interviewed more than 170 families (Hoover-Adams–Maple-Adams Neighborhood 1993). Member groups of this cluster, El Rescate and the Central American Community Center, launched a door-to-door campaign. In Mid-Cities, the Korean Youth Center addressed the ethnic mix by holding meetings with Latinos, Koreans, and Filipinos separately and drew on a needs-assessment survey by the American-Thai Education and Research Institute (ATI).

Other aspects distinguish the cluster reports from each other. For example, I was asked to help the Boyle Heights cluster to meet a tight deadline. I talked with staff, drew from relevant existing surveys, fashioned a report that identified multiple development issues facing Boyle Heights (from the CRA, the MTA, and the Housing Authority of the City of Los Angeles), and tied coalition-building to historical examples in which organizing had failed to prevent plans from physically dividing the community.[14] The report drew on existing interviews to summarize needs; rather than being an end product of an organizing approach, the document was viewed as a reference that organizers might use, especially after it was translated into Spanish.

In another example, the Dunbar Economic Development Corporation (Macauley and Chapple 1994), already undertaking the concept of the Historic Renaissance, educated the larger CND audience about its particular strategy. Reclaiming the sites of the earlier African-American community—such as the Ralph Bunche house (Bunche was the first African-American representative to the United Nations), and the original offices of the Golden State Mutual Insurance Company and the *California Eagle* newspaper—was discussed within the context of being "sensitive to the current demographics of the Vernon-Central community." In yet other examples, cluster plans assembled the results of long-standing organizing efforts and needs assessments, such as those of CHARO (Community and Housing Resources, Inc., November 1994) and the Lincoln Heights Organizing Committee (LHOC) in East L.A.

SOME CND OMISSIONS AND PROBLEMS

The CND reports convey an implicit optimism about the planning process, and it is easy to second-guess what could have been included. For example, although neighborhood histories are available, most CND reports do not identify the known obstacles to implementation. That is, their thrust is to promote investment although it might have been helpful to cite issues that arise when the neighborhood planning process moves to implementation as well as alternative responses to external pressures from agency proposals, politicians' deals, private-sector negotiations over land use, cutbacks in state funding, and the general public's lack of sympathy for poor communities. Most if not all of the member groups shared this background, having frequently formed to fight an "outsider's" plan that typically had government's blessing.

Other more immediate organizational problems surfaced. Within any coalition, tensions exist between balancing individual and collective obligations. Member CDCs had to raise funds for their own survival, pay attention to reporting requirements for existing projects, meet construction schedules, and respond to the daily needs of residents, businesses, and so on. Different groups had different agendas and priorities. In part, CND recognized the distinction by including targeted neighborhoods that were not directly affected by the 1992 riots but that had a history of neglect and underdevelopment. Yet some communities had been more affected than others, even though the unrest left behind a more level playing field. For example, half the 607 properties that were severely damaged or destroyed in 1992 had not been rebuilt by 1994; the rebuilding that occurred was outside the harder hit South Los Angeles or Pico Union neighborhoods. Roberto Barragan, director of the Community Financial Resource Center in South Central, reflected two years after the 1992 disturbances: "Watts never fully recovered after the 1965 riots. If something is not done, we'll be the Watts of the 1990s" (Feldman 1994).[15]

The long-term coalition-building project that the CND promised was inherently vulnerable to criticisms leveled at individual CDCs, which are pulled by numerous demands: service delivery, support staff, efficiently managing property, following the money trail in order to survive, and responding to new programs. Even in its most remarkable moments of cross-cultural activities, CND did not and could not monopolize community rebuilding initiatives after the unrest. Other actions were under way that relied less on place-based neighborhoods and more on class groupings or common interests.

The California Mutual Housing Association (CMHA) was in its beginning stages, mobilizing around housing but attempting to reach tenants in private as well as in public housing. For a time, CND and CMHA shared the same suite of offices, along with Communities for Accountable Reinvestment (CAR), facilitating communication among them. RLA, although criticized for taking credit for projects that others had brokered, was involved in bringing supermarkets (Ralph's and Von's) and job-training facilities to parts of the underserved communities. At the very least, board members of CDCs that belonged to CND were involved with some of these negotiations. The Bloods and the Crips, the umbrella groups for gangs throughout the country, negotiated a truce and undertook a separate planning process that reflected their ideas for rebuilding. Their recommendations included proposals that were remarkably similar to that of the cluster reports.

The CND, like most CDCs, did not have a fully articulated vision or political philosophy about empowerment, participation, rebuilding, revitalizing, and economic development. Its clearest concept was that it recognized the lack of authentic community voices within the established planning process; and despite the admitted frustration, it can be argued that people who might not otherwise have been heard were engaged. That the CND reports did not stretch the bounds of traditional planning or provide sufficient answers to fulfill the requirements needed in the case of the empowerment zone application should not have been a surprise, even to its advocates. Neighborhoods with little power but whose leaders value increased participation in decisionmaking processes are embarked on long and complicated struggles.[16] This type of community building differs from government bureaucracies, which process applications for federal dollars to meet arbitrarily set deadlines, or from private corporations, where decisions may be made quickly and hierarchically.

An unanticipated set of problems emerged for CND when Los Angelenos were violently awakened at 4:41 A.M. on 17 January 1993. The Northridge earthquake upstaged the civil unrest; government agencies shifted attention to the epicenter in the San Fernando Valley where buildings had suffered the greatest damage. It was as if victims of the natural disaster were "truly worthy" recipients of federal aid, as HUD made available special Section 8 vouchers for emergency housing.

Be that as it may, CND provided a structure for going beyond rhetoric, for place-based coalition-building at a time when ideas about place had shifted and neighborhood boundaries had become blurred. South L.A. was considered as anyplace in the metropolitan area where fires were set, looting occurred, poverty conditions existed, and police remained on tactical alert. After 1992 CND provided one of the few grassroots forums for talking about commonalities. Many of the participants, previously unknown to each other, met in different parts of L.A. and came to hear and learn about the issues in their several neighborhoods. At a time when race and ethnic differences were particularly explosive, neighborhoods were being treated as if they were homogeneous, and the media was playing catch-up, CND provided a structure that permitted people with "differences" to talk about a collective response from the grassroots.[17]

Although the analogy may seem farfetched, CND may be likened to a country that undergoes a revolution only to stumble in setting up new structures and in ensuring the equality promised during the struggle. CND was neither in charge of leading a revolution, nor did it have unlimited resources. Planning control was not formally transferred from the city to the neighborhoods. Planners within the City Planning Department were not permanently assigned to work in the offices and out of the homes of CND participants. The neighborhood planning process by itself is not a revolutionary tool, and despite the ties to and involvement of the grassroots, it is still time consuming, perhaps more so when outsiders are in charge. Unless the state pledged and targets implementation monies before the planning process, the efforts can only be frustrating. If CDCs are to direct community sentiment to a peaceful reconciliation of needs and resources, a deal has to be made beforehand with the political and economic institutions. A transfer of power away from official planning agencies, perhaps as a special overlay district, would have had to occur. Lacking that or some similar assurance, the answer to the question about the adequacy of planning as a tool for responding to civil unrest is that it falls short. Were the CND plans then in vain? The answer is a qualified no.

The qualification is based on the conclusion that the reports can still be used effectively as an organizing device. One outlet is to resurrect an initial idea to produce position papers, including a public policy agenda to be targeted toward legislative and other policymaking bodies. The survey data in individual reports can be more closely examined as responses to particular policies, such as questions about immigrants and their long-term residency in communities. Neighborhood planning and organizing can be evaluated in order to determine what worked, what did not, and why. The other, more immediately evident, application is to direct attention to the opportunities and pitfalls of the Community Redevelopment Bank.

THE COMMUNITY REDEVELOPMENT BANK

It can be argued that the federal government should have acknowledged Los Angeles' special situation of "police brutality–trial–a verdict–racial conflict–a riot" with greater understanding about the need for process, either through a separate funding package or within the empowerment zone competition. Instead, the Los Angeles riot became indicative of the response (or the lack thereof) from a leaner, meaner government and a subordination of the general welfare to the market (Warren 1995; Wood 1995). The consolation prize, the Community Redevelopment Bank, is clearly market-driven. Safeguards that permeate the official documents are aimed to protect the city from bankruptcy and to ensure safe loans. Conflict-of-interest protections will probably be waived for potential bankers in an effort to get the bank started, even though outreach efforts are not yet slated to begin.

The bank will select different community intermediaries to make microloans, and business loans and to set up a revolving venture capital fund. This latest vehicle for economic development is aimed at job creation and retention, especially for jobs that pay more than the minimum wage and that offer training opportunities for higher positions. But benefits probably will be greater for or reach more established businesses, financial institutions, and CDCs as well as individuals with good credit histories, equity, or both.

Safeguards for people who will otherwise be left out were articulated somewhat at a meeting of the Los Angeles City Council's Community and Economic Development Bank Committee on 2 October 1995. Council members Mike Hernandez (District 1 and committee chair) and Richard Alarcon (District 7), in different ways, questioned the types of intermediaries in the bank's pool.[18] Alarcon argued that empowerment should be not just at the level of a "community but block-by-block . . . not [for] just a few select groups that may have lived in poverty before but don't live there now." Unless empowerment is seen otherwise, he continued, the CDB will be "an old boy network getting the same old thing." Alarcon emphasized the need to provide the up-front impetus for partnering, or the funds will be "all sucked up by existing intermediaries." Hernandez repeatedly asked spokespersons for the mayor, city government, and HUD about the request for qualifications from intermediaries, pointing out that groups that started only after the unrest or the earthquake would be refused on the basis of their length of existence. Finally, Alarcon argued out that "the drive to get money on the street may be subordinating the creation of new intermediaries."

Frequently, Hernandez and Alarcon and members of the bank's bureaucracy were not speaking the same language as the city council members considered their accountability to their community constituencies and the respondents their bureaucratic responsibilities. The respondents, in regard to expanding the pool of community intermediaries, repeatedly explained that new organizations would not be turned aside as long as they hired a management staff with a certain number of years of experience. Hernandez countered by pointing out that there were people in his district who questioned whether their prior experience in banking in Nicaragua and Mexico would be recognized at all.

To the extent that opportunities reach less established individuals and businesses, the CDCs and the CND cluster reports may offer a basis for organizing at the grassroots level. They may also help to create new worker-owned institutions. This approach might be a way to precipitate a united neighborhood front. For such action to occur, however, far more attention needs to be paid to the collective rather than to the individual CDCs. CDCs and CND clusters must agree on a collective plan and strategy so that their plans can be funded and adopted by the city; otherwise, visions "from the ground up" get ground down.

NOTES

1. Los Angeles, unlike New York City or Chicago, has had a much thinner history of neighborhood-based organizations in poor communities. After the 1965 Watts rebellion, numerous organizations were begun, but only three community developers have sustained any growth, two of which are more widely known.

2. Two better-known groups are the Watts Labor Community Action Committee (WLCAC) and the East Los Angeles Community Union (TELACU). Both survive in 1995 as successful entrepreneurs, with WLCAC having built more than 500 units of low- and moderate-income housing for families and seniors, and TELACU having produced 1,000 units of low-income housing. Both organizations have weathered criticism regarding their continued ties with the grassroots. For example, during the 1992 unrest, part of the WLCAC center was burned, although the estimated loss of $4.5 million did not stop the agency from serving members of the community while the fires and looting occurred. Afterward, Ted Watkins, founder and leader of WLCAC, led the rebuilding effort and in 1993 oversaw the groundbreaking for a 35,000-square-foot building that houses various of the organization's programs. Watkins died in October 1993 but his work is being carried on. TELACU has withstood allegations since 1976 that concern its transformation from an antipoverty agency into a business empire and political base. The U.S. Department of Labor and the Small Business Administration challenged expenditures, asked for but did not receive documentation, and accused TELACU of self-dealing and conflicts of interest with a subsidiary. The Los Angeles County Board of Supervisors terminated all TELACU's social service contracts in 1982 and in 1983 placed a lien on portions of an industrial park.

In 1987 Housing L.A. brought together new and old activists in a coalition of "individuals and organizations concerned with the growing housing crisis." The range of participants included the twenty-two-year-old Coalition for Economic Survival; Concerned Citizens of South Central Los Angeles, a nonprofit housing and economic development corporation that formed in 1985 to successfully fight the siting of a solid-waste incinerator in its neighborhood; the Venice-based Lincoln Place Tenants Association, which was newly formed in response to the owner's decision to sell the 800-unit apartment complex; and the Little Tokyo Service Center (LTSC) Housing Committee, which was starting its renovation of forty-three units of low- and very low-income housing. Housing L.A. tackled Mayor Tom Bradley's proposal to lift the Community Redevelopment Agency's (CRA) spending cap, spend an anticipated $2.1 billion in downtown private development, and make available another $2.1 billion for housing and day care. Under state law, CRA was permitted to recoup property taxes generated by new development "in excess of the amount previously collected" (Coalition of Neighborhood Developers, *Housing LA* 1989, 3). In 1977 a court decision had ruled that the CRA could receive only $750 million in subsidies; the remainder of an estimated $5 billion was to go to the county, the city, schools, and governmental agencies in the same proportion as other property tax revenues. Housing L.A. worked with health advocates in staging a public hearing and spun off a Campaign for Critical Needs. Ultimately, the cap was not raised (a 1995 court decision has once again sustained the cap).

In another issue, advocates successfully strengthened the rent control law through a post-card campaign that flooded council members' offices (it was negated in 1994–1995 by changes that weakened state rent control legislation).

3. Three years later, following Ueberroth's resignation and changes in leadership at the top, RLA's usefulness as a broker for economic development remained an open question.

4. The panel included a majority of developers and planners strongly interested in imple-mentation: Smedes York, Raymond Brown, Rick Cohen, Paula Collins, Fritz Duda, James Goodell, Dennis B. Martinez, Naomi Porat, F. Terry Schnadelbach, Michael A. Stegman, and Roslyn M. Watson.

5. The panel included Robert Mier, professor of urban planning at University of Illinois at Chicago Circle and the director of development under Chicago's mayor Harold Washing-ton; Ed Blakely, at the time a professor at the University of California at Berkeley and chief of staff to the mayor of Oakland; Henry Cisneros, HUD secretary; Norm Krumholz, a pro-fessor at Cleveland State University and former planning director for the City of Cleveland; Weiming Lu, director of the Lowertown Redevelopment Corporation in St. Paul; and Bon-nie Turner, deputy director of Economic Development for Denver. The only person from Los Angeles was Gene Grigsby, a professor at the UCLA Department of Planning and director of the Afro-American Center. The cities of L.A., Inglewood, Long Beach, Comp-ton, and Culver City were represented.

6. The winning proposals were from Detroit, New York City, Chicago, Atlanta, Balti-more, and the combined cities of Camden, New Jersey, and Philadelphia.

7. Unlike South Shore, the Los Angeles Community Development Bank is not a private commercial institution that offers savings and checking accounts, and its investments are directed toward economic, not residential, uses.

8. In 1992 the designation South Los Angeles, now common, was new to many of the individuals who study the city. Areas known informally as South Central turned out to be part of the officially designated planning area of South East. South Central and South East, roughly divided by the Harbor Freeway (Interstate 110), are the two planning areas that make up South Los Angeles. Watts is a substantially smaller area in the southeasternmost corner of South Los Angeles.

9. Both women share a commitment to institution-building at the community-based level. Each holds a planning degree: Landecker received a master's degree from the Massachu-setts Institute of Technology and Fairchild a doctorate from the UCLA Graduate School of Architecture and Urban Planning. Each has strong connections to neighborhood groups, Landecker from her days as head of the Los Angeles Community Design Center and Fairchild as an activist whose résumé includes a run for a city council seat. In 1994 Fairchild chose to leave LISC and is currently working on projects on economic develop-ment and employment training at the community college level. She remains influential in the community development movement in Los Angeles.

10. For example, the Los Angeles County Commission on Human Relations played a key role in forming the Black-Korean Alliance and the Black-Latino Roundtable. Although about thirty community groups participated, Regalado found that membership was "without the community," and the Alliance and Roundtable disbanded after the uprisings of 1992. Of the groups that Regalado reviewed, the Multicultural Collaborative (MCC) was the only one formed after the unrest. Its key staff represents the African-American, Latino, and Asian-American communities who are involved in outreach and networking programs that reflect their boards' interests as well as the strengths of the lead organizers. The New Major-ity Task Force (NMTF) regrouped after 1992 around "inclusive economic development strategies and planning," but Regalado criticizes its lack of ideas about implementation of policies.

11. CND is not the only left-out group. AGENDA, also relatively new, with a con-stituency based in South Los Angeles, has concentrated on influencing the Los Angeles

Police Department's community policing experiment. As part of this focus, AGENDA was influential in redirecting federal "weed 'n seed" monies to a Youth Empowerment Project.

12. City Planning's existing Southeast/South Central Task Force included "about 20 planners (many of whom grew up in the community) who were already authorized to spend 10% of their time on a special work program for that area" (Bernstein 1992, 7, 9).

13. For insight about visionary plans, see Mier 1994, 61.

14. When I was asked to write a report for Proyecto, the CND's *From the Ground Up* was already published, and the need was less critical to adhere to one particular format. Proyecto's administrator and organizers wanted to convey the underlying organizing philosophy that is rooted in liberation theology and in establishing base community groups that translate teachings from the Bible to everyday issues.

15. Not surprisingly, quake repairs have followed the same pattern. Recovery is reported to be stalled from Hollywood to south of the Coliseum, which is the South Los Angeles area. These neighborhoods have a high percentage of loans that have been rejected or withdrawn. See Doug Smith (n.d.).

16. If there is confusion among newcomers to the planning process, the planning literature certainly reveals the differences between scholars and practitioners.

17. In part, the cluster reports are CND's legacy, and they may avoid the typical death of storage in file drawers. More critical is the expanded network of people who may be able to regroup in various other ways. For example, in Los Angeles, a citywide popular education center (similar to Highlander in Tennessee) is in the process of developing. The intention is to provide a place where ideas are exchanged, debated, translated, and strategized among neighborhood activists, union organizers, base community organizers, academics, youth workers, service workers, and practitioners—in general, people committed to helping create better neighborhoods and higher quality working conditions.

18. Update, 2 October 1995, by Keith Comrie, city administrative officer, Ron Deaton, chief legislative analyst, and a representative from the Mayor's Office to the City Council Community and Economic Development Committee.

9

Faith-based Community Development and African-American Neighborhoods

June Manning Thomas and
Reynard N. Blake, Jr.

> *A community whose life is not irrigated by art and science, by religion and philosophy, day upon day, is a community that exists half alive.*
> —Lewis Mumford, *Faith for Living*

> *Any religion that professes to be concerned with the souls of men and is not concerned with the slums that damn them, the economic conditions that cripple them, is a spiritually moribund religion in need of new blood.*
> —Martin Luther King, Jr.

Individuals involved in neighborhood development in distressed central-city neighborhoods in the United States must confront, sooner or later, faith-based community development. Particularly in majority African-American neighborhoods, community activists will need to assist faith-based groups, to work in collaboration with them, or at least to understand their role.

"Neighborhood development" has little meaning without reference to location, class, or race. For white professional areas, neighborhood may simply mirror exclusionary home rule, complete with strong mechanisms for social exclusion (Larry Bennett 1990, 76). For areas peopled by suppressed minorities, neighborhood may represent a trap, created by segregation, poverty, and neglect.

Neighborhoods in distressed central-city areas face a dizzying array of forces of devastation, including population decline, job disappearance, racial segregation, financial disinvestment, institutional loss, and social disintegration. With global economic trends, the situation may get worse before it gets better. Neighborhood development would have to be a powerful tool to succeed in areas caught between the nexus of economic disintegration and inner-city decline.

Faith-based community development has the potential to become such a tool, particularly in African-American neighborhoods. Faith-based development offers considerable strengths, although it also confronts major challenges.

131

In order to absorb the lessons offered here, readers will have to overcome the tendency to dismiss from the dialogue of social reform anything that has to do with religion. Those who do so may react negatively (and appropriately) to repressive religious fundamentalism yet fail to understand the important role religion plays in the culture of oppressed people. Secular, mainstream traditions of liberal logical positivism have yielded few lasting results. It is time to reevaluate the role of religion in social change, as social activists have already begun to do in several countries in Latin America, Asia, and Africa (West 1993, 19).

OPPORTUNITIES

Faith-based community development, particularly in African-American neighborhoods, offers several opportunities for neighborhood improvement. Religious institutions have a strong presence within inner-city neighborhoods; they operate within a coherent value system, providing the conceptual framework necessary to undertake social reform; and they offer ready-made leadership and possibilities for strategic cooperation.

Presence

Faith-based organizations are often among the last institutions to remain in poor neighborhoods. Surveys have shown that nonprofit organizations vary substantially across cities; their numbers dip sharply in very low income areas, but religious institutions exist in virtually all neighborhoods (Vidal 1994, 37). It is precisely for this reason that neighborhood organizers associated with Saul Alinsky's Industrial Areas Foundation often begin their work by organizing churches, whether in Chicago, Texas, or New York.

Describing the South Bronx, where he built an effective coalition of forty-five churches, IAF's Jim Drake noted that he organized churches because "the only other organization that is viable is the drug one. . . . There is no Kiwanis; there is no Elks. There are no PTAs" (Rooney 1995, 223). There were, however, churches, some of them supported by majority-white, mainstream religious denominations that were loath to abandon their substantial investments in buildings and people. Alinsky, according to Drake, tried to organize neighborhood groups in severely depressed areas. These groups did not work because they had no institutional base, "like the church that survives when somebody moves away" (Rooney 1995, 224).

African-American churches are a cultural phenomenon born in a society that more carefully observed racial separation in the religious sanctuary than it did anywhere else. Arising as a response to the racist practices found in many white churches, these churches let African Americans worship God based on their cultural traditions, without reprisals or challenges from white society. They offered a spiritual structure to black lives and provided avenues for self-determination (Lincoln 1984).

Historical circumstances made black churches particularly visible in northern city neighborhoods. The churches provided important support for the rural southern emigrants, but their culture tended to support a relatively high number of churches per capita; therefore when blacks moved into formerly white areas, they found insufficient numbers of church buildings. Small storefront churches filled the gap (L. N. Jones, 1982–1983, 42).

Some churches in predominantly black neighborhoods contain minority congregations belonging to larger mainstream Christian denominations. Other churches are affiliated with one of the eight largest historically black denominations,[1] or with nonaffiliated, independent congregations. And still other African Americans have left Christianity altogether to become Muslim, through either the Nation of Islam, the more inclusive American Muslim Mission, or other Islamic groups (Lincoln 1984). If one adds in the smaller groups affiliated with other global religions, such as Buddhism or the Bahá'í faith, the variety is staggering.

Values and Ideology

Religious groups possess a fairly cohesive set of values and a strong ideological basis supporting social and economic development. Those values rest largely upon Judeo-Christian traditions, although they may be translated into Afrocentrism or other cultural or religious dialects. Their conceptual framework for social reform is grounded in persuasive credentials. To complete a quotation, partially cited above, from the IAF organizer Jim Drake: "In places like the South Bronx, [churches] are the only entities that have a genuine claim on people. The only other organization that is viable is the drug one. I would say that the only set of values that is as strong as the Judeo-Christian set of values [is the one] around drugs. There is no Kiwanis" (Rooney 1995).

Judeo-Christian values might be summarized as belief in the Ten Commandments, the work ethic, and lifestyles informed by biblical moral teachings.[2] The fact that these values are battered and frayed, particularly in neighborhoods of concentrated poverty, does not mean that they do not still hold power. They provide a platform from which religious communities can help protect families and youth from the ravages of inner-city life or launch rescue missions into the city at large.

Several biographies/accounts tell of Christian and Muslim protection and retrieval in cities across the nation. Among the most powerful are the stories of Rev. Cecil Williams, in San Francisco, and Rev. Johnny Youngblood, in Brooklyn, New York (Williams and Laird 1992; Freedman 1993; Haley 1973; Bird 1990). Both men rescued people from addiction, destitution, and anomie by evoking those Judeo-Christian values that center on personal redemption. From that basis, furthermore, Youngblood developed an extraordinary record of physical community development.

The ability to "protect" youth and families, or to "rescue" those who have stumbled, is an important skill: much of the crisis facing distressed black neighborhoods has to do with a complex morass of dilemmas that is, though economic in origin, social and spiritual in its manifestation. The problems include widespread susceptibility to addiction, crime, violence, and family dissolution. These dilemmas go far beyond the problems of poor housing conditions or inadequate community facilities. The disintegration of social controls in some areas has made even veteran organizers afraid to live in their own neighborhoods (Boggs and Boggs 1994).

To ignore these conditions, or to pretend that only massive economic or political reforms can address them, provides little hope for today's victims. As eloquently argued by Cornel West, "liberals" have rightly fought against "conservative" tendencies to overemphasize religion and blame the victims for "moral" failures. Although it is important to avoid doing so, it is also important to develop effective solutions to the deadly "nihilism" afflicting many black communities (West 1993; 1994).

Social reformers understand that successful social movements usually rest upon a strong conceptual framework for judging social conditions and planning action. Marxism provides a powerful example of such an ideology, as does socialism, black nationalism, or modern conservatism. Among activist urban Christians, a comparably strong ideology is based on an interpretation of the Bible that comes close to Latin American liberation theology in its social implications. This ideology provides the motivational imperative necessary to spur action. Martin Luther King, Jr., believed that faith-based community development is morally right and even mandatory for those people professing to be true believers: "We are gravely misled if we think the struggle [for economic and social justice] will be won only by prayer. God who gave us minds for thinking and bodies for working would defeat his own purpose if he permitted us to obtain through prayer what may come through work and intelligence" (Cone 1991, 147–48). King, a leading theoretician of faith-based action, elucidated the connection between social justice and socioeconomic reform, and his teachings still ring true.

Other individuals have also made significant contributions. During the 1970s, Italian-American priest Geno Baroni, best known for promoting white ethnic neighborhoods, linked Catholics supportive of civil rights with those motivated to resolve urban problems and helped to form coalitions among the races. Baroni's short but cogent "Agenda for the '70s" identified urban problems as a moral issue and helped redefine the modern "urban mission" movement, linking it as well with national urban policy (O'Rourke 1991, 73–82).

Princeton University professor Cornel West is probably the most influential African-American intellectual of aggressive Christian ethos since King. Possessed with strong academic credentials and theoretical boldness, he calls courageously for "prophetic" social change, cogently articulates the spiritual dimensions of urban decline, and denounces the moral crisis facing African-American and middle-class white communities (West 1993; 1994).[3] Robert Linthicum's *City of God, City of Satan* is as complete an explanation of biblical references to the need to rebuild the social, economic, and spiritual infrastructure of today's distressed cities as one could expect to read. His "urban theology," furthermore, is well seasoned by his practical experiences in Detroit, Chicago, Milwaukee, and Calcutta, India. His book compels Christians to accept salvation of the city as a sacred religious obligation (Linthicum 1991).[4]

Muslim religious leaders have also promoted faith-based community development. Elijah Muhammed and Malcolm X built African-American Muslim communities renowned for their social and economic development activities and successful retrieval of "lost souls," including prisoners. Both men laid the theoretical groundwork for continuing community development, now carried out by diverse kinds of Muslim congregations (Muhammad 1965; Malcolm X 1992).[5]

The complex nature of problems facing black neighborhoods means that holistic approaches to community development, involving political, spiritual, social, and economic strategies, may be the only hope for success. Neighborhood solutions require both a recognition of the importance of community (T. M. Smith 1984; Cochran 1994) and the planning and development of holistic community intervention strategies (Shiffman 1992). Religious institutions—keepers of social values, and communities in their own right—are particularly well suited for such work. And the best institutions use a holistic approach to neighborhood residents' needs, helping people to address their individual and collective challenges and to build communities beyond "bricks and sticks" (Kriplen 1995, 10).

Note, however, how different it is to base social action on "urban theology" rather than on social science. Believers in the social science tradition, such as ecological models of invasion/succession, would label "hopeless" some of the neighborhoods that faith-based groups target. Faith-based community development, in contrast, taps powerful spiritual visions of success. According to Linthicum, the key New Testament paradigm is the Kingdom of God on earth, in the city; the key Old Testament paradigm is the reconstruction of Jerusalem. As Ezekiel proclaims, "The name of the city from that time on will be: The Lord is There" (Linthicum 1991, 80).

Leadership and Social Reform

Faith-based community development also benefits from ready-made leadership, opportunities for new leadership, and the possibility of building strong, multifaceted coalitions. African-American religious organizations arose in part in order to enable independent leadership. This situation has roots in the Reconstruction Era, when "new seeds, scattered by the plowmen of three great institutions—the black church, the black lodge and the black college—were sending down shoots. The focal point of these developments was the black church, which quickly established itself as the dominant institutional force in Black American life" (Lerone Bennett

1987, 286). Many African-American social movements and organizations were connected with faith-based institutions or leaders: the Nation of Islam, so-called Black Muslims; King's civil rights organizations, including the Montgomery Improvement Association, Southern Christian Leadership Conference (SCLC) and Student Non-Violent Coordinating Committee; the SCLC's Operation Breadbasket, which Jesse Jackson headed before starting People United to Save Humanity (PUSH); and the Opportunities Industrial Center, begun by Rev. Leon Sullivan (L. N. Jones 1982–1983, 47–48).

Black religious leaders have a long history of political and social involvement, a tradition that has continued into the present. According to one study of Atlanta's Concerned Black Clergy, formed in 1983, member churches first met to discuss their own homeless shelters and soup kitchens but went on to lobby for government shelters, welfare benefits, and affordable housing. Their efforts significantly supported the needs of the community (H. Newman 1994, 26). Yet all the key religious leaders in black neighborhoods are not black. Whites have played important roles in the community development efforts that have succeeded in the South Bronx, East Brooklyn, Detroit, and other cities. Joining activist white and black religious leaders together creates powerful partnerships.

The Lilly Endowment began to fund religious institutions involved in community development in 1989. Its study of twenty-eight U.S. religious institutions or partnerships that had received its funds included twenty in urban areas and twenty serving large populations of people of color. These groups had developed many kinds of partnerships to implement community development, mostly through housing programs. The partnerships that worked best were those with common visions and goals, a high level of trust and respect between partners, and a structure that "promotes inclusiveness and has bridged ecumenical, racial, cultural, geographic or economic differences." When religious institutions became active partners, access to resources improved (Scheie et al. 1991, 64).

One of the most widely publicized coalitions, the Nehemiah Project in East Brooklyn, has illustrated the power of partnerships among faith-based institutions. There, and in the South Bronx, groups of such institutions used the services of professional IAF organizers to get an array of congregations to work together. A coalition of fifty African-American churches in Baltimore, BUILD, has also had great success (Clemetson and Coates n.d.; McDougall 1993).

RESULTS

It is beyond the scope of this chapter to describe the array of cases in which faith-based community development has worked in inner-city, predominantly African-American, neighborhoods. We will briefly mention a few major sources of information and then proceed to draw a brief picture of the effects of faith-based development on one city, Detroit.

Exceptional work has been carried out under the Nehemiah project in East Brooklyn, where a church-based coalition built, in one development project, 2,300 single-family rowhouses. The IAF helped organize that effort and another one described in *Organizing the South Bronx.* Essential to the full story of Nehemiah and the South Bronx are both Rooney's book and Freedman's *Upon This Rock,* the story of Rev. Johnny Youngblood. Rooney beautifully explains the IAF and the organizational story, but Freedman reveals the power of motivation and spiritual renewal, from the perspective of one black church (Rooney 1995; Freedman 1993).[6] Another excellent case study is *Black Baltimore,* a holistic account of the rise and fall of community among that city's African Americans. Upon his account of the role of community institutions, including a black church coalition (BUILD) and a Muslim group, McDougall builds a theory of "base community" that has great potential for black neighborhoods (McDougall 1993).

World Vision, Inc., a global Christian organization with which urban theologian Robert Linthicum is affiliated, has published a compendium of organizational case studies entitled *Rebuilding Our Communities.* The studies come from a wide range of cities, including Bethel New Life, Inc., in Chicago; Ecumenical Social Action Committee, in Jamaica Plain, Massachusetts; and Heart of Camden, Inc., in Camden, New Jersey. Other important cases appear in Clemetson and Coates (n.d.), which focuses specifically on African-American churches, and in Joel Lieske's account of Jubilee Housing in Washington, D.C. (Shabecoff 1992; Lieske 1984).

These accounts offer important pieces of a story, but the literature about them tends to be scattered, disjointed, and descriptive rather than conceptual or analytical. The impact of these activities emerges somewhat more fully when we consider their effects upon one city. By briefly describing such efforts in Detroit, home to several faith-based groups, our purpose is not to present Detroit as exceptional but to describe some of the effects of faith-based development upon one sample city's community development culture. There, faith-based initiatives have created some of the most impressive community development organizations in the city.

A prominent example is Focus:HOPE, which has remade its predominantly black neighborhood, largely through the efforts of two Catholics with conscience, Fr. William Cunningham and Eleanor Josaitus. A biracial civil rights group that formed after the 1967 civil rebellions, Focus:HOPE began with a food distribution service that now serves 85,000 people a month. Its machinist-training institute trains eighty youth at a time and places 98 percent of them in jobs; a Montessori day-care facility serves sixty-five children; and a new Center for Advanced Technologies provides training in high-technology manufacturing. Its Fast Track program offers accelerated programs in reading and math that give poorly prepared public school graduates a second chance. The programs are located in several buildings on one street, forming a twenty-five-acre complex that has transformed the surrounding neighborhood (Chargot 1992, 1A).

Another exceptional organization is the Warren-Connor Development Coalition, founded in 1984. This biracial development group is not faith-based but received its start through the financial support of Catholic Mercy Hospital, on the city's East Side. The coalition has developed pioneering initiatives for its African-American neighborhood, including crime prevention, youth enrichment, support for chronically jobless families, and a new shopping center.

Several black churches in Detroit have also developed strong initiatives. Hartford Memorial Baptist Church, a 7,000-member congregation led by Rev. Charles G. Adams, used more than $1 million in church funds "to purchase land in an eight-block wasteland in the heart of northwest Detroit's black community." The "wasteland" now includes a McDonald's and a Kentucky Fried Chicken restaurant and several small auto shops. The church is building a $3.5 million one-stop car "mall" for automobile services, which will hire local residents (Henderson and Hays 1992).

Black churches helped construct housing in Detroit as early as the 1960s. During the urban renewal era, three displaced black churches forced the City of Detroit to sell them land within the Detroit Medical Center. During the 1960s and 1970s, when subsidized housing funds were easily available, they built three substantial multifamily rental housing complexes that complemented the medical center hospitals (J. Thomas 1996).

Modern examples of housing efforts by nonprofits associated with black churches include REACH, Inc., housed in the Twelfth Street Missionary Baptist Church, which has opened a restaurant (now closed) and rehabilitated several housing units. Church of the Messiah Housing Corporation, started by Episcopal churches in Detroit, has used funds such as the Lilly Endowment and Section 8 to rehabilitate four large apartment buildings and to build new low-income townhouses. An umbrella organization to which the Church of the Messiah belongs, Islandview Village, has rehabilitated and constructed housing and plans to build a new shopping center. One indication of such groups' importance to neighborhood and housing improvement is apparent in Table 9.1, which lists successful Detroit applicants for the state of Michigan's most important neighborhood improvement program.

Detroiters have also contributed to the general literature on faith-based community development, largely through the work of Linthicum and of attorney Gregory Reed. Reed's book, *A Blueprint for Progressive Community Development*, is based on his work with Detroit churches and includes the basic legal documents necessary for faith-based organizational development, sprinkled with biblical references. The Public Broadcast Service (PBS) film "A Neighborhood Redeemed" is a stirring account of one Detroit neighborhood's transformation, as assisted by Rev. Eddie Edwards, founder of Joy of Jesus, Inc. (Linthicum 1991; Reed 1994; PBS c. 1991).

More mature Detroit organizations have taken the lead in training less mature groups in the basics of community development. They have sponsored a training program, funded by World Vision, in which June Thomas has participated as a trainer. The sessions began in 1992 and 1993, and trained, in three years, thirty

Table 9.1. Neighborhood Partnership Program Designees, Detroit 1990–1995

Michigan State Housing Development Authority			
Organization	Faith-based nonprofit	Early faith-based support	Percentage black in target area
Cass Corridor Neighborhood Development Corporation	No	Yes	54.3
Core City Neighborhoods, Inc.	No	Yes	66.3
Corktown Redevelopment Committee	No	No	33.1
Islandview, Church of the Messiah Housing Corporation	Yes	Yes	72.3
People in Faith United Housing Corporation	Yes	Yes	72.5
Pilgrim Village: REACH, Inc.	Yes	Yes	98.0
Vital Neighborhood	No	No	
Woodbridge Citizen District Council	No	No	60.4

Source: Document in author's possession, mailed from Michigan State Housing Development Authority, 14 December 1992; phone interviews, Dave Mehelich, Margaret Alant, Lillian Randolph, February–April 1995.

Detroit faith-based groups in organizational growth and community development techniques. Although most of the organizations were Christian churches, trainees have also included one Muslim group and one Buddhist.

Faith-based efforts in Detroit have also succeeded in engaging the black middle class. In many low-income neighborhoods, professional blacks have moved out (Wilson 1987). Yet they may come back for religious services. Serving on the board of one organization in Detroit are two black professional urban planners who do not live in the neighborhood but belong to the sponsoring church. Their organization contracted with a mixed-race team of faculty and students from Michigan State University's Urban and Regional Planning Program, on an at-cost basis. The church-sponsored organization thereby funneled black human and financial resources into a distressed neighborhood.

The sum total of these efforts: faith-based institutions or their nonprofit affiliates or offspring are major players in community-based development in Detroit. They have created some of the most persistent and innovative community development programs in the city, they have organized significant resources for the benefit of the poor, and they have contributed to the national dialogue about faith-based development.

CHALLENGES

Work with these organizations has raised a number of concerns, however. The challenges facing faith-based community development include the magnitude of the problems, the nature of the work, and the nature of faith-based organizations.

The Problems

The most obvious challenge is to overcome the devastation facing the people who would remake inner cities. Most distressed U.S. neighborhoods are facing an extensive array of social, economic, and political problems that are entrenched and long-standing. Some of the problems have stymied the most capable mayors as well as numerous intellectuals and bureaucrats.

While it is heartening to see the visionary efforts of faith-based groups, which have made a place for themselves upon the landscape of cities, how much impact can these groups reasonably expect to make? It may be unfair to expect them to triumph where better-financed enterprises have failed. Although many of these groups do succeed, others have attempted to "save" neighborhoods that have been so deteriorated that little successful impact was possible.

Even the "protection" and "rescue" operations already mentioned, targeted toward people caught in the web of economic and social disintegration, have limits. The forces of negativism can be overwhelming. The air waves send out compelling messages of destruction, disrespect, and nihilism, and the drug culture entices with the promise of material wealth. This environment has made retrieval of people difficult; so too is the retrieval of abandoned, burned-out neighborhoods (West 1993; 1994).

The Work

Community-based development is slow, frustrating, and complex, circumstances no less true for faith-based organizations than for others. For example, community-based housing development has a number of conceptual contradictions and difficulties that slow down whatever progress might be made (Bratt 1990). For its twenty-eight funded groups, the Lilly Endowment found that "lack of planning expertise and skills hampered project planning in several partnerships" (Scheie et al. 1991, 69). Some staff were relatively inexperienced in housing or economic development. Sometimes the problem was high staff turnover, due to low salaries and staff benefits.

Organizers of World Vision's training program in Detroit found it necessary to train groups in organizational basics, including how to set up accounting systems, choose suitable board members, develop mission statements, and apply for foundation grants. That portion of the training took several months; only then could trainers approach more complex topics. Getting an organization fully equipped could easily take—and has taken—years. Though many groups handle social services well, the work of actually building housing or financing commercial development is much more difficult. Some groups have fallen by the wayside.

The Organizations

The work of community development is new territory for many faith-based organizations. In addition to learning the mechanics of the development process, some groups need to make major philosophical changes. They may also need to overcome the handicaps of personalized leadership and to transcend the fragmentation and disunity that face religious communities.

In Rooney's account of the South Bronx, one organizer explained how hard it can be to organize people who make a living preparing for the afterlife. As he put it, "We make a strong distinction between the 'World As It Is' and 'The World As It Should Be.' A lot of [ministers] are very trapped in just thinking about the World As It Should Be. They have given up on this one. They are going to wait for the next" (Rooney 1995, 114).

African-American religious leaders can be either passive conservatives or social activists. Even during the civil rights era, not all of them supported Martin Luther King's social activism; only in hindsight did King become universally popular among black leaders. In Atlanta, as a contemporary example, black clergy have been more likely to support the current "urban regime" than to challenge governmental and social injustice (H. Newman 1994, 24).

Most religious organizations depend upon a minister to be the leader. Typically a church, mosque, or other congregation wanting to undertake community development sets up a separate nonprofit organization, but the initiative to do so often comes from a religious leader, whose continuing support may be crucial. If a particular leader does not support social and economic development, the likelihood that someone else within that congregation would do so diminishes.

Another problem is that sharing power goes against the strong-leader culture in some faith-based communities. Yet the most effective community organizations depend on a collaborative effort by several people, both between organizations and within. The patriarchal nature of some groups may hinder full participation by women, but women can be some of the most successful community leaders and organizers.

Furthermore, the religious community is, by its nature, fragmented, which sets up barriers to collaborative effort. It is not uncommon to find many churches in relatively small black neighborhoods: thirteen exist in the Detroit neighborhood of 1,000 homes already mentioned, which has two planners on the nonprofit organization's board (Michigan State University 1994). Protestant denominations have succeeded in fostering independent thought and worship at the cost of unified action.

Add to this lack of unity the natural fragmentation that occurs even within the same denomination, by race and class, and the situation worsens. In most of this chapter we have addressed faith-based community development by central-city groups. But what about suburban religious communities? Although a few of these have arisen as supportive partners—in Detroit, for some coalitions, such as Focus:HOPE and People in Faith United, or for ameliorative activities such as paint projects or soup kitchens—the overwhelming majority of suburban worshipers has done little to help. Indeed, they fled the black central city along with their nonreligious neighbors.

A BETTER FUTURE

In spite of the challenges—working with an intractable situation, carrying out difficult development activities, and overcoming problems of apathy, disunity, and fragmentation—the possibilities for faith-based community development are many. Faith-based organizations, which exist in even the most devastated neighborhoods, provide an institutional foundation upon which community-development groups and coalitions can build. They are firmly connected with the culture of the community because residents retain strong attachments to their religious organizations despite social chaos. Religious groups possess the ideological framework necessary to promote social development, encouraged by powerful spiritual teachings. Such communities offer ready-made leadership structures, and the possibility of partnership with like-minded organizations.

To close, it might be useful to offer a few thoughts on the challenges of fragmentation and neglect. Religious history and American culture have built faith-based communities that reflect the social wrongs of racial segregation, class exclusion, and middle-class apathy toward social justice. Congregations in cities and suburbs seem quite happy to remain the most segregated places in America. Religious people within black neighborhoods seem content to support several churches, large and small, within the same neighborhood area.

It is important to address the continuing fragmentation of the metropolis and of the religious community and the tendency for many national leaders to promote religious values without acknowledging moral responsibility for the poor. Spiritual writings that directly address these issues need more attention. The ones quoted below come from the Bahá'í faith, a multiracial religious community best known for its support of racial and global unity, but they echo the teachings of Christianity and Islam.

The heart of the problem is the tendency to divide, rather than to unite, along political, racial, or religious/denominational lines. Yet "The world of humanity is one race, the surface of the earth one place of residence, and these imaginary racial barriers and political boundaries are without right or foundation" (Bahá 1986, 2). Indeed, "Since We [God] have created you all from one same substance, it is incumbent on you to be even as one soul, to walk with the same feet, eat with the same mouth and dwell in the same land" (Bahá'u'lláh 1986, 2). This precept challenges the very notion of African-American neighborhoods or cities, which exist because of oppression rather than free choice. Similarly, excessive division of the faith-based community is counterproductive and unjustified.

Another universal teaching that needs further attention is the moral obligation to care for our neighbors. Inner-city people and groups deserve to receive support from their suburban neighbors. Yet many suburban voters passively support exclusion and elect politicians who call for traditional religious values even as they ignore the plight of the oppressed. In contrast, important spiritual teachings suggest that "the poor in your midst are My [God's] trust; guard ye My trust, and be not intent only on your own ease" (Bahá'u'lláh 1986, 43). Faith-based groups should not have to struggle alone, trying to rectify the wrongs of decades of disinvestment and neglect. All people of conscience have a responsibility to support their efforts and to help build good cities, perhaps even the City of God.

NOTES

1. African Methodist Episcopal (A.M.E.); African Methodist Episcopal Zion (A.M.E.Z.); Christian Methodist Episcopal (C.M.E.); Church of God in Christ; National Baptist Convention of America, Inc; National Baptist Convention, U.S.A., Inc.; National Missionary Baptist Convention of America; Progressive National Baptist Convention, Inc. (Mukenga 1983).

2. Islam basically accepts the authenticity of Christianity and manifests a value system that includes (but supplements) Judeo-Christian values.

3. On the back cover of *Prophetic Fragments,* Henry Louis Gates, Jr., called West "the preeminent African-American intellectual of our time."

4. Black liberation theologians, a related but different category of thinkers, include Prof. James Cone, at Union Theological Seminary, and Rev. Albert Cleage, of Detroit's Church of the Black Madonna.

5. Those individuals who have chosen the Koran to supplement the Bible—for example, Imam Warith Deen Muhammad's American Muslim Mission—have access to a religious tradition that strongly encourages the complete transformation of society. The Nation of Islam relies on the social teaching of both Elijah Muhammad and the Koran, and those teachings strongly emphasize the social and economic development of inner cities.

6. The reader might also find it helpful to read the Book of Nehemiah in the Old Testament, or at least to read Linthicum's interpretation of it, in *City of God,* chapter 9.

Part Three
The Community Development Movement

The authors in Part Three take a close look at the rise of the community development corporations, their impact on the community development movement, and the challenges faced by these relatively new organizations. The community-based organizations have emerged as a new player in efforts to revitalize neighborhoods and have often been a key catalyst for neighborhood change.

The CDCs are nonprofit (501(C)3) organizations, that are neighborhood-based and with boards that are representative of the community. They are involved in various development activities in order to re-create the market within their neighborhoods. Most CDCs focus on housing as their initial activity; however, they also are involved in commercial development, economic development, industrial retention, and neighborhood planning. Some organizations have gained enough clout to be granted control over all land-use planning in their neighborhoods. The corporations are recognized as important players in neighborhood revitalization; thus 1990 federal housing legislation, as well as state legislation, included set-asides of funds earmarked for CDC-sponsored projects.

The organizations are examples of public/private partnerships that provide services within neighborhoods that are no longer attractive to the private market. They leverage resources and try to remove barriers in order to allow private reinvestment to occur.

The use of nonprofits as an appropriate vehicle to address community problems is not new. The historical underpinnings of these organizations can be found in the long-standing American tradition of the association or mutual aid society, the rise of the social settlement-house movement, and early efforts of nonprofits to meet the housing needs of low-income residents, as described in Chapters 1 and 3.

At the turn of the century, progressive leaders created housing trusts and limited dividend corporations to develop housing to meet the needs of the working poor. It was the inability of these organizations, given market realities and the drastic decline of private housing production during the Great Depression, that led to the first federal government-sponsored housing. The public housing program was developed to create jobs, eliminate slums, and provide housing to people who could not find housing in the private market. Even after the early success of public housing, however, there was never widespread support for the program, and it was continually attacked by the real estate industry.

The 1960s tested another solution to the nation's housing problems. Rather than direct involvement, the federal government would provide a subsidy to the private market to develop housing to meet the needs of low- and moderate-income Americans. Housing was built and managed by private developers and the mortgage was subsidized in order to make the rental rate more affordable. These programs were generally not successful.

Based on these historical precedents, community organizations that had often fought to have vacant and vandalized housing demolished came to the realization that they were tearing down their own neighborhood housing, which was actually a potential asset for revitalization. Housing development corporations were formed by these community organizations to redevelop housing in their neighborhoods. These new entities avoided one of the major problems of the past since it was the community, not people outside the neighborhood, who was deciding on the development of the housing. However, these groups faced problems similar to those at the turn of the century in terms of finding the capital for renovations.

The new neighborhood development organizations were initially staffed by community organizers who had to learn real estate development from the bottom up. In addition to learning about financing and acquisition, they also learned about rehabilitation, construction management, and property management. The greatest challenge was to find the means to finance the deals. These new nonprofit development organizations had to be creative and innovative to support their housing projects.

The CDCs have initiated innovative strategies in all aspects of the development process. They have created mechanisms to acquire property through receivership and tax foreclosure. They devised means to lower the cost of money through the use of linked deposits (deposits made by charitable organizations and churches that are paid a reduced interest rate, which allows the bank to lend at a reduced interest rate); through program-related investments from foundations (funds loaned to a project rather than a grant); by tapping existing sources of funds in new ways, such as the Community Development Block Grant program; and by lobbying for changes in federal tax policy that resulted in the creation in 1986 of the Low Income Housing Tax Credit. These efforts helped to build the confidence of organizations to accomplish projects that had an impact on the neighborhood and gave them a significant stake in the project and community.

Unlike previous approaches, CDCs included neighborhood residents on the boards who decided on the type of housing development that would take place. The development corporations have become important institutions because of their deep roots in the community. However, CDCs face significant challenges. The shortage of financing has meant that projects take a long time to develop and often are very complex; the number of units developed is usually fairly small and does not have immediate impact on much larger housing needs. Sometimes, tensions arise because of differences between the types of projects that can be financed and the types of projects the community needs. Avis Vidal looks at the status of CDCs in Chapter 10, considering where they have come from and what they are called upon to do. She documents their changing and expanding role, the present status of the movement and some of the challenges that the organizations face.

The rise of CDCs has been parallel in some communities with the development of housing coalitions, which often include CDCs as well as other advocates for the production of housing to meet the needs of very low-income citizens. Edward Goetz has studied the rise of these housing coalitions and in Chapter 11 describes the impact that they have had on neighborhood revitalization. He finds that housing coalitions are more likely to emerge in cities with a significant history of involvement in federal housing and urban development programs. Goetz concludes that much of the positive local response results from local governments being prodded by the low-income housing coalitions.

Rachel Bratt explores some of the broader issues that are raised by the community-based housing movement in Chapter 12. She looks at "ethical dilemmas" that exist within the community-based housing development organizations and that affect the types of services and housing they provide. These issues reflect the long-standing debate about how as a nation we are to meet the housing needs of low-income citizens. Bratt outlines these ethical dilemmas in detail and suggests that the issues must be faced and resolved. The rise of the mutual housing association (MHA) is one model that has attempted to respond to the dilemmas, and Bratt's analysis of MHAs helps to frame the issues that organizations involved in neighborhood revitalization must address.

10
Cdcs as Agents of Neighborhood Change: The State of the Art

Avis C. Vidal

THE COMMUNITY DEVELOPMENT MOVEMENT

Organizing at the local level, either for cooperative self-help activities or to promote civic improvements, is a strong tradition in the United States that goes back to the colonial period. In the 1960s, however, a new type of grassroots organization entered the neighborhood scene. Products of their communities, these groups were formed and are controlled by community stakeholders (residents, business proprietors, clergy, service providers, and so on). Although some groups serve a community that is defined by ethnicity, e.g., Hispanic Housing, most serve a neighborhood or cluster of neighborhoods.[1] Known generically as community development corporations, these groups are typically organized as nonprofit 501(c)3 corporations whose mission is the revitalization of poor or at-risk communities, including many communities of color.[2]

Spawned amid the activism of the War on Poverty in the 1960s, some early CDCs got their start with federal funding under the Equal Opportunity Act's Special Impact Program. Others are deeply rooted in the civil rights movement, often linked (at least initially) to a church with an activist ministry. During the 1970s new CDCs commonly sprang from neighborhood-based advocacy and protest activities, e.g., against construction of the inner-city portions of the interstate highway system or encroachment by large urban institutions such as universities and hospitals. In the 1980s sharp declines in federal support for affordable housing and a corresponding increase in corporate and philanthropic support for community development led to the formation of a new generation of organizations initially focused on housing issues.

Despite the dramatic changes that have occurred in the nation's urban neighborhoods and in the national political and fiscal climate since the community development movement began thirty years ago, the number of CDCs has expanded dramatically—testimony to their adaptability and their generally entrepreneurial character. Originally isolated from one another, they have increasingly found com-mon ground—forming local associations, working with public/private partner-ships, and tied into national networks by a new constellation of financial intermediaries and technical assistance providers that support their work.

In this chapter I profile the current state of this rapidly evolving system of com-munity development organizations and activities. I begin by describing the activi-ties and accomplishments of CDCs and outlining major factors that contribute to successful performance. I focus next on the support network of nonprofit, public, and private entities that has developed to strengthen CDCs and facilitate their work. I conclude with a discussion of major policy issues and challenges con-fronting CDCs and their supporters.

THE MOVEMENT HAS COME OF AGE

The community development movement has now matured into what many people consider a fledgling industry that includes more than 2,000 community-based development organizations (National Congress for Community Economic Devel-opment [NCCED] 1995). CDCs are now active throughout the United States, par-ticularly in cities. A survey conducted in 1989 of 133 U.S. cities with populations above 100,000 (75 percent of all cities) found one or more CDCs operating in 95 percent of them (Goetz 1993, 117). As CDCs have become better established, they have moved away from the protest actions that gave many early groups their start in favor of a wide range of activities and programs that provide direct benefits to their neighborhoods. Significantly, both their numbers and their level of activity continue to grow.

The vast majority of CDCs (90 percent) are involved in creating affordable housing. During the period from 1960 to 1990, CDCs produced an estimated 14 percent of all federally subsidized housing units, excluding public housing (C. Walker, 1993); by 1993 they had produced a total of 400,000 units (NCCED 1995). Their role in low-income housing production has become institutionalized in recent federal legislation. For example, the Cranston-Gonzalez National Afford-able Housing Act of 1990 mandates that at least 15 percent of each participating jurisdiction's funds under the HOME program be earmarked for use by qualified nonprofit housing producers, or Community Housing Development Organizations (CHDOs). Similarly, states are required to set aside 10 percent of their low-income housing tax credits for use by nonprofit providers.

In addition to housing production, CDCs are engaged in a wide variety of com-munity improvement and community-building activities. Resident services such as homeowner and tenant counseling, weatherization assistance, and housing for homeless people are common CDC programs. About two-thirds conduct advocacy and organizing activities. Over 60 percent provide some type of human services (emergency food pantry, job placement, child care, teen pregnancy counseling, and so on). Eighteen percent are active in commercial and industrial real estate development, and 23 percent engage in small-business lending or other types of business development work. The mix of activities conducted by any given CDC depends on perceived community needs, staff capacity, and the availability of funding and any needed technical assistance.

Although increasingly numerous, most CDCs remain relatively small, with a median staff size of seven people (C. Walker 1993). Even among larger CDCs, the median annual budget is substantially less than $1 million (Vidal 1992). Walker (1993) estimates that those CDCs active in housing produce about 23,000 units a year—roughly 13 percent of all federally subsidized units built annually (a combination of new construction and rehab)—and a majority manage the rental units they have built. Yet annual housing output varies greatly across organizations, with one-half of all CDCs sponsoring fewer than ten housing units a year, and 10 percent produced more than fifty per year, roughly twice the number produced by the typical small, independent, for-profit developers who constitute 75 percent of U.S. homebuilders (Vidal 1992; (C. Walker 1993). Production of commercial real estate is modest in scale—typically consisting of the rehabilitating of small convenience shopping centers or stores (perhaps with associated offices) on the main neighborhood shopping street. Some experienced CDCs are becoming more ambitious, however; those serving communities long underserved by major supermarket chains are beginning to fill this gap by developing local shopping centers anchored by a full-service supermarket.

A number of factors contribute to successful performance by CDCs. Since the corporations serve poor communities, outside resources and other types of support are critical (the role of the external institutional environment in supporting CDCs' work is discussed later in this chapter). But resources alone do not ensure success. Community development is a difficult endeavor, and resources continually fall short of community need. The CDCs that have been most productive over a sustained period have had the benefit of stable, capable leadership. They act strategically, e.g., rehabilitating a highly visible deteriorated building and then doing smaller supporting projects nearby, and set clear priorities. They seek to make their varied activities mutually reinforcing and to expand their range of activities in ways that enable their growing experience to increase the capacity of the organization.

Several older CDCs illustrate the varied mix of activities in which these organizations engage and the potential of strong organizations working over a sustained period on a strategic community improvement agenda:

Inquilinos Boricuas en Accion (IBA) is typical of the CDCs born out of community opposition to urban renewal plans. In 1966, a group of neighborhood residents and a local parish priest organized in response to plans by the City of Boston to raze an historically integrated neighborhood. Implementation of the plan would have displaced all residents of the targeted area. This group, which eventually evolved into IBA, won designation as the developer of the area and has completely rebuilt it. The group now manages the more than 850 units of housing it developed, has developed a small commercial center, runs a human services program (including counseling, advocacy, and legal services), rehabilitated a church as a cultural center, and incubated and spun off a child development center and a credit union.

New Community Corporation emerged in Newark's Central Ward after the 1967 riots in this poor, mainly African-American neighborhood. Originally supported by a network of churches active in the civil rights movement, it has become one of the nation's largest CDCs, managing 2,400 units of assisted housing and 100 units of transitional housing for formerly homeless families who receive a comprehensive package of services. It built and holds an equity interest in a large new supermarket, and its chain of day care centers provides for more than 600 children. New Community and its growing network of subsidiaries provide employment for over 1,100 people.

East Bay Asian Local Development Corporation (EBALDC) is a successful developer and manager of residential and commercial property in downtown Oakland, with over 600 housing units under management and development. In addition to providing child care, job training, and referrals to a variety of service providers for some of its tenants, the group operates a small-business revolving loan program and is a strong advocate for the interests of Oakland's Asian community. EBALDC's proficiency has led the city of Oakland to encourage the group to undertake housing activities in other neighborhoods. Within its own neighborhood the group seeks to add the growing Latino population to its constituency.

Project for Pride in Living [PPL] has concentrated its activities in the south Minneapolis neighborhood where it got its start in 1972 but develops and manages housing in a number of neighborhoods in both Minneapolis and St. Paul. Emphasizing the goal of helping low- and moderate-income people to become self-sufficient, PPL's many activities include a multifaceted Self-Sufficiency Program for families, youth programming, a tool lending library, and two small businesses, one of which is housed in the group's neighborhood shopping center.

Cities differ greatly in the amount of CDC activity they support and the pace at which that activity is growing. A few, like Boston and Chicago, are well known for their strong neighborhoods and active CDCs; more common are cities like New Orleans and Detroit where community-based development activity has only recently begun to take hold.

The number and strength of CDCs in a locality depends heavily on the willingness and ability of local political and business leaders to make neighborhood development a priority. Cities with an active group of effective CDCs tend to be places where the local business community has a strong tradition of civic activity and has made neighborhood development a priority; the long-term participation of business in the Allegheny Conference in Pittsburgh is a good example. Local government in these cities is more likely than government in other places to have gained experience and expertise in community development and to devote more resources and attention to strengthening neighborhoods. This combination has resulted in and been reinforced by a higher incidence in these cities of the public/private partnerships that are increasingly important providers of support for community-based development.

Cities with distinct, identifiable neighborhoods have developed more CDCs than have those without clear neighborhood structures; hence the cities of the Northeast and Midwest have tended to generate more CDCs than cities of comparable size in the South and the West. Developing and sustaining a grassroots organization presumably is easier when a group's turf is readily recognizable. However, a paucity of clearly defined and recognized neighborhoods does not preclude CDC development any more than the presence of such areas ensures their formation. As the CDC movement has grown stronger and as a national system of support has developed, the number of CDCs is increasing throughout the country, even in cities where they were few or nonexistent fifteen years ago. Thirty percent of the CDCs that have completed development projects were founded after 1985 (NCCED 1995), testimony to the movement's rapid recent expansion.

Support for the remarkable growth of CDCs derives both from growing recognition of their accomplishments and promise in strengthening poor communities and from the gradual withdrawal of other actors. This trend is clearest in the area of housing. With the demise of deep-subsidy federal production programs, developing affordable housing in poor inner-city communities has become financially unattractive to most for-profit developers. In many places CDCs are the only organizations willing and able to assemble the many sources of funding—so-called creative financing—necessary to produce low-income housing (Vidal 1995). One recent study found that the average CDC-sponsored housing development required funding from seven different sources, each with its own terms, restrictions, and requirements (Hebert et al. 1993). Equally important, state and local governments value the CDCs' goal of permanent housing affordability (Mayer 1990, 366; Goetz 1993, 116).

More generally, CDCs are credited with initiating a broad array of activities aimed not only at improving community life but also at strengthening the sense of community itself. Supporters most frequently cite the fact that CDCs are doing the difficult job of providing service and leadership in communities that need help and that other agencies cannot or will not serve: they have the ability to operate in complex environments where others cannot and a willingness to do projects that others will not because the projects are too small or too risky. They are also commonly praised for articulating a vision of the community's future and helping local people help themselves (Vidal 1992).

This is not to say that CDCs are without their detractors. Some critics argue that CDCs do not operate at great enough scale to have a meaningful impact on the fundamental problems of the inner cities. Others feel that their heavy involvement in housing has distracted many CDCs from their broader goals (Shiffman and Motley 1990). Some voice concern that CDCs are commonly vulnerable because they are small and undercapitalized (C. Walker 1993). And those concerned with governance issues have raised questions about whether CDCs are adequately accountable to their communities.

Despite these occasional reservations, CDCs have clearly come into their own. The political right sees in them the traditional virtues of self-help and bootstrapping, and the left views them through the community control lens of the l960s. Although federal funding for the needs of poor neighborhoods has declined from 1980 to 1992 and is likely to continue to do so, CDCs appear increasingly well positioned to take advantage of whatever funds are available. Federal policies support their active participation in major neighborhood-serving programs, and they continue to gain support from states, localities, foundations, and corporations.

PROFILE OF THE INSTITUTIONAL SUPPORT SYSTEM

On the front lines in working to strengthen distressed inner-city neighborhoods, CDCs make much of their impact by leveraging resources from sources outside the community. Their accomplishments are thus the product of the combination of their own efforts and the resources and support of other institutions: government agencies, intermediaries, foundations, banks, education and training institutions, trade associations, and technical assistance providers.

These institutional supporters have increased rapidly in number and sophistication since 1980. Their growth in tandem with the growth of the CDCs themselves is no accident. A dense network of CDCs both requires and attracts support; most CDC successes require some outside support, and they in turn increase the reputation of community-based development and reflect well on supporters. The relationship between a system of support for community development and level of CDC activity (number of groups and what they accomplish) is thus reciprocal; success breeds success.

As a result, in places like Boston, Chicago, Cleveland, Minneapolis, New York, and San Francisco, where CDCs have become strong and numerous, supportive institutions have learned to work effectively both with the CDCs and with one another, providing complementary types of assistance and coordinating their activities. In other places, particularly cities in the South and Southwest (e.g., Miami, Dallas, and New Orleans), this learning process is more recent, and support for CDCs is more fragmented and uneven.

Most national supporters and local support systems initially focused on housing production. Seriously distressed neighborhoods often need to be stabilized residentially before other types of development can occur. Equally important, housing is less difficult and less risky than other types of development CDCs undertake; starting with housing reduces the difficulty of raising needed financing and increases the likelihood that early activities will be successful.

Once the CDCs' ability to succeed with housing was established, attention shifted to getting CDC production "to scale." A central concern was and remains the capacity of small community-based organizations to produce and rehabilitate units at a level that will have a significant impact on inner-city neighborhoods. In this vein, a number of local intermediaries have mounted capacity-building programs that seek to make CDCs better managed and technically stronger. Most recently, supporters are turning their attention to helping CDCs undertake a wider range of activities (the challenges involved in doing so are discussed later in this chapter).

Regardless of the activities being undertaken, CDCs need three basic types of assistance from their supporters: funding, technical assistance, and political support. When the support system is at its best, these key elements are designed and coordinated into programs that meet the particular needs of CDCs and their communities.

Financial support is best organized and most widely available for housing construction and rehabilitation. The system has recognized the primary financial barriers to low-income housing development, including the availability of predevelopment funding, mortgage funds, equity capital, and gap financing (Goetz 1993; C. Walker 1993). It has responded by making available to CDCs a combination of mortgages, tax credit equity, and grants (which are necessary to subsidize production to keep unit rents affordable)—although the CDC's task in piecing these elements together into financially viable deals often remains formidable.

The major sources of financial support for project development are federal, state, and local governments, foundations, and banks and corporations. The public sector typically makes its funding available directly to the CDC developer. Other partners commonly channel their dollars through national intermediaries or local partnerships.

Technical support is most important to smaller, younger groups that have not become large enough to support specialized in-house expertise or to help groups of any size expand into an unfamiliar line of activity. Availability of technical assistance, like funding, is broadest and deepest in support of housing development. Commercial, industrial, and business development and property management are much less widely supported. Consultants (both individuals and nonprofit or for-profit firms) and educational institutions are the primary providers of technical assistance and training.

Finally, many members of the support system are in a position to provide less tangible—but quite valuable—kinds of assistance. These include networking, advising, coordinating activities and resources to make them readily available and mutually supportive, building a local culture conducive to charitable giving, and advocating community-based approaches as the preferred vehicle of social and economic development. Public agencies are the most ubiquitous potential supporters whose mission is consistent with the goals of community-based development. Hence, public-sector participation in the support system at all levels of government is especially important.

Most broadly, public policy establishes the legal framework within which community development takes place. At the national level, the tax-exempt status of CDCs and federal income tax provisions applicable to real estate, i.e., the low-income housing tax credit, depreciation rules, and deductibility of interest payments, are critical to the financial viability of CDCs and their projects. Policies at the state and local level can be comparably important:

> Seven states have legislation or constitutional provisions that restrict the use of public funds for housing (Berenyi 1989)—provisions that clearly inhibit CDCs' work. Conversely, state enabling legislation for limited equity cooperatives, like Minnesota's, enable CDCs to provide home ownership opportunities to low-income households. Progressive city practices, such as San Francisco's ordinance to preserve the low-income housing stock by restricting condominium conversion and the destruction of SROs, can also facilitate CDCs' work. (Vidal 1992)

The public sector is the largest provider of financial support for community development—a natural result of the fact that improving the well-being of poor urban communities is an acknowledged public purpose. Despite consistent declines in new federal funding for housing during the 1980s and early 1990s, the federal government remains the single largest financial supporter of CDCs; its support includes a number of programs, such as Community Development Block Grants and Home Ownership Made Easy (HOME), that are actually distributed by states and localities.

Partly in response to federal withdrawal and partly in response to growing recognition of the efficacy of CDCs, states and localities have been expanding their support for affordable housing programs used by the development corporations. Before 1980 there were only forty-four state-funded housing programs and most of these were in just three states—California, Connecticut, and Massachusetts. Over the next decade, however, state spending on housing and community development more than quadrupled, jumping from $621.6 million in 1980 to $2.9 billion in 1990 (Goetz 1993, 78).

Cities expanded their support as well. By 1990, 82 percent of the cities with populations of at least 100,000 that had active nonprofit housing developers provided them with project financing, as did 63 percent of the states. More than half of these cities also provided nonprofits with administrative funding, predevelopment loans, and technical assistance, with a similar proportion of the states also providing such assistance (Goetz 1993, 122).

Cities also provide support in a variety of other forms, including some opportunities, such as tax abatements, low-cost land and buildings owned by the city (e.g., because prior owners failed to pay property taxes), or project-related infrastructure, not available from other sources. These types of support are commonly tied to locally designed programs tailored to local circumstances. For example, New York City's housing agency administers a program under which local nonprofit groups develop multifamily low-income housing in conjunction with LISC and the Enterprise Foundation. The city provides vacant, publicly owned buildings and low-interest mortgages, and the intermediaries bring in equity capital through the syndication of Low Income Housing Tax Credits. The intermediaries provide these groups with extensive technical assistance throughout the development and operation of the buildings. The program has produced abut 6,000 low-income housing units from 1989 through 1994.

Although many CDC supporters such as state and local governments are familiar organizations taking on new roles or adopting new programs, the intermediaries are an institutional invention of the community development field. They have played a central role in expanding the base of financial, technical, and political support for the community development movement since 1980. Functioning as specialized community development banks, the intermediaries receive grants and low-interest loans from foundations, banks, corporations, and public-sector agencies and use the resulting financial pool to provide grants, loans, and credit enhancements to CDCs.

The success of the intermediaries derives from their ability to meet the distinctive institutional needs of both financial supporters and community organizations. CDCs work in weak markets—marginal neighborhoods where property values and resident incomes cannot support debt. This means that CDCs do high-risk work, making their projects less secure investments than conventional developments. Intermediaries are critical because they facilitate risk-sharing and enable all participants, especially those in the private sector, to reduce risk exposure. Funders benefit from intermediaries' experience and expertise in assessing risk and in structuring projects and financial packages that avoid unnecessary exposure. Funders also save the administrative costs of dealing with individual CDCs and evaluating individual funding proposals. For their part, CDCs benefit from the technical and program-design expertise of the intermediaries. Finally, intermediaries serve as quality control guarantors.

The best-known intermediaries are national in scope. The three largest, described below, have expanded their range of programming to support a growing array of community development activities and to provide technical assistance to the CDCs with which they work. The oldest of the major national community development intermediaries is the Neighborhood Reinvestment Corporation (NRC), a public nonprofit corporation established by Congress in the 1978 Neighborhood Reinvestment Corporation Act "to revitalize older urban neighborhoods by mobilizing public, private, and community resources at the neighborhood level." NRC and its companion organization, Neighborhood Housing Services of

America, along with over 180 local Neighborhood Housing Services organizations, form the NeighborWorks network. Funded annually by Congress, NRC provides local NHS groups with direct financial assistance, technical assistance in developing local lender pools or acquiring low-cost financing, and assistance in starting local revolving loan funds (Neighborhood Reinvestment Corporation 1994).

Founded in 1979 by the Ford Foundation, the Local Initiatives Support Corporation seeks to build the financial and technical capacity of community development corporations to sponsor and shape community development. LISC has helped more than 1,000 CDCs in thirty-four cities and regions of the country build or rehabilitate 53,000 affordable homes and develop over 9 million square feet of commercial and industrial space. LISC programs support economic development, social service delivery, and job creation. Since its inception, LISC and its affiliate, the National Equity Fund (NEF), has raised more than $1.3 billion in donations and investments from more than 1,200 corporations and foundations, individuals, and public agencies (LISC 1994).

The Enterprise Foundation was founded in 1981 to develop affordable housing in low-income neighborhoods and to move people out of poverty and into mainstream American life. Working in over 150 locations and with over 500 neighborhood groups in the Enterprise Network, the Enterprise Foundation has helped develop more than 36,000 homes. In addition, the Jobs Network has made over 21,600 placements for hard-to-employ individuals. The Enterprise Foundation and its financial subsidiary, the Enterprise Social Investment Corporation (ESIC), have raised over $655 million to finance low-income housing through loans, grants, and tax credit investments (Enterprise Foundation 1994).

Significantly, the major national intermediaries have often acted as catalysts in forming local intermediaries, sometimes in the form of local housing partnerships that eventually incorporate as nonprofit organizations, broaden the base of local financial and political support for community-based development, and take on a locally developed support agenda. One of the oldest and best known is the Metropolitan Boston Housing Partnership, which has a

board of directors composed of representatives of its members: major banks, insurance companies, and utilities, and other local businesses; the city of Boston; the state housing finance agency; local universities; and local housing and community development organizations. The Partnership's professional staff structures and arranges financing for discrete "programs" in which varying numbers of CDCs are selected to participate. These programs use state and local housing money as well as other sources of funding, sometimes including equity participation by local corporations. The centralized structuring of these programs through the Partnership facilitates access to resources, relieves individual CDCs of some of the burdens of assembling complex project financing, and effectively leaves the Partnership with some of the responsibility for long-run program success. Although created to support low-income housing production, it has become increasingly concerned about and involved with helping participating CDCs to address housing management problems and related tenant services issues. (Vidal 1992: 132–33)

Most recently, the Partnership has begun doing strategic planning to cope with anticipated declines in federal funding for housing.

National and local intermediaries have helped CDCs to tap substantially increased levels of corporate and philanthropic support. Total grant support from these sources was $179 million in 1991—up 72 percent from only two years earlier (Council for Community-Based Development 1993). Further, the national intermediaries and the organizational networks they represent have undoubtedly been an important force behind the federal government's moves to give CDCs and other nonprofits a growing role in providing affordable housing.

CHALLENGES CONFRONTING THE COMMUNITY DEVELOPMENT SYSTEM

CDCs and their support system confront a number of serious challenges in the years ahead. Some of these are the product of changes in their environment that are likely to make their work more difficult. Others derive from the way in which the system has grown and matured and the "natural" growth pressures it will face in the future.

Difficulty Ahead for Community Development

Three major trends in housing policy and central city housing markets signal that community development—already a daunting task—is likely to become more difficult: reduced availability of public funding, greater federal reliance on block grants as the preferred form of funding, and the combination of the continuing shift to demand-side subsidies and on-going weakness in the housing markets where CDCs work.

First, public-sector funding for poor communities shows all signs of becoming significantly tighter. To the extent that changes in programs that provide direct assistance to poor households (e.g., Aid to Families with Dependent Children, Food Stamps) impose tighter eligibility guidelines or receive funding streams that do not keep pace with household need, the problems of poor communities will increase. Federal efforts to shift responsibility for many programs to state and local governments will surely place greater pressure on their budgets, rendering them less able than they were in the 1980s to make up for federal spending cuts in housing and other programs commonly used by CDCs. At the same time, federal funding for those programs CDCs use appear likely to face continuing reductions. Although CDCs can continue to develop rental units using the Low Income Housing Tax Credit, they must combine it with other sources of subsidy if they are to keep rents low enough to be affordable to moderate-income people, and those other sources of subsidy will be in increasingly short supply.

Second, the program structure of federal programs CDCs can use for housing and other community development activities is changing in ways that connote a mix of good news and bad news. Federal housing and community development funds are increasingly being consolidated into block grant programs.[3] This gives states and localities greater flexibility to design programs that are sensitive to local needs and circumstances (like the New York City program already described). The shift may benefit housing groups operating in robust institutional settings. Those state and local governments that already rely on nonprofits to carry out their housing programs and that provide them with financial and technical assistance to do so will probably treat new housing block grants in the same manner as they did CDBG and HOME block grants. However, in places where CDCs are fewer, weaker, or have limited city support, they may face serious funding problems since public agencies in these places may simply lack the requisite capacity to handle the new planning and program design responsibilities being handed to them—much less have the experience needed to fashion programs that can be effectively accessed by community organizations.

At the same time, the shift to block grants will mean that funds traditionally used by CDCs will be combined with funds that have been supporting other types of organizations and programs. This shift creates uncertainty among diverse constituencies about whether, and at what level, they will be served. It will be a major challenge for CDCs and their supporters to develop effective relationships both with city and state agencies and with other advocacy coalitions to avoid unproductive conflict over shrinking funding pools among the various advocates for the poor. Further, block grant programs are generally politically easier to scale down than categorical ones since it is less clear exactly whom funding cuts will affect.

Finally, a constellation of factors are combining to make CDC-sponsored housing developments financially vulnerable. Most housing developments subsidized through the federal CDBG, HOME, and Low Income Housing Tax Credit programs and through state and local programs do not offer subsidies for ongoing operating costs (Connerly 1993; Stegman and Holden 1987). Instead, they provide up-front subsidies to projects in the form of grants and low-interest loans. Although these subsidies make housing initially affordable to low-income families, they are not structured to cover such operating costs as utilities, maintenance, and taxes. In the absence of operating-support subsidies, developments encounter serious financial trouble if vacancies increase or if costs rise more than anticipated (Bratt et al. 1994).

Federal housing policy has been undergoing a continuing shift from project-based subsidies to housing vouchers; tenants receiving vouchers can use them to rent any apartment they choose (as long as the landlord is willing to accept a subsidized tenant). This demand-side subsidy approach has the virtue of giving subsidized households greater choice—but it also increases the financial risk of owners of rental property, who must retain and attract recipients of rental vouchers if they are to receive federal subsidies.

These subsidies are essential to the financial health of many CDC-sponsored developments. Unfortunately, in many cases CDCs are likely to find it difficult to attract adequate numbers of subsidized tenants (i.e., voucher holders). Many central-city housing markets are quite weak as a result of continued population loss. In general, the weaker the market, the more choices households have in selecting apartments and neighborhoods because of lower rents and higher vacancy rates. CDC-owned developments in neighborhoods widely viewed as being "less desirable," particularly those in high-crime neighborhoods, will find it increasingly hard to attract and retain subsidized tenants. Without them, the housing itself will be progressively more difficult to maintain in good condition—and decline in the physical and financial condition of the housing bodes ill not only for the residents but also for the viability and reputation of the CDCs that own it.

Challenges Related to Growth and Maturation

The rapid growth of the community development movement is properly seen as evidence of the potential of this approach to addressing some of the problems of poor urban neighborhoods. At the same time, this growth and the sense of accomplishment that accompany it present three strategic problems for the movement. These are the continuing uneven geographic distribution of CDCs and related systems of support, the risk of overburdening CDCs by pressing them to expand too quickly, and the need to develop support for a broader community-building agenda without overselling the promise of CDCs, thereby setting them up to fail.

The number and sophistication of CDCs vary sharply across cities and regions because CDCs form in response to local events and circumstances. The institutional support system is correspondingly uneven. Some cities and states host more, and more vibrant, CDCs and have richer institutional support systems than others. Smaller cities and areas lacking in local foundations and traditions of institutional collaboration are less likely to nurture strong support systems.

The geographic unevenness of CDC activity underscores the central role of the national intermediaries. They are crucial in providing CDCs located in institutionally barren environments with the necessary financial, technical, political, and moral support for fostering a viable low-income housing industry. With the national government reducing its support for CDCs it is increasingly up to the intermediaries to standardize and simplify the development process and find ways of disseminating their assistance as broadly as possible. It is also incumbent on the intermediaries, with their strong corporate and foundation backing, to try to cultivate supportive local networks for CDCs. LISC, Enterprise, and NRC have already taken up this challenge—as evidenced by their growing roster of local offices, their engagement in the National Community Development Initiative, and their joint sponsorship of the Consortium of Housing and Asset Management to help CDCs achieve become better property management. Much remains to be done, however, to give the movement truly national presence.

Second, in some settings, the support system sees CDCs as the best (or sometimes the only) organizational vehicle for strengthening poor neighborhoods. Since very poor neighborhoods commonly suffer from a paucity of strong institutions, successful CDCs may be pressed by agencies that see no other capable neighborhood partners to take on more challenging responsibilities. In some cities, e.g., New York and Boston, CDCs have—with the encouragement and help of the city and intermediaries—have assumed ownership of substantial inventories of low-income housing that is in poor condition, inadequately financed, or both. The federal government increasingly sees community-based nonprofits as preferred purchasers for publicly owned assisted housing, much of which is quite troubled. But there are signs that without careful organizational development, sufficient resources, and in some cases "growth control," community organizations can become overwhelmed. This greatly increases the risk that their work will decline in quality, undermining both the quality of service they deliver to local residents and their credibility within and outside the community.

More broadly, the maturation of the CDC movement is expanding the CDC agenda. As CDCs establish themselves as developers, they simultaneously acquire a portfolio of property that must be managed. Many CDCs choose to manage that housing themselves, either out of the conviction that they should control and be responsible for this community resource or because they lack good alternatives. Housing management in the inner city is notoriously difficult, however, and it requires a different set of organizational skills than development—skills that many CDCs are still in the process of building.[4]

Housing ownership, and the direct daily contact it brings with residents, also makes CDCs more acutely aware of their communities' needs. In response, foundations and intermediaries are taking the lead in devising a variety of new programs to support CDCs in expanding the range of services they offer (to include such activities as child care, job placement, or youth programs) and in becoming more effective brokers and advocates on behalf of their neighborhoods.

These programs are clearly an effort to address pressing community issues, and most CDCs have always had this holistic notion of community development and service at the core of their mission. Housing was the "point of entry" because it was the sphere of activity in which it seemed most likely that CDCs could demonstrate clear successes and thereby gain credibility and access to additional resources, both financial and intangible. Expanding the agenda will require careful attention to the challenge of expanding the funding base (which requires asserting that positive results can be achieved) without promising more than CDCs can actually deliver. Even if organizational capacity issues can be dealt with (and building capacity itself requires resources), the problems facing inner cities are not primarily of their own making. They are the product of strong national, sometimes even global, trends in the nation's economic, social, and political life. Addressing them requires more than the work of even the strongest network of CDCs—and the community development movement bears part of the responsibility for keeping that central fact prominent in the discussion of national urban policy.

NOTES

1. Rural CDCs typically serve a much larger area, e.g., one or more counties, and assist low- and moderate-income people throughout that area. They are not discussed in this chapter.

2. I use the term "community development corporation" generically to refer to the full range of community-based development organizations, which may have a variety of names, e.g., Neighborhood Housing Service (NHS), neighborhood improvement association, local development corporation. Their common characteristics are that they are incorporated as nonprofit (usually 501[C]3) organizations and are engaged in physical or economic development, or both, in their communities.

3. Many federal-housing subsidy programs were initially created to meet public housing, housing for the elderly or for people with disabilities, units for formerly homeless families and individuals. Over time, such programs are being consolidated into block grants that recipient cities spend for a variety of specified purposes.

4. Like their for-profit counterparts, CDCs create legally separate entities for each real estate development they build so that if it encounters financial trouble the funds of the parent corporation will not be at risk. Non–real estate activities may also be legally distinct, e.g., small businesses, revolving loan funds, credit unions.

11

The Community-based Housing Movement and Progressive Local Politics

Edward G. Goetz

From roots in the neighborhood movement of the 1970s, a community-based housing movement became an important force during the 1980s in triggering the expansion of local government involvement in housing policy. This local housing movement was made up of neighborhood activists, social service professionals, tenant activists, and low-income housing advocates who attempted to get state and local governments to respond to the growing housing problems in the 1980s and to a shrinking federal commitment to housing assistance. The movement is notable for its focus on local governments, for the blending of neighborhood activists with service professionals, and for a coherent agenda of community-based housing policy that focuses on nonmarket housing, nonprofit development, and community-based planning as means of solving local housing problems.

Prior to the 1980s, the federal government was the dominant actor in U.S. housing policy. State and local governments spent a minuscule amount of money on housing assistance, relying almost completely on implementing a range of federal housing policies. Housing advocates who wanted to have an impact on policy during these years focused lobbying efforts in Washington. Indeed, the neighborhood movement, a federation of local community organizations, did this during the 1970s when it mobilized around the issue of neighborhood disinvestment. The neighborhood movement was able to achieve national legislative success in the form of the Home Mortgage Disclosure Act of 1975 and the Community Reinvestment Act of 1977 (Squires 1992). Both acts required lending institutions to disclose where their loans were going and provided an opportunity for community activists to challenge the lending practices of local banks. The neighborhood movement culminated in the creation of a national organization of neighborhoods and a presidential commission convened to analyze the conditions of the nation's urban neighborhoods. During the Carter administration a number of HUD housing and economic development programs were created or modified to incorporate an explicit neighborhood orientation.

The political environment for neighborhood-based urban policy changed dramatically at the end of the 1970s. President Carter's Commission for a National Agenda for the Eighties recommended facilitating the movement of jobs and capital out of "obsolete" inner cities and, on a regional level, increasingly out of the Northeast and Midwest (Squires 1994). This policy was carried out in the name of enhancing the nation's economic competitiveness. President Ronald Reagan slashed housing and other domestic programs, reduced the level of federal aid to local governments, and reoriented federal urban policy to focus on facilitating regional economic restructuring rather than on ameliorating the social impact of that restructuring (Harrison and Bluestone 1988). Urban policy, such as it was, came to be focused on facilitating the movement of labor to pursue jobs that were increasingly being created in the Sunbelt or in suburban and nonmetropolitan areas. In housing, the Reagan administration attempted to limit significantly the role of HUD, preferring to leave housing in the realm of the private sector (Hays 1985). The HUD housing budget was reduced by more than 80 percent from 1978 to 1986. The community development block grant, the major federal urban program and a main source of housing assistance for local governments, was also reduced during this time. As Congress went along with Reagan budget cuts and the reordering of national priorities, local governments became more important actors in delivering housing and social services.

The reordering of national priorities coincided with the deterioration of housing conditions in most urban areas. Rents rose at a rate higher than the increase in personal income (Leonard et al. 1989). A large portion of the affordable housing stock was lost to downtown revitalization, a trend that was at least twenty years old at the time but that peaked during the early 1980s (Hoch and Slayton 1989), and to the "filtering up" of a significant portion of affordable housing units through gentrification, condominium conversions, or price inflation (Turner and Edwards 1993).

The local housing movement emerged in this environment of federal budget cuts and deteriorating local conditions. During the 1980s advocacy coalitions for low-income populations organized to focus political pressure on state legislatures and city councils. At first the coalitions reacted to Reaganomics and the slashing of social programs early in Reagan's first term. Gradually, from this initial response, a growing housing movement emerged and incorporated not only social service advocates but neighborhood groups and community development corporations who had been working on urban poverty issues for years. These advocacy coalitions incorporated a wide variety of organizations, some neighborhood-based and some service-based.

In this chapter the emergence of these coalitions and their impact on local housing policy and planning will be described. The data come from three primary sources: a national survey of local housing officials conducted in 1991, a survey of local planners from 1992, and case studies of three U.S. cities—Knoxville, Tennessee; Hartford, Connecticut; and Oakland, California. The 1991 survey of 173 cities with populations over 100,000 resulted in 133 responses, a 77 percent response rate. The survey of planners (using the same population of 173 major U.S. cities) generated 140 responses, or an 81 percent response rate. The profiles of the respondents to the 1991 questionnaire, the 1992 questionnaire, and the full population of cities with populations over 100,000 are virtually identical by region, size, and type (central city or suburb).[1]

THE EMERGENCE OF THE LOCAL HOUSING MOVEMENT

The extent of the local housing movement can be measured by the existence of low-income housing advocacy coalitions (LIHACs) in most large cities and states in the United States. Most of the LIHACs in large U.S. cities formed during the 1980s, with the greatest increase occurring after 1984 (see Figure 11.1).[2]

The survey evidence suggests that these groups exist in every region of the United States, from over half of the large cities in the South to more than three-

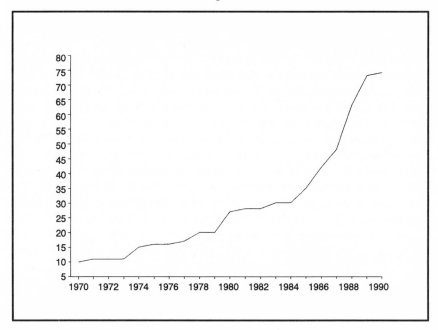

Figure 11.1. Number of Local Housing Advocacy Groups in Sample Cities, Through 1990 (Source: Adapted from Goetz, *Shelter Burden: Local Politics and Progressive Housing Policy* [Philadelphia: Temple University Press, 1993])

quarters of northeastern cities (see Table 11.1). LIHACs were more likely to emerge in central cities than in large suburbs (72 percent of large cities had a LIHAC compared to 32 percent of suburbs in the sample).

Table 11.1. Regional Low-income Housing Advocacy Coalitions in U.S. Cities, Populations over 100,000

	Northeast	Midwest	South	West
LIHAC	14	20	26	26
	(78 percent)	(74 percent)	(53 percent)	(68 percent)
No LIHAC	4	7	23	12
	(22 percent)	(26 percent)	(47 percent)	(32 percent)
n = 133				

Among the cities in the sample, community-based housing coalitions were more likely to exist in larger cities; the nineteen cities with populations over 500,000 had housing advocacy coalitions. Housing coalitions were also more likely to emerge in cities with a significant history of involvement in federal housing and urban development programs; 79 percent of the cities with a high degree of prior experience with federal urban programs had a housing coalition compared to only 37 percent of cities with little or no experience.[3]

Discriminant analysis, using a series of demographic and housing stock measures, allows a multivariate profile of cities with LIHACs. The coefficients listed enable us to determine the housing market and economic conditions that distinguish between cities with LIHACs and those without. Higher standardized coefficients mean that those variables have greater discriminant power. Thus, we see that a number of variables distinguish the two types of cities; cities with LIHACs have greater problems with the cost and availability of affordable housing, have larger populations (though lower rates of population growth), had significantly higher rates of poverty in 1980, and lower rates of overcrowded housing. The canonical correlation indicates that 55 percent of the variance is explained by the variables listed.

Standardized Coefficients

Cost and availability	
of affordable housing	.443
Substandard housing	−.035
Old housing stock	.253
Overcrowdedness	−.811
1984 population	.529
1985 unemployment	.052
1983 per capita income	.328
Municipal debt-to-	
revenue ratio	.281
1980 poverty	.805

1970–1980 population
growth   −.284
Canonical correlation   .5489

THE POLITICAL IMPACT OF THE LOCAL HOUSING
MOVEMENT

The local housing movement has advocated a series of community-based or "progressive" policies as a means of addressing urban housing problems. The particular solution put forward by the movement includes greater regulation of the private-sector development process, leveraging resources for affordable housing from the private development market, greater reliance on nonmarket actors (such as nonprofit CDCs) and alternative property ownership models, and community-based planning. Research has indicated that the housing movement has been effective at the local level in enacting these particular progressive policies and also in triggering a greater housing policy activism by state and local governments more generally (Goetz 1991; 1993; 1994).

Moreover, the housing movement was seen by local officials as an influential actor in local housing policy debates. In those cities where LIHACs exist, local officials were significantly more likely to perceive the movement as influential (see Table 11.2).

Table 11.2.   Public Officials' Perception of
Local Housing Movement Influence

	LIHAC	No LIHAC
Widely influential (pct.)	26 (31)	3 (8)
Sporadically influential (pct.)	41 (48)	8 (22)
Not influential (pct.)	11 (13)	9 (25)
Not involved in policymaking (pct.)	7 (8)	16 (44)

n = 121, 12 missing cases

Note: X^2 = 29.12
$p < .001$

A separate survey of housing planners confirms the findings listed in Table 11.2. In 1992 planners from cities with populations over 100,000 were sent questionnaires related to the process of creating their first Comprehensive Housing Affordability Strategy (CHAS).[4] The strategy was required of local governments by the 1990 National Affordable Housing Act and was intended to ensure a comprehensive and inclusive process of housing needs assessment and policy strategizing by jurisdictions receiving federal housing assistance. Respondents were asked to rate the influence of different actors in the development of their local CHAS. Included among the actors evaluated were CDCs, neighborhood groups, and low-income housing advocates.

For the mean responses to these questions, broken down by cities with a formal low-income housing advocacy coalition and those cities without one, see Table 11.3. The survey responses of local housing planners listed in Table 11.3 are consistent with the perceptions of local housing officials reported in Table 11.2. Planners perceive a greater level of influence for community-based housing advocates in cities with a formal coalition. They attributed a significantly higher level of planning influence to CDCs and low-income housing advocates in those cities where a formal LIHAC exists. Though respondents also attributed a slightly higher level of influence to neighborhood representatives in cities with a LIHAC, the difference is not statistically significant.

Table 11.3.   Influence of Groups in CHAS Planning Process, Difference in Means

	Cities with LIHAC	Cities without LIHAC	Sig.
CDCs	3.26	1.57	**
Neighborhood representatives	2.77	2.50	n.s.
Low-income housing advocates	3.33	2.60	*

Note: Measured on a scale of 1 to 5, 1 = no influence, 5 = very influential
  * p < .05
 ** p < .001

Actual CHAS documents filed with the federal government allow an analysis of the impact of LIHACs on housing expenditure plans. The strategy requires city officials to list anticipated resources and an expenditure plan for housing programs in which officials estimate revenues from private, local, state, and federal sources. The influence of the local housing movement goes beyond the perceptions of local officials, as already described. Previous research has shown that the movement has been able to prod local governments into adopting a range of innovative programs. We can also hypothesize that LIHACs will have an impact on spending levels and the degree to which local governments support housing assistance with their own revenues.

Cities with housing coalitions are compared to those without for their reliance on local funding sources and for their planned per capita expenditures on housing (see Table 11.4). The data show that cities with a LIHAC use a significantly higher proportion of nonfederal funds in their housing programs (33 percent to 24 percent). In addition, the overall level of housing expenditures, on a per capita basis, is significantly higher for cities with LIHACs ($175 per capita to $101). Indeed, across all categories, cities with LIHACs show a greater per capita effort in housing. Especially significant are the nonfederal sources of funds, almost three times larger per capita in cities with LIHACs.

Table 11.4. Anticipated Housing Revenues from 1991 CHAS

	Cities with LIHACs	Cities without LIHACs	Sig.
Percentage of housing revenues from nonfederal sources	33.12	23.76	*
Per capita revenues from			
federal government	107.58	74.63	*
own sources	28.15	6.92	*
private sector	24.5	9.80	*
all nonfederal sources	69.22	24.5	**
all sources	174.58	100.60	**

Note: * p < .05
      ** p < .01

The results of these national surveys show the local housing movement to be influential in local housing policy development. It has had success in enacting the progressive agenda of local housing policies, and it is perceived by local officials to be central to the policymaking and planning process. The three case studies that follow provide examples of how the local housing movement was created and how it operates in cities.

CASE STUDIES

Knoxville

In late 1987 a coalition of thirteen community organizations in Knox County, Tennessee, including neighborhood groups representing the near-downtown neighborhoods in Knoxville, launched a community reinvestment campaign by wrapping a red ribbon around First Tennessee Bank's downtown office tower to symbolize their allegation that the bank had systematically disinvested (redlined) low-income neighborhoods in the city. The coalition called itself the Community Reinvestment Act Regional Steering Committee, and it had completed a three-year analysis of lending practices by the region's top banks. First Tennessee, according to the group, was the worst; from 1984 through 1986 the bank had loaned less than $300,000 in low-income neighborhoods compared to $6.75 million in the highest-income areas of the city. In 1988 the coalition challenged First Tennessee's status as the depository institution for city funds while simultaneously broadening its target to include other banks in the area. After individual negotiations, the coalition coaxed lending agreements from all of the targeted banks by January 1989.

The banks, neighborhood representatives, local government officials, and other local community-based organizations formed an ad hoc committee to explore systematically the reinvestment needs of the city's neighborhoods. The committee was able to identify projects of common interest in neighborhood lending that would help banks satisfy Community Reinvestment Act requirements and be leveraged by the city's CDBG funds. The negotiations were assisted by the new mayor (elected in late 1987), who was more responsive to neighborhood concerns than his predecessor. The mayor's office committed the director of community development to the reinvestment negotiations. The adhoc committee investigated forms of partnership taking place in other cities, and shortly afterward the city announced a neighborhood revitalization program, the Partnership for Neighborhood Improvement (PNI). It had three components: housing development and reinvestment to be coordinated by a new entity called the Knoxville Housing Partnership (KHP), small business and job creation to be coordinated by the Small Business Action Council, and capacity building for community-based organizations to be provided by a third new entity, the Center for Neighborhood Development.

The KHP board of directors is made up of neighborhood representatives, bankers, representatives from the homebuilding and real estate industries, and local and county officials. The director of the Knoxville Department of Community Development regards KHP as the lead agency for local housing efforts. As such, KHP is more than simply an advocacy group; it is, simultaneously, an implementation organization for local public and private affordable housing programs. KHP has created its own program, FirstHomes, that provides mortgage assistance, rehabilitation loans, and homeownership counseling for first-time homebuyers. The program is available countywide and is restricted to households earning less than 80 percent of the area median. Nine area banks serve as lenders for the program. KHP also coordinates affordable housing development activities in the county, channeling resources to existing community-based developers. Although a 1992 KHP-sponsored initiative to create a local housing trust fund was voted down by the city council, the continuing support of the mayor, the city housing agency, and the continued efforts by the Partnership did persuade the council to accept a scaled-down demonstration program the next year.

More recently, KHP has taken on the role of developer for multifamily housing. Though KHP officials insist that the role has been assumed reluctantly and only in those areas in which no suitable local developer exists, some community activists are concerned that KHP may neglect its coordinating role and the support of existing neighborhood groups as its own development agenda increases. A community advocate said, "I'm trying to look at KHP from the point of view of not just housing production, but how can housing production be an empowering experience for low-income people and community-based organizations in the neighborhoods." The tension between KHP's role as an advocate and a means of neighborhood empowerment and its responsibilities as a developer and implementation agency for local housing programs has not been fully resolved by its members and supporters. The Partnership is considering offering technical assistance to neighborhood groups interested in developing affordable housing as a way of increasing capacity at the neighborhood level. Potentially the most lasting accomplishment of the movement is the increased level of cooperation between community-based organizations, lenders, and city officials. The cooperation began with the reinvestment strategies that emerged from the CRA battles in 1987–1988 but has extended into more recent collaborations on housing projects and into the planning by the city and local service agencies in social program development.

Hartford

The Hartford Neighborhood Housing Coalition (NHC) began in 1979 as an ad hoc group organized to provide input to the city council on neighborhood-level development priorities. There was a feeling among neighborhood leaders at the time that the corporate sector in Hartford was much more organized and unified in its perception of the development priorities for the city. The creation of the ad hoc neighborhood-based organization was an attempt to bring together neighborhood-based groups from across the city to articulate a single vision of the city's development needs from the perspective of the neighborhoods. One of the issues of primary importance to the neighborhood organizations was the manner in which the city distributed housing and community development funds. From these early meetings a more permanent structure was created and quickly became an important political actor in Hartford.

The coalition is an umbrella organization; its members are organizations themselves. Initially, NHC was made up of a range of community-based groups, including nonprofit development organizations, tenants' rights organizations, neighborhood advocacy organizations, and social service and legal advocacy groups. After a few years, in the mid-1980s, the organization went through a phase in which it included more social service agencies and CDCs than community organizing groups. Currently, NHC is a wide mix of CDCs (six), tenant associations (four), church-based groups (five), ethnic/race-based community organizations (three), legal services (three), and neighborhood organizations (six). The board of directors is chosen from representatives of the member organizations; the full membership meets once a month. Though the board directs policy and advocacy campaigns, final decisions are ratified by the full membership.

The coalition boasts a number of local policy successes and a long history of political advocacy. NHC began sending questionnaires to city council candidates in 1982 requesting their positions on neighborhood and community development issues, a practice that lasted ten years. Among its policy successes are the Housing Preservation and Replacement Ordinance (HPRO), an Antiblight Ordinance, and state funding for nonprofit housing development. The HPRO was passed in 1985 as a result of a major lobbying effort by NHC. The ordinance requires property owners or developers who wish to demolish or convert a housing unit to either physically replace the units within eighteen months, pay an in-lieu fee to the city's Housing Preservation Loan Fund, or appeal to a Board of Administrative Review. In the early 1980s, Hartford was experiencing a significant reduction in its stock of affordable housing units. Between 1981 and 1985, developers were converting or demolishing an average of 51 units each year, or two-and-one-half times the number of units being added through new construction in the city (Maine 1987). Since HPRO became effective, 47 properties, including 171 dwelling units and 106 SROs, have been converted or demolished; $736,000 has been paid into the fund and subsequently loaned or granted by the city for affordable housing development; an additional $588,565 in letters of credit has been channeled into the fund; and 127 units have been directly replaced.

The Antiblight Ordinance, which prevents landlords from intentionally holding units empty for the purpose of speculation, also originated with NHC. Under the terms of the law, landlords are subject to fines if they do not actively try to rent their units while their buildings are substantially vacant. NHC was also successful in the state legislature (located in Hartford), in conjunction with the Connecticut Housing Coalition, in getting programs passed that provided development financing for smaller-scale housing projects (the type most typically sponsored by Hartford CDCs) and in creating state programs for limited equity cooperatives, mutual housing, land trusts, and land banks.

The political success of NHC partly stems from the fact that it has acted in the context of a larger progressive movement that has had a large impact on Hartford's city politics. One of the first issues taken up by the movement in the early 1980s was a housing linkage program patterned after the San Francisco and Boston programs. The groups created a downtown development strategy that involved the use of revenues from downtown growth to meet neighborhood revitalization needs. However, the city council, faced with the combined opposition of business and labor leaders, ultimately rejected the idea in 1986 (Stegman and Holden 1987).

Though on opposite sides of the linkage issue, labor and community groups forged strong ties during this time. Labor leaders reached out to community activists during the 1986 Colt Firearms strike and created the Community-Labor Alliance (Simmons 1994). After other community-based organizations joined the effort, a new political party, People For Change (PFC), emerged and successfully ran candidates for the city council. Among those elected from the ranks of community organizers were board members of NHC-member organizations. Activists suggest that this community activism created a fertile environment for even more effective electoral campaigns by neighborhood activists. Though not all were elected on the PFC ticket, other activists won state legislative seats and city council seats as Democrats.

The movement also placed a number of its members in appointed positions. The former director of NHC was appointed director of housing for the city in 1987, and she was succeeded in office by another activist who had been on the board of NHC. In addition, the city's Fair Housing Officer has become an active member of NHC. The electoral strategies of NHC and the progressive movement were complemented by numerous direct actions, including, for example, shutting down the interstate leading into Hartford from the suburbs to highlight the linkage issue. The former director of NHC said that while the community groups filled the confrontational role, NHC leaders would position themselves as the more rational experts, ready with a policy solution to the problems identified by community organizing groups.

For a number of years in the late 1980s, NHC enjoyed a close relationship with the city council, because of the electoral success of neighborhood activists. During this time NHC and the city worked cooperatively on a number of initiatives, and as one activist said, "Everyone was trying to work in the same ways, and when they [the city] said 'no' it was because they really couldn't." Recently, that situation has changed. PFC has no members on the city council, which currently has a conservative majority, leaving NHC on the outside for the first time in many years. The organization is having to rediscover its past in confrontation and challenge.

In 1994 the conservative majority on the council attempted to weaken HPRO by providing generous exemptions for developers, arguing that the law hinders economic development by imposing costs on developers. NHC was able to defeat the effort to repeal the ordinance in August 1994 by a margin of one vote.

Oakland

East Bay Housing Organizations (EBHO) grew out of meetings that took place in the early 1980s in which housing advocates expressed the need for a single coordinating organization that could facilitate the exchange of information among providers and advocates and that could go to local funders and request assistance for housing production. Originally called Oakland Housing Organizations (OHO), it was formalized in 1984 after a sustained effort to support a housing project proposed by an Oakland CDC. Though the project was ultimately unsuccessful, the groups involved in the campaign decided to continue meeting monthly to discuss common issues.

In 1986 the organization formed a partnership with OCCUR (Oakland Citizens' Committee for Urban Renewal), a forty-year-old citizens' organization that served as the fiscal agent for funds received by the coalition. OCCUR staff also supervised the coalition's first staff person. Since then, the coalition has grown, become independent, and widened its focus to include all of Alameda County. The coalition's financial support has come from private foundations and from membership dues; it receives no government funds.

Most members of the coalition are nonprofit housing developers active in Alameda County and the East Bay. In addition to these developers, the organization includes local fair housing groups; tenants' rights organizations, professionals in housing development, such as architects, consultants, and legal firms; and representatives from local governments, such as the Oakland Housing Authority and the City of Oakland.

The coalition engages in networking for its members, advocacy of affordable housing issues and of particular affordable housing projects, and in supporting the development of affordable housing through management of specialized development funds. For example, one of the largest projects undertaken by the coalition is replacement housing for units lost in the 1989 Loma Prieta earthquake, which left approximately 1,100 of the East Bay's older SRO hotels and apartment buildings in uninhabitable condition. The coalition convened nonprofit developers and other individuals interested in responding to the housing issues resulting from the earthquake, and the replacement plan emerged. Twelve developers and service providers worked together to purchase the damaged properties or other properties that could be used to replace the damaged ones. The coalition's goal was to replace 750 of the lost units, make them permanent housing, and to add services for residents.

Funding for the replacement housing effort came from four sources: (1) a consortium of private foundations that provided $.25 million for project management and $40,000 for administration; (2) the Red Cross, which provided $.5 million to set up a revolving fund that was first used as predevelopment assistance by the nonprofits, then paid back and reused for social services in the projects; (3) the California Disaster Assistance Program, which provided permanent financing in the form of 3 percent loans that are forgiven if the housing remains affordable for thirty years; and (4) an $11 million lawsuit settlement of a Legal Aid case against the Federal Emergency Management Administration for discriminating against SRO dwellers. A total of ten hotels have been completed, affecting over 1,000 units.

The coalition has operated as a networking and advocacy organization on a wide range of issues related to affordable housing. One of its more active areas is in responding to criticisms of affordable housing projects. EBHO has formed a task force to create anti–NIMBY strategies. The affordable housing projects sponsored by EBHO organizations have encountered often fierce resistance from neighborhood and business groups in parts of Berkeley and Oakland. The opposition has spread from its traditional base in the more affluent hill districts of the cities to include working-class and lower-income neighborhoods in the flatlands, which feel they already have an overconcentration of social services and low-income residents. The opponents of subsidized housing have grown more sophisticated in recent years, challenging EBHO with lawsuits and political campaigns. The coalition has attempted to counter the opposition's negative imagery and currently is considering becoming more proactive earlier in the planning process by engaging neighborhood organizations at that stage rather than fighting them at the approval stage.

The organization also has task forces focusing on reducing utility rates for affordable housing, rezoning to accommodate affordable housing, strengthening eviction protection for tenants, and legalizing secondary units as a low-cost means of providing affordable housing.

EBHO has enjoyed a good relationship with city staff in Oakland, and the directors of the relevant city agencies have been supportive of the coalition. Though Oakland residents elected a progressive slate to the city council in 1992, EBHO still organizes actions at city council meetings to support affordable housing issues.

The case studies highlight a number of characteristics shared by many groups in the local housing movement. Perhaps most notable is the high degree of professional participation in the peak organizations of the movement. EBHO, for example, is an organization of and for CDCs and nonprofit housing developers. The 1991 survey of city officials revealed that 26 percent of the larger cities surveyed had such a coalition (Goetz 1993). CDCs play an important role in the Hartford coalition and the Knoxville Housing Partnership as well. But housing developers are not the only professional organizations involved in the local housing movement. The Oakland, Hartford, and Knoxville coalitions also include tenants' organizations, social service agencies, and various legal assistance and advocacy groups. In Knoxville, the Housing Partnership incorporates the involvement of local officials (as in Oakland) and private-sector actors such as lenders and builders.

The local housing movement in each of the cities has been successful in enacting policies or initiating projects that are focused on housing improvements in lower-income neighborhoods. The progressive policy agenda, illustrated by the replacement housing ordinance in Hartford, the housing trust fund in Knoxville, and replacement SRO housing in Oakland, has been a major part of the movement's political advocacy. In each city, the movement has benefited from the support of elected and appointed officials sympathetic to its progressive objectives. In Knoxville the coalition was supported by a progressive mayor and local bureaucracies. In Hartford, local housing advocates played an important part in a larger progressive movement that resulted in significant political changes in the city. Yet the Hartford example also illustrates how fleeting such political support can be. The NHC has had to fight in recent years to protect policy gains made during the 1980s. In Oakland, the election of progressive council members has not been enough to counter vocal criticism of affordable housing programs. EBHO still finds it necessary to organize groups of people to attend council meetings in support of their interests.

In most of the cities there is a strong connection between the housing movement and neighborhood organizations. The efforts of the local housing movement are generally focused on the viability of lower-income urban neighborhoods. Thus, in Knoxville, the Housing Partnership emerged from a prolonged community reinvestment fight. In Hartford, the coalition's advocacy of linkage, the Antiblight Ordinance, and replacement housing has resulted from a neighborhood-oriented political movement. The exception, in this instance, is in Oakland, where the coalition has fought with neighborhood organizations whose leaders feel that their communities are already too concentrated with low-cost housing and social services. Though the coalition hopes to improve its relationship with neighborhood organizations, it still identifies NIMBYism as its primary challenge.

The vacuum in U.S. housing policy innovation created by the federal withdrawal during the 1980s was filled, in part, by local governments that committed greater resources to housing assistance and created innovative housing assistance programs. To a large extent, local governments have been prodded into that response by a community-based housing movement that has combined long-standing neighborhood concerns about disinvestment and gentrification with the interests of tenant organizations, community-based social service agencies, and affordable housing developers. The movement is facing numerous obstacles, including a continued reluctance from the federal government to fund housing assistance programs, the historical reluctance of local governments to fund social programs, budgetary retrenchment at all levels of government, and the current dominance of conservative political ideology. In an era when government programs are considered to be problems more than solutions, the local housing movement has been attempting to expand local government programs for housing. The obstacles the movement faces make its successes all the more remarkable.

NOTES

1. For details of the questionnaire respondents, see Table 2 in E. Goetz 1991.
2. Existence of a LIHAC was determined by the response to the question: "Is there a city-wide low-income housing advocacy group in your city?"
3. Level of prior program experience is defined by the average annual amount of funds received under the seven categorical programs folded into the Community Development Block Grant program during the period 1968–1972. The programs were: Urban renewal, model cities, water and sewer grants, open space grants, public facility loans, housing rehabilitation loans, and neighborhood facility loans (Rich 1985, 330).
4. The 1990 National Affordable Housing Act (NAHA) required local governments to undertake a comprehensive planning process related to housing needs. Jurisdictions wishing to receive HOME and CDBG program funds were required to complete a Comprehensive Housing Affordability Strategy (CHAS) document. The CHAS eclipsed the Housing Assis-

tance Plan (HAP) that had been in place until 1990, and was to include a wider range of policy outcomes and a more systematic plan for allocating anticipated revenues from various sources, including the private sector and all levels of government. Housing advocacy groups regarded the CHAS as an opportunity to make a formal impact on long-term housing assistance goals at the state and local government level.

12

Community-based Housing Organizations and the Complexity of Community Responsiveness

Rachel G. Bratt

Promoting a sense of community is clearly at the heart of the community-based housing strategy. Although at first glance this goal appears straightforward and unlikely to generate much conflict, it is, in fact, complex and inherently contradictory. The core of the issue is that any given community is not a monolithic, single entity, with completely shared visions and goals. Instead, community and neighborhood are very much in "the eye of the beholder," and individuals often identify with multiple communities and interests.

For example, in a mixed residential and commercial area, there may be one set of shared interests among the residents and another set among the business people. Also, within the residential population, interests may diverge between homeowners and renters, and, further, between resident owners and absentee owners. In attempting to meet "community" needs, a planning entity or community-based organization is likely to run into such conflicts and concerns (see, for example, Davis 1991; Heskin 1991). Nevertheless, the unique problems encountered by community-based housing organizations (CBHOs) in attempting to respond to multiple constituencies has been little studied.

In this chapter I continue earlier work in which I explored six dilemmas facing CBHOs (Bratt 1989; 1994), by developing a typology that is aimed at clarifying the broad kinds of challenges facing these groups. By acknowledging these dilemmas, CBHOs should be better able to navigate their way through the tasks that confront them while attempting to mitigate the conflicts inherent in their mission and operation. Also, from a policy perspective, it is important that realistic expectations be placed on these groups and that the obstacles they are facing be reduced through public action, whenever possible.

In this chapter I am primarily concerned with a group of dilemmas that arise from the difficulties associated with CBHOs trying to meet community needs, a category I call "ethical dilemmas." Before exploring this particular group of concerns, I provide a brief overview of the community-based housing strategy, introduce another class of dilemmas—those arising from the nature of the CBHOs' professional practice, examine some broad issues concerning competing values in public policy, and describe the unique characteristics of a particular type of CBHO—the mutual housing association—that offers many rich examples of how ethical dilemmas in community-based housing present themselves. I conclude with some observations about the importance of policymakers and advocates paying close attention to the professional and ethical dilemmas confronting CBHOs.

OVERVIEW OF COMMUNITY-BASED HOUSING STRATEGY

Over the past few years nonprofit community-based housing has gained increasing recognition as a viable strategy for producing affordable housing. This is due partly to a long-standing negative public image about the public housing program, a growing awareness that the public subsidy programs that depend on for-profit developers have some major problems (i.e., expiring-use restrictions), and the recognition that rental certificates and vouchers do not generally stimulate the production of affordable housing, especially in those markets where such housing is lacking. Moreover, the reputation of the community-based housing strategy has been enhanced by the positive record of community-based nonprofit housing developers themselves (Mayer 1984; Pierce and Steinbach 1987, 1990; Vidal 1992; Bratt 1989; NCCED 1989; Zdenek 1990; Goetz 1993).

In addition to their growing track record as affordable housing producers, CBHOs usually have a commitment to promoting a sense of community, both among residents and between residents in the housing development and the surrounding neighborhood, and to fostering individual and community empowerment. Community-based housing programs are

> efforts in which members of a local group or a group of tenants join together to produce, rehabilitate, manage or own housing. With multifamily housing, the central feature is that control and often ownership of the housing is in the hands of individuals who live in the housing or the community. Community-based housing that is rehabilitated or produced for sale, either as single-family homes or as cooperatives, is often (although not always) provided with restrictions attached concerning the amount the owner's equity is allowed to appreciate. These efforts can be distinguished from other forms of community action that have resulted in legislative or regulatory initiatives (e.g., Community Reinvestment Act, local rent control, and condominium conversion ordinances). Community-based housing programs provide housing or services or resources needed for housing; other initiatives prompted by community action usually depend on other actors to change their mode of operation to make housing more available or affordable. (Bratt 1989, 171–72)

Nonprofits recently have gained visibility in policy debates and have even won some important legislative victories. For example, the Financial Institutions Reform, Recovery, and Enforcement Act of 1989 (FIRREA, known as the S & L bailout legislation) provides nonprofits the first right to purchase distressed S & L properties from the Resolution Trust Corporation (RTC). A similar provision, aimed at properties owned by failed commercial banks, was included in the Comprehensive Deposit Insurance Reform Act of 1991, the legislation that bailed out the Federal Deposit Insurance Corporation. Further, the Cranston-Gonzalez National Affordable Housing Act of 1990 requires each jurisdiction receiving funds under Title II, the HOME program, to set aside 15 percent of its allocation for nonprofit community housing development organizations. Additional funds are authorized for technical assistance for nonprofits. Also significant in this legislation is the provision under Title VI, which provides nonprofit organizations and other "priority purchasers" the first right to make a bona fide offer to purchase a federally subsidized development whose owner has announced an interest in prepaying the mortgage. Such priority purchasers thereby commit to maintain the low-income use restrictions for the remaining useful life of the property.[1]

Although the accomplishments of community-based housing have been gaining recognition, it is also important to acknowledge the shortcomings of this strategy. Criticisms include the relatively small number of units produced, particularly in relation to the overall need; the uncertain ability of nonprofits to increase production and management capacity; the long lead-times needed to get groups ready to develop housing; the complexity of financing; and the difficulty of trying to attack problems whose roots are regional, national, or even international at a local level (Bratt 1989). The first four objections could be more fully addressed if there were adequate financial resources and technical assistance for community-based housing developers, but the last is potentially the most problematic. Nevertheless, where housing needs are acute or affordable housing nonexistent, we do not have the luxury of bemoaning larger economic trends that may be beyond the reach of local nonprofits. The only reasonable response is to work at the margins of the economic system and to do whatever is possible to try to meet the need and alleviate human suffering. In addition to the most overt difficulties facing community-based housing groups, also face a series of dilemmas, the resolution of which is not always readily apparent. The first group can be classified as Professional Dilemmas.

PROFESSIONAL DILEMMAS

Professional dilemmas relate to the internal workings of the CBHO, at either the staff or board level; the day-to-day operation of the organization; and the ways in which the CBHO interacts with other public, private, and nonprofit organizations in the locality.

Six main challenges facing CBHOs fall under this category:

1. Maintaining a community and tenant orientation while functioning as a developer and landlord. Any landlord, whether nonprofit or for-profit, must be concerned with the overall economic viability of the development. The tenants' goal—to keep rents as low as possible, while services are adequately provided— may be at odds with that of the owner, who must cover the expenses associated with operating the housing, even if this requires a rent increase. A sensitive CBHO may be caught between economic realities and human needs.[2] Another aspect of this dilemma may involve the desire by tenants to participate in management decisions, and the CBHO may be uncertain about the possible costs or savings that might result from such activities.

2. Balancing advocacy and project development work. Many CBHOs, which were originally organized around advocacy issues, became frustrated with the limited gains they achieved through protest and became involved with development work. Although some groups appear to have combined advocacy and development, many others have found that protest, on the one hand, and cultivating good relationships with city hall and the real estate and banking communities, on the other, are contradictory.

3. Maintaining good staff in the face of low salaries and burnout. The success of a CBHO is closely linked to the experience and quality of its staff. However, with the low pay and long hours that generally are part of community development work, even the most dedicated worker can become frustrated and leave the agency. According to Avis Vidal, "Salaries of CDCs' executive directors and other senior professional staff are generally low compared to those paid in other types of organizations" (1992, 47).[3] Further, Vidal points out that although the executive directors of the CDCs sampled held their positions an average of seven years, the median number of years that staff at lower levels had been in their jobs ranged from about three to three-and-a-half years.[4]

4. The possibility of professional staff of CBHOs becoming out of touch with community residents. Executive directors and staff of CBHOs are frequently from the same racial or ethnic group as the community being served (Vidal 1992, 42–43). Moreover, "Regardless of their own characteristics and backgrounds, executive directors and other senior staff know their communities well and are strongly motivated by the desire to improve the life in those communities" (Vidal 1992, 43). Yet this affinity with the community can be lost in a haze of administrative and programmatic details. In view of the complexity of inner-city housing development, CBHO staff have had to master a host of professional skills. This complexity has increased with the loss of deep federal housing subsidies and the current need to patch together financing deals from numerous public, private, and nonprofit funders (Bratt et al. 1994). Although it appears certain that most staff members of CBHOs have their hearts in the right places, the need just to get the job done can produce some degree of separation and even alienation from the organization's constituents.

5. Potential for conflict between the original objectives of the agency, as expressed by its first board, and goals of newcomers—and new board members.

As a community changes, possibly upgrading in response to the efforts of the CBHO, new residents may move into the area and attempt to alter the mission of the original group, including converting any housing owned by the CBHO into market-rate units or condominiums. Unless the low-income housing has been safeguarded through long-term use restrictions, existing tenants may run the risk of being displaced. Even without a change in board and neighborhood composition, CBHOs invariably find themselves debating which groups within the community to serve. Should the groups with the greatest needs and lowest incomes receive top priority or, instead, should preference be given to households who are somewhat better off but who could use a helping hand and who would require less subsidy money?

6. Desire by both the CBHO and other public, private, and nonprofit institutions in the local area to effect development, even though there is an awareness that budgets may not be adequate. There are numerous examples of nonprofit sponsors of affordable housing embarking on development deals with full knowledge that construction, rehabilitation, or operating budgets were possibly or certainly insufficient. CBHOs often embark on a project under these circumstances because of their desire to build legitimacy in the local development community and in order to be responsive to board and resident demands for the organization to produce. But whatever the reasons, the decision to proceed with a project that is inadequately funded at the outset is certain to create long-term management challenges for the CBHO. The organization will constantly be confronting the need to respond to problems with additional resources, which are probably difficult to raise (Bratt et al. 1994).

Unfortunately, there are no clear-cut, easy answers to these dilemmas. For each, convincing arguments can be raised on either side. But the challenges posed by the professional dilemmas notwithstanding, the conflicts raised by the second set of dilemmas—those that pit individual needs against the larger community and those that pit one part of the community against another—are even more daunting and provocative. Before exploring these ethical dilemmas more fully, it is first important to reflect briefly on the larger context of how different values often compete in policy debates. Although it is only recently that CBHOs have found themselves confronting dilemmas related to individual versus community needs, as well as the various needs of subgroups within a community, such conflicts are extremely common in other domains.

COMPETING VALUES IN POLICY DEBATES

What are the relative merits of individual and community needs and how should they be assessed? For example, should individuals be checked at airports for weapons or other dangerous objects? Should airplane pilots and train engineers be required to undergo mandatory drug testing? Staunch civil libertarians oppose both these measures on the grounds that they infringe on individual rights. Communitarians, in contrast, argue that both measures enhance security for the larger community and that these values should take priority (Etzioni 1991).

A second group of concerns relates to the way in which the needs of one group within a community should be weighed in relation to the needs of another group. For example, what criteria should be used to site unwanted facilities such as nuclear reactors, hazardous waste, and sewage treatment plants? Should the needs of the larger community to develop such facilities take precedence over the likely opposition of the adjacent community?

Again, quick or simple answers to such questions are not possible. But it is important to recognize how widespread questions of this type are and to be prepared for such dilemmas to permeate virtually every aspect of American life. CBHOs have not been immune to such controversies. The particular CBHO used in this study, the mutual housing association, provides particularly fertile ground for examining the two classes of ethical dilemmas: the individual versus the community and community versus community.

UNIQUE CHARACTERISTICS OF MUTUAL HOUSING ASSOCIATIONS

There are three major forms of community-based multifamily housing that involve some form of resident or nonprofit organizational ownership—community development corporations, limited equity cooperatives, and mutual housing associations. Of the three, CDCs are by far the most common.[5] In limited equity cooperatives, although the housing may have been developed by a community-based nonprofit, which may or may not have a continuing relationship with the project, the key attribute is that residents of the housing own shares of the development and generally have significant involvement in management decisions.

Mutual housing associations present a third model of community-based development. Although a variety of organizations have adopted the name Mutual Housing, in this chapter I draw on the experiences of those MHAs that were created with assistance from the Neighborhood Reinvestment Corporation. Since the early 1980s the NRC has been promoting the concept of mutual housing and, since then, some fifteen associations have been formed, which own nearly 3,800 units of housing.[6]

MHAs are similar to limited equity cooperatives in that residents are encouraged to think and act more like homeowners than renters. However, MHA residents, unlike those in limited equity cooperatives, do not have any legal ownership of the development. In promoting the feeling of ownership, MHAs have experimented with a number of issues that address how residents can be made to feel more like owners than renters. These efforts include charging a flat rent to all residents as opposed to fixing rents as a percentage of resident income; providing security of tenure despite rising incomes, and providing preferential rights for a qualified heir or family member to occupy an MHA unit when the original resident vacates it. Despite the potential for this bundle of rights to promote the feeling of homeownership among MHA residents, it turns out that each one comes at a price and raises some interesting ethical dilemmas.

At the outset, it is important to note that there is not a single model of an MHA and that the following dilemmas have been addressed and resolved in a variety of ways. Each local group has had to grapple with the issues and come up with solutions that seem to best suit the residents' needs. Also worth underscoring is that these dilemmas arise in virtually every MHA, and many of them also arise in other types of community-based housing development initiatives as well. Thus, in view of the overall effectiveness and popularity of community-based housing, ethical dilemmas are fertile ground for study, analysis, and deeper understanding.

ETHICAL DILEMMA NO. 1—THE INDIVIDUAL VERSUS THE COMMUNITY

This group of dilemmas is specifically associated with ways in which individual needs, such as the provision of more rights (which may approximate a homeownership situation), may also conflict with the needs of a broader community.

Entrance Fee Appreciation

Limited equity cooperatives, buyers of homes from CBHOs, and MHAs typically cap the amount of money that the required down payments or membership fees are allowed to appreciate. The result is that purchasers of property developed by CBHOs are unable to gain as much of a foothold in the economy as other comparable property owners. In MHAs, residents are charged a one-time buy-in fee upon moving into the development, which can range from a few hundred dollars to as much as $2,500. Unlike cooperatives, mutual housing residents are not owners, and this fee does not represent equity in the development. However, when the resident leaves the development, the money is returned. It is up to the MHA whether and how much the fee is permitted to appreciate. Thus, upon the resident's departure, the original amount is returned, plus whatever amount it is allowed to rise, based either on a fixed rate of interest or some other standard.

By limiting equity appreciation, the units stay permanently affordable and available as a community resource. The ability of a neighborhood to maintain its population by providing units that are not subject to market forces and that will continue to be affordable to other comparably low- and moderate-income people, even if neighborhood housing values increase, is certainly a community-stabilizing goal. On the other hand, the policy of equity caps could be viewed as unfair to the individuals involved, since wealthier owners are able to take full advantage of the appreciation of their property. One could further argue that the latter group is also subsidized since they are able to enjoy the tax benefits from the homeowners' deduction. Thus, why should residents of mutual housing and other types of limited equity housing be penalized from enjoying appreciation of their property, when even higher-income households, who are subsidized to an even greater degree by the IRS, are entitled to the full appreciation on their homes?

Security of Tenure

There are two considerations related to security of tenure. The first involves the goal of virtually all CBHOs to provide long-term affordable housing. This objective does not have any apparent conflicts with equity issues. However, a second aspect, which entails providing a guarantee against displacement to all residents, regardless of income levels or need, may result in serious inequities.

None of the MHAs that have been developed so far require tenants whose incomes rise to leave their homes. In attempting to remedy one of the classic problems associated with the public housing program, MHAs could find themselves subsidizing residents who are not the most needy in the community. On the other hand, to the extent that MHAs and other CBHOs are committed to building a sense of community within their developments, security of tenure is obviously an important component of such an effort.

Another interesting dilemma related to providing security of tenure can arise if an empty-nest household is occupying a unit with more bedrooms than it needs. Obviously, in a homeownership situation, the family would have the right to remain in the larger unit. But in a mutual housing development the question arises whether the association should insist or strongly encourage a household to leave that unit so that a family needing it can move in. To the extent that such a request is made, the individual's right to the unit is relegated to a lower position than the needs of the overall community.

Inheritance Rights

The issue of inheritance rights is very similar to security of tenure. In most MHAs, residents can nominate another family member to succeed them upon their death or departure from the development. Although this is key in helping residents to feel more like owners than renters as well as important in developing a sense of community, the policy can also be problematic. If the new household is not among the neediest awaiting affordable housing or has not been waiting the longest for a unit in the development, allowing them to assume the rights to the unit could be viewed as inequitable.

An interesting subproblem that arises as a result of the provision that mutual housing residents can nominate a qualified heir to their unit is that the new family may have a need for a different-sized unit. For example, the prior resident may have been a single person occupying a one-bedroom unit, but the new household may have several family members and require two or three bedrooms. Clearly, the right of that family to a specific unit, as in the case of homeownership, would not be in the best interest of either the MHA or of the new family. But again, that household's needs take precedence over others waiting for a unit, the policy could come under attack for being unfair to the broader community.

ETHICAL DILEMMA NO. 2—COMMUNITY VERSUS COMMUNITY

This second group of ethical dilemmas pits one segment of the community against another.

Variable Rents and Fees Versus a Flat Amount

Although public housing residents, Section 8 tenants, and occupants of most types of community-based housing are required to pay 30 percent of their incomes for rent, many mutual housing residents are not required to pay a fixed percentage of income. In the more traditional subsidized housing situations, if incomes rise, a greater sum must be paid in rent, regardless of whether there is an increase in the development's costs. The subsidy amount is reduced as a tenant's contribution increases.

Most MHAs have opted for residents to pay a flat rent for a given size unit, as opposed to levying the charges based on percentage of income.[7] Whenever mutual housing residents pay a flat amount of rent, some pay more than the federal standard of 30 percent of income, and others pay less. In a study done of the Neighborhood Reinvestment Corporation's first MHA, Baltimore's Alameda Place, all units of a given bedroom size command the same rent. As of 1 September 1988, 25 percent of residents paid less than 20 percent of income for rent, but another 47 percent paid between 21 percent and 30 percent. Thus, nearly three-quarters of the residents carried a rent burden below the federal standard. At the same time, 28 percent paid more than 30 percent of income (Bratt 1990, 36).

The policy of raising rents only if development costs increase is, understandably, enthusiastically endorsed by the people in the community who are most likely to be positively affected. In a survey of thirty-nine Baltimore MHA residents, the greatest number of respondents (65 percent) rated this policy as one of the three best features of living in the development out of eight other attributes they were asked to rank (Bratt 1990, 42).

Nevertheless, the policy can be viewed as inequitable. One part of the MHA community benefits while another does less well. Residents with the highest incomes make the least sacrifice in paying rent; those with the lowest incomes feel the burden of the rental payments and increases the most. When rents increased in 1988, 12 percent more of the MHA's households fell into the group of those paying in excess of 30 percent of income for rent. One could argue that it would be more equitable if all members of the MHA community—all the residents in a given development—were required to contribute to the costs of operating the development according to each household's ability to pay. Either everyone would be asked to contribute a fixed percentage of income toward rent, as in the federal subsidized housing programs or, even more equitable perhaps, there would be a progressive rental scale: wealthier households would be required to pay a larger percentage of income toward rent than their lower-income neighbors.

A similar dilemma arises in connection with the way in which the membership fee, paid when the resident moves into the development, is set. In the Baltimore MHA, all residents occupying the same size unit, in terms of number of bedrooms, pay the same fee. In contrast, the MHA of Southwestern Connecticut, based in Stamford, levies a flat membership fee of $2,500 for all residents. And, in New Haven, the MHA of South Central Connecticut's membership fee varies by income.[8] Although the last method may appear to be the most equitable arrangement, it is important to note that in each case the residents themselves devised the plan that they felt best suited their needs.

Marketing

A significant aspect of community-based housing development work involves providing improved housing to the organization's clients. Yet this effort may conflict with various laws that require housing to be marketed on an open-occupancy basis.

Clearly, there is a need for a community organization to develop its base of support within its community, to enhance its position of leadership, and to legitimize itself as a positive force in the community. But in the quest of building community, by extending preferential treatment to neighborhood residents, the organization may be unfair to others who are equally, or even more, needy. This situation is particularly troubling and, moreover, possibly illegal, if those who are excluded are racial or ethnic minorities.

Another twist to this dilemma was confronted by the MHA of Southwestern Connecticut. Working in a predominantly minority community, the MHA was required to market a portion of its units to residents living outside the local community. In this case, they were required to recruit white households.

All CBHOs and MHAs invariably confront the marketing issue and need to figure out an equitable plan for renting their units. And, if the housing is subsidized with federal or state dollars, the plan probably must be approved by the appropriate agency.

Alternative Use of Funds

One of the goals of NRC-sponsored MHAs is generally to encourage the production of affordable housing as long as there is a need for additional units in the community or until a threshold number of units under management is achieved, thereby allowing management income to cover operating costs.

Building additional affordable housing units would strengthen the surrounding community and assist households in need of such housing. Yet, to achieve this goal, existing MHA residents must constantly weigh their needs, either to keep their own costs down or to add new services of programs, against the commitment to ongoing production. Since some residents may be carrying a relatively light rent burden and others a heavier load (given that rent generally is not based on percentage of income), it may be difficult to advocate uniform policies about how much money should be committed by any particular MHA for ongoing production, because the financial burden of such a decision will be borne in different ways by the various groups of residents. For example, if a household is paying 40 percent of income for housing, is it "fair" that a portion of that household's rent be earmarked for a new production fund, if what that tenant needs most is to pay less rent? Thus, in this dilemma, not only do we have one community's needs (people who lack affordable housing in the larger community) in potential conflict with that of another's (existing residents), but we also see that the needs of some individuals may be at variance with other members of the community. The more one delves into these dilemmas the thornier they seem to become.

Mutual housing and other types of community-based housing programs are oriented toward promoting a sense of community among residents within their developments as well as between those residents and neighbors in the surrounding area. However, some of the provisions of MHAs that work toward building community and that are viewed as major improvements over more traditional federal subsidy programs, such as public housing, clearly are replete with ethical dilemmas. For policymakers the question emerges, "What do we really want—equity or community—if it seems that we can't have it all?" In the current context of retrenchment from housing, certainly at the federal level but for many states as well, the question may be totally irrelevant. Instead, we may need to ask, "How can we sustain support for affordable housing?" Contemplating issues of community and equity may be nothing more than academic self-indulgence.

NOTES

1. This chapter was completed in early spring 1995, just as the U.S. House of Representatives voted for major rescissions in domestic programs, including over $7 billion for housing assistance. The buyout provisions under Title VI could be in jeopardy as a result of these cutbacks as well as congressional disaffection with the program on the grounds that it is too costly. HUD's proposed budget for FY 1996 does not include any funds for this program. Nevertheless, for purposes of underscoring the ways in which nonprofits have gained national attention, it is relevant that they were given a prominent role in the original legislation.

2. In a recent study of management challenges confronting nonprofit owners of affordable housing, we found numerous examples of the difficulty of groups meeting what we

called "the double bottom line," fulfilling both the social and economic mission of operating community-based housing (Bratt et al. 1994).

3. CDCs are the dominant type of community-based housing organizations (see note 5).

4. Vidal also points out that "for positions below that of the executive director, these tenure figures reflect not only the level of turnover, but also the rapid growth of many CDCs, which has created new positions" (1992, 47).

5. In addition to CDCs, there is an array of other types of groups that often become involved with housing development, such as Neighborhood Housing Services, social services agencies, religious groups, and unions. For purposes of this chapter, however, all such entities are being grouped together under the general heading CDC.

6. Interview with Diane Gordon, Field Service Officer, Neighborhood Reinvestment Corporation, Boston office, 22 March 1995.

7. Ibid.

8. Ibid.

Profiles of Leading
Neighborhood Figures

The following profiles highlight some of the people who have made significant contributions to the preservation of neighborhoods and who have fostered urban neighborhood-based initiatives. The list is not exhaustive but offers a sampling. Some individuals are nationally recognized for their contributions, but in every community there have been other organizers and leaders who should also be recognized.

These sketches document the early reformers such as Mary Simkhovitch, a pioneer in the settlement house movement; community organizers like Gale Cincotta and Ernesto Cortes, who recognized the power of neighbors acting together; critics such as Jane Jacobs, who challenged the antineighborhood bias in urban renewal planning; people like Msgr. William Linder and Mary Nelson whose faith brought them to work in and with neighborhoods; the directors of successful Community Development Corporations who have led community building initiatives; and visionaries such as Mitchell Sviridoff and James Rouse, who developed unique institutions called intermediaries to support the emerging field of community-based development in the 1980s.

GALE CINCOTTA
*National Training and Informa-
tion Center (Chicago)*

Gale Cincotta believes that money is the lifeblood of communities and neighborhoods and that the death of a neighborhood is not a natural phenomenon. She has
dedicated her career in community organizing to bringing resources back to neighborhoods and to holding accountable the people who have the power and
resources to revitalize neighborhoods. In working to form partnerships, she has
found that confrontation is a good way to bring together people who might not
otherwise sit down at the negotiation table. She has used this approach since her
early work as a PTA mother battling the education system in her West Side
Chicago neighborhood.

After working to bring together community organizations in Chicago, she saw
the opportunity for a national organization of these groups that would demand
accountability on the national level as was occurring on the local level in Chicago.
She helped to form National People's Action, a multiissue, broad-based coalition
of over 300 community organizations that collectively fights for issues affecting
neighborhood revitalization nationwide. Two of her most acclaimed victories were
the Home Mortgage Disclosure Act in 1975 and the Community Reinvestment Act
in 1977.

Her efforts did not end with the passage of these laws. She has spent nearly
twenty years using this legislation in building partnerships for neighborhood revitalization. Her efforts have challenged the assumption of financial institutions that
investing in city neighborhoods was no longer profitable. In March 1995 Chicago
banks committed $4 billion over five years to the neighborhoods. The president of
First Chicago Bank, which made a $2 billion commitment, credits Cincotta with
starting the productive partnership that now exists between banks and low- and
moderate-income neighborhoods.

In 1972 she cofounded the National Training and Information Center to assist community organizations around the country. Cincotta is chair of National People's Action.

ERNESTO CORTES, JR.
Communities Organized for Public Service
(San Antonio)

In 1973, Ernesto Cortes, Jr., returned to his hometown of San Antonio after two years in Chicago to find the poor neighborhoods on the West Side even more degraded than when he left in 1971. He had returned after receiving Industrial Areas Foundations training, the program founded by Saul Alinsky to train associates to form People's Organizations to assist poor and working people in exercising power to improve their social and economic conditions.

Cortes went to the parishes in the West Side to see how he could use the training the IAF had given him. Physically segregated, the primary low-income and minority population was ignored by the media and neglected by city leaders. As Cortes conducted over a thousand individual meetings with the residents, he brought forth the energy and political will integral to building a new citizens' organization. The group would act on the interests expressed in the meetings—safety, family, education—through identifiable problems such as deteriorating schools, dangerous junkyards, flooding, and unsafe streets.

A year later, Communities Organized for Public Service (COPS) was born. After an intensive period of leadership development, exhaustive research, and action, Ernesto Cortes and COPS embarked on the path to becoming the oldest and most powerful of the forty IAF organizations nationwide.

To date, COPS, with its sister organization the Metro Alliance, has brought over $1 billion in streets, parks, housing, sidewalks, libraries, clinics, streetlights, drainage, and other infrastructure to the poor neighborhoods of the inner city. COPS and the Metro Alliance have organized San Antonio's Community Development Block Grant process into an effective, accountable, nationally recognized project.

"Organizing is a fancy word for relationship building," Cortes has said. "No organizer ever organizes a community. What an organizer does is develop leadership. And the leadership builds the relationships and the networks, and following that, does the organizing."

Cortes has successfully used the strategy of "no permanent enemies, no permanent allies" to rebuild the physical infrastructure and to reorganize the political power of San Antonio. "In the IAF we teach that it is important to polarize people—with business leaders and elected officials—to get their attention, to gain recognition. . . . Yet what is even more important is to depolarize the situation in order to provide both you and your opponent with room to negotiate and develop a relationship. If you cannot have a real conversation with your opponent, he or she will never become your ally. In the same vein, it is important to help your enemies recognize their self-interest in developing a relationship with you."

DENISE G. FAIRCHILD

Denise G. Fairchild is an urban planner with over twenty years of experience in housing and community development. She began her education in planning at Fisk University, a black college in Nashville, where she was first introduced to community organizing. Subsequently, she earned her master's degree in urban planning at the University of Pennsylvania and her Ph.D. in 1987 from UCLA. She is now executive director of the Community Development Technologies Center at LA Trade Technical College, where she provides training and technical assistance on community development.

Before joining the college, Fairchild was program director of the Local Initiatives Support Corporation in Los Angeles, where she managed a $25 million neighborhood revitalization program for community development corporations. She is among the many dedicated community advocates who helped to structure a creative, grassroots response to the 1992 uprising in South Central Los Angeles.

JANE JACOBS

Considered by many to be one of the most influential writers on planning in North America, Jane Jacobs is neither a planner nor an academic. Her observations and criticism come from outside the field, from a perspective that challenges the notion of planning in the formal sense. Among Jacobs's many books and articles, her most notable work is *The Death and Life of Great American Cities,* a critique of urban renewal planning and the efforts to replace old, small-scale neighborhoods with large-scale development in the 1950s and 1960s. She argues for managing cities from a community base, preserving diverse neighborhoods as a necessary resource for urban vitality. Jacobs's original reference for neighborhoods is Greenwich Village in New York City, where she was both an activist and a writer.

In her attack on the urban planning mindset that favored slum clearance and vast new complexes over old neighborhoods and diverse buildings, she introduced concepts such as neighborhood preservation, scale, street life, and mixed-use districts as alternatives for planning practice. In 1969 she argued in the *Economy of Cities* that cities are the primary forces that drive national economics. Great cities have grown through flexibility and innovation.

Originally from Scranton, Pennsylvania, she came to New York to be a writer in 1934. It was while working as an associate editor at *Architectural Forum* that she began to solidify an opinion about neighborhood survival, favoring diversity and density over planned uniformity. Even though she has written a great deal about American cities, Jacobs is no longer an American citizen, having left the United States in 1968 with her husband and children in protest of the Vietnam War. She currently resides in Toronto. Her latest book, *Systems of Survival,* is a conversation among five characters exploring two value systems that basically shape the world.

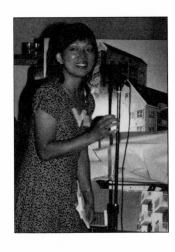

LYNETTE LEE
East Bay Asian Local Development Corporation

In 1975 several college students and residents of Oakland, California, decided to buy and fix up a deteriorated warehouse to collect under one roof social services supporting a growing Asian community. Eight years later, the Asian Resource Center was completely renovated and the East Bay Asian Local Development Corporation had expanded its efforts to better the community.

In 1982 Lynette Jung Lee became EBALDC's executive director. Although her previous experience as a case worker and teacher did not formally prepare her for real estate development, Lee has led EBALDC in taking a comprehensive approach to community and economic development. She has helped the organization move beyond its first project to give attention to land-use and advocacy issues, particularly housing preservation and production.

As of 1995 EBALDC has built or rehabilitated 550 housing units in several projects. Along with economic development activities, EBALDC also plans and organizes activities that benefit Asian immigrants and refugees and other low-income people in the East Bay. Lee is president of the board of the National Development Leadership Network.

MONSIGNOR WILLIAM LINDER
New Community Corporation (Newark)

Civil unrest in 1967 left much of Newark's Central Ward in ruins. Rather than leave the community to deteriorate further, Msgr. William Linder set an ambitious grassroots agenda, envisioning a new community many people did not think possible for an inner-city neighborhood. In addition to housing, Linder's vision encompassed providing employment, day care, education, social services, job training, and health care to urban residents.

After developing a holistic twenty-year plan for the Central Ward, the next obstacle was financing. When banks would not take the risk, Linder convinced the New Jersey Department of Community Affairs to provide a $13,000 seed loan to get New Community Corporation (NCC) started. With a local parish as a backup corporation and the Jaycees selling "shares" in the Central Ward, NCC was able to acquire a 45-acre tract and build 2,400 housing units.

Today, NCC is the largest community development corporation in New Jersey, providing affordable housing to nearly 7,000 individuals and owning and operating more than 3,300 units in four cities. In addition to housing, NCC has developed commercial and educational facilities and provided employment opportunities. Today, NCC activities include day care, social services, job training, and health care for the Central Ward. Among the many economic development projects is the Neighborhood Shopping Center and the Pathmark Supermarket, which attracts 50,000 shoppers each week.

New Community Corporation's 1,426 employees are 94 percent African American, Hispanic, or other minorities, and over 60 percent live in Newark. A career-ladder concept has been developed, and additional education and training leads both to personal advancement and promotions.

In 1994 Msgr. William Linder received the Entrepreneurial American Leadership Award, presented once every decade by Partners for Liveable Communities. He was cited for "faith and hard work in restoring the inner-city neighborhoods of Newark."

MARY NELSON
Bethel New Life

When Mary Nelson offered to help her brother move to Chicago's West Side in 1965 to become the new pastor at Bethel Lutheran Church, she did not expect to stay. Three days later, after driving through the middle of a riot, Nelson decided she could not leave. Rather than fleeing from the bricks and bottles thrown that day, she committed herself to working with the Bethel congregation to improve the lives of poor residents in the West Garfield Park community.

Nelson credits her faith and her belief in working for justice to her upbringing. She was inspired both by her father, a minister, and her mother, an activist. Through 1978 Nelson was director of planning and development for an ecumenical community-based organization composed of thirteen churches, developing an alternative high school, eight day-care centers, and a nursing home.

In 1979 Nelson and other members of the church formed Bethel New Life, Inc., to tackle the serious housing shortage and abandoned property in West Garfield Park. Since then, under Nelson's direction, the church-based community development corporation has found creative ways to develop affordable, low-cost housing units as well as services and support aimed at reducing poverty and unemployment. Bethel is credited with innovative ways to link projects together that meet the needs for employment and services. In 1995 Bethel New Life, Inc., had an annual operating budget of $10 million and employed nearly 500 people.

JAMES ROUSE
Enterprise Foundation

James Rouse spent his adult life working in American cities, beginning with his development work at the Rouse Company, which he founded in 1939. When he retired from his post as board chairman forty years later, he and his wife Patty launched the Enterprise Foundation, a charitable corporation that works with neighborhood groups focused only on providing fit and affordable housing for the very poor. Most recent and notable among the many Enterprise projects throughout the United States is the transformation of Baltimore's Sandtown neighborhood, where a comprehensive plan has been initiated to improve not only the housing but also the lives of its residents.

Among his many activities over the years, Rouse was a member of President Eisenhower's Task Force on Housing in 1953 and President Reagan's Task Force on Private Sector Initiatives in 1982. In 1987 he served as chairman of the National Housing Task Force which made proposals to Congress in 1988 for a new housing program that later formed the basis for the National Affordable Housing Act of 1990. Until his death in 1996, Rouse was the chairman of the Enterprise Foundation and of the Enterprise Development Company, the for-profit commercial real estate development company that provides dividends to support the foundation's charitable work.

MARY KINGSBURY SIMKHOVITCH

Mary Kingsbury Simkhovitch is often described as a housing reformer and settlement house worker. Like many woman activists of her time, however, she pursued a wide range of social justice issues, including woman suffrage, economic reform, and progressive politics. Simkhovitch's work with the settlement house movement began while she was in graduate school in 1897. She lived at the College Settlement House on New York City's Lower East Side, where the women believed in working with residents in the neighborhood and experimenting with new economic and social ideas.

It was here that she also began her work with tenants to seek housing reform and social change. Simkhovitch's next position was chief resident of Friendly Aid House. Within a short time, she established Greenwich House, where she was able to act on her belief in indigenous leadership and stress the limited benefits of one class acting on behalf of another class of people. During this time, Simkhovitch's efforts to reform housing continued as she emphasized the widespread problems caused by overcrowding.

Her seminal work, however, was in the 1930s in her efforts to get federal support for housing needed as a result of the Great Depression. From 1931 to 1943, Simkhovitch served as president of the Public Housing Conference, during which time she achieved support for low-income housing in the National Industrial Recovery Act. She was also appointed vice chairman of the New York City Housing Authority in 1934, where she drafted the Wagner-Steagall Housing Act to mandate construction of public housing. In 1946 Simkhovitch retired from her position as director of Greenwich House and died there five years later.

REVEREND LEON SULLIVAN
*Opportunities Industrial Center
(Philadelphia)*

As pastor of Zion Baptist Church from 1950 to 1988, Rev. Leon Sullivan made a significant mark on North Philadelphia. He began by confronting discrimination that prevented African Americans in his neighborhood from getting well-paid jobs, by organizing boycotts against employers, and by starting a training program to build youth work skills. At the same time, Sullivan began collecting donations from his congregation to start the Zion Non-Profit Charitable Trust, a capital base for housing, education, and economic development programs.

Today, as pastor emeritus his efforts continue to positively affect urban areas worldwide through an array of economic development activities. Most notable is the Opportunities Industrial Center (OIC) of America, which sponsors training and retraining on a massive scale. Since its inception in 1964, OIC has trained more than 1 million persons with more than 80 percent placed, representing approximately $15 billion a year in annual income.

In 1969 Sullivan founded OIC International to help workers in African countries. More recently, he worked with corporate leaders to establish the International Foundation for Education and Self-Help (IFESH) as a means to lead American companies, institutions and individuals in improving conditions of people primarily in Africa but also in other developing countries. In 1991 he was awarded the Presidential Medal of Freedom for service to the poor and needy of America and Africa.

MITCHELL (MIKE) SVIRIDOFF

Best known for his leadership in helping launch the CDC movement, Mike Sviri-doff began as a metal worker at Sikorsky Aircraft in Connecticut. He then served as regional director of the United Auto Workers until President Kennedy appointed him special assistant to the administrator of Latin American Aid in 1961.

Sviridoff returned to Connecticut in 1962 to take responsibility for neighbor-hood renewal in New Haven. As director of Community Progress, Inc., one of the five Grey Areas projects founded by the Ford Foundation, Sviridoff developed innovative programs in community-based employment, education, and social ser-vices in New Haven's poorest neighborhoods.

In 1966 Sviridoff became New York City's first commissioner of the Depart-ment of Human Resources. He then served as vice president for the National Affairs Division at the Ford Foundation until 1980. During this time, he initiated the first generation of CDCs, helping to set up the Bedford-Stuyvesant Restoration Corporation as a means of getting investment dollars back into the disinvested Brooklyn neighborhood. In 1981 Sviridoff helped found the Local Initiatives Sup-port Corporation, a successful strategy to foster partnerships focused on neighbor-hood reinvestment between private businesses, financial institutions, and foundations. Under his leadership as president, LISC emerged as one of the nation's most successful of all intermediaries encouraging neighborhood lending. In 1986 Mike Sviridoff joined the New School for Social Research, where he cur-rently is professor emeritus and senior fellow.

TED WATKINS
Watts Labor Community Action Committee
(Los Angeles)

In August 1965 the Watts neighborhood in Los Angeles flared up in an outburst of arson, killing, and looting. The fundamental causes included joblessness, poverty, and discrimination in this poor minority section of the city.

The Watts Labor Community Action Committee, founded by Ted Watkins, was one of the organizations that emerged from the riot. It responded with a comprehensive, grassroots-based program of social and economic development. Watkins was the founder, president, and administrator of WLCAC until his death in 1993. Under his leadership, the organization became one of the leading minority, self-help development corporations in the United States.

Ted Watkins, who was a native of Mississippi and came to Los Angeles when he was fourteen, achieved numerous national and international honors. Most important to him, however, was the change he inspired in Watts and the respect and admiration of his neighbors.

BOB WOLF
Famicos Foundation (Cleveland)

In the late 1960s, Bob Wolf started his second career—helping poor families in Cleveland's neighborhoods. A chemical engineer with a Ph.D., he began working with Sister Henrietta, a charismatic nun, in the Hough neighborhood to help residents rebuild their lives after the 1966 riot left whole blocks burned and vacated. After seeing first-hand the widescale effects of poverty, Wolf shifted his attention from providing food and clothing to providing residents with decent and affordable housing. Sister Henrietta started Famicos (Family Cooperators) in 1970 as a way to provide homeownership opportunities in Hough.

Initially, Dr. Wolf helped raise money to purchase and rehabilitate homes that could be leased with an option to buy. After retiring from his post as vice president of development at B. F. Goodrich in 1973, he came to work at Famicos as its full-time, volunteer director. He developed a program that involved substantial rehabilitation as well as sweat equity. Weatherization was included in each house to help keep the housing affordable. Since then, the Famicos lease-purchase program has become a model for other groups wanting to create homeownership opportunities for low-income families.

After recruiting five other neighborhood groups to replicate the Famicos model, Wolf helped form the Cleveland Housing Network (CHN) to pool resources and expertise for its members. Working with the Enterprise Foundation, CHN used the Famicos model as the basis for the low-income housing tax credit. Since 1981, CHN has expanded membership to thirteen neighborhood-based housing development corporations and added a family development component to help families move out of poverty and become self-sufficient. The Network to date has developed more than 1,000 units of affordable housing for low-income families throughout Cleveland.

Part Four
Urban and Metropolitan Development Policies

In Part Four we examine metropolitan forces and federal policies that have in the past and undoubtedly will in the future impact urban neighborhoods. The antiurban bias that often runs through the fabric of American culture is revealed in the process of suburbanization, one of the great population migrations in American history, in which millions of middle- and upper-class households, overwhelmingly white, moved out of central-city neighborhoods to low-density, largely single-family areas in the suburbs. The process, significantly under way since the 1920s, picked up in speed and numbers after World War II. In the 1970s, for the first time in history, more Americans lived in suburbs than lived either in cities or in small towns and rural areas. During the 1980s population continued to sprawl in ever-widening suburban areas around the core cities, and the process continues into the 1990s.

The magnitude of the size of the shift to the suburbs was striking, but the racial dimension was profound as well. In the twenty largest cities of the Northeast and Midwest, for example, the white population fell by over 2.5 million, or 13 percent, between 1960 and 1970 and by another 4 million, or 24.3 percent, by 1980. The black population in the same cities grew by almost 2 million, or about 38.8 percent, during the same period. In the process, older central cities and their neighborhoods become significantly African-American and poorer in relationship to their surrounding suburbs.

Compared to those in the rest of the world, American suburbs are unique in terms of lower population densities, higher rates of homeownership, more use of personal automobiles, and higher degrees of race and class segregation. Conventional wisdom holds that this pattern was the inevitable result of changing technology and consumer choice in a free economy. Yet the sharp difference of the American pattern from that of other countries suggests that there is much more to the story than changing technology and individual tastes.

In the 1920s suburban growth began to compete with the growth of the industrial cities. Although almost 5 million people were added to the suburbs in the 1920s, that fact did not seem to represent a threat to the vitality of cities or urban neighborhoods. Most of the people who lived in the suburbs still worked in the city, and almost all white-collar people worked and shopped in the old downtowns. The Great Depression and World War II brought suburban growth to a near standstill and created a huge backlog of demand for housing. The pent-up demand erupted after the end of the war when single-family housing starts rose from only 114,000 in 1944 to 1,692,000 in 1950. Almost all of this new construction took place in the suburbs. Before World War II, suburbanization was mainly an upper- and middle-class phenomenon, but it has now filtered down to include working-class families.

For most families, owning their own home in the suburbs became a better economic bargain than trying to stay in their old neighborhoods. Federally insured home loans, cheap energy, federal highways and other transportation policies, and new building technologies made it cheaper to build a new house in the suburbs than to rehabilitate a home or rent an apartment in older urban neighborhoods. The Federal Housing Administration, which provided basic home mortgage insurance and overwhelmingly emphasized new housing construction in the suburbs, shared the real estate industry's belief that racial segregation was preferable to integration. That belief, translated into FHA policy, help cast racial segregation and city-suburban economic disparities in cement. Meanwhile, the interstate highway program and the lack of strong land-use controls opened up the urban fringe for new suburban development.

As the authors of the following chapters make clear, these and other federal policies were heavily weighted toward the needs of the suburbs. Rather than being an inevitable outcome of anonymous forces of technology and the market, the pace and shape of suburban growth in the United States was shaped and sustained by public policies and private institutions.

In Chapter 13, Norman Krumholz points out that support for urban neighborhoods has run through the rhetoric of every president, liberal and conservative, since the 1960s, yet all the rhetoric falls far short of a coherent program. Instead, federal policies have frequently been contradictory, with few assisting revitalization and many assisting outmigration and suburbanization. After describing the metropolitan nature of neighborhood change, he points out general shortcomings in present revitalization efforts, observing that many problems that manifest themselves at the neighborhood level did not originate there and cannot be solved there. He then suggests a set of more comprehensive strategies within a metropolitan context to help revitalize older urban neighborhoods.

In Chapter 14 Gregory D. Squires examines the history of race in the mortgage-lending market and the impact of neighborhood-based groups in organizing protests and other activities to improve community reinvestment. He makes explicit the long-term contradictory role of the federal government in neighborhood investment. In addition, Squires reviews components of recent specific lending agreements in cities throughout the United States to illustrate the nature and extent of community lending efforts.

An analysis of public policies is the subject of Chapter 15, "Neighborhood Revitalization: Future Prospects," by Norman Krumholz and Philip Star. These policies were aimed at America's most obvious problem: the physical and social deterioration of severely depressed inner-city neighborhoods. Yet the decline of many urban neighborhoods continues unabated. Krumholz and Star discuss the shortcomings of many past federal programs, point to some successful approaches, and discuss needed future federal initiatives in urban neighborhood revitalization.

13

Metropolitan Development and Neighborhood Revitalization

Norman Krumholz

At an early stage, the American industrial city was making its living by manufacturing and exports. Like all cities of the time, it was a self-contained political unit surrounded by a hinterland that had few people and little economic activity outside of farming. The city contained rich and poor, employers and employees, and identifiable neighborhoods of different ethnic groups and classes. Rich or poor, native-born or immigrant, all city residents worked and lived in the same small space and under the same political administration. The major spur for the growth and development of the industrial city was jobs. Americans did not deliberately plan or build a city as much as agglomerate a mass of jobs. Everything else came after that.

The early industrial city was successful; that is to say, production and profits were high, and workers were educated, urbanized, and moved into the economy. But the industrial and residential density of the city made it increasingly difficult for manufacturing firms to receive or ship goods or to expand. Owners began thinking of moving their plants to outlying sites where they could take advantage of cheap and open land. As private investors, they were free to ignore the harm to the social and fiscal integrity of the central city that their suburbanization would bring. Wealthier residents also became aware of the city's limitations, especially with respect to crowding and deteriorating environments. They considered moving further out as well, but locational choices were constrained by limited transportation technology. That soon changed. First the trolley, then the train, and then the automobile opened up suburban areas for both industry and middle- and upper-class residents, and the growth of the suburbs and metropolitan regions began in earnest.

SUBURBANIZATION

The process of suburbanization has been under way since at least the beginning of the twentieth century. Studies indicate that over its first sixty years the density of population and economic activity has continuously decreased with distance from the center of the city (Mills 1970). The movement of the upper and middle classes to the suburbs, however, did more than "deconcentrate" densities in the central city. It also began to produce polarization of social and economic classes since each suburb enjoyed political autonomy and could determine the use and regulation of its land. As the suburbs developed, they used their zoning and other development regulations to keep the poor out in order to maximize land and housing values (Downs 1994). Racial discrimination was also employed as a means of developing and maintaining high-status and high-income suburbs.

Suburbanization is both a spatial and a class process; we have middle- and high-income classes and middle- and high-income suburbs. As one author has pointed out, the pleasures of living in a prestigious area away from the noise, congestion, and crime of the central city were benefits realized early and were available to those who could afford them (Suttles 1975). Suburban land-use control, racial discrimination, and the law of the housing market impacted central cities and determined early on that the lower-income population—especially the lower-income minority population—would live in the older, deteriorating neighborhoods of the central city.

METROPOLITAN GROWTH PATTERNS

One of the fundamental realities of metropolitan development is that regional growth is highly interdependent. Although the new communities and urban core may be miles apart spatially and light-years apart in status, the viability of inner-city neighborhoods is tightly related to the development of newer, expensive neighborhoods on the urban fringe and to the entire metropolitan development process.

Consider one example: a new highway is built connecting the urban core to the fringes of the metropolitan area. The highway causes manufacturing firms to reconsider their land-locked locations in the central city and to relocate to the suburbs. Workers follow their jobs to the suburbs and buy houses there. Housing developers take advantage of the access conferred by the highway and build new subdivisions on land that was formerly considered too far out for profitable development. Middle-class city families move into these new suburban subdivisions and their vacated houses are occupied in turn by families with more modest incomes. Housing continues to filter down from higher- to lower-income groups (Quigley 1979; Downs 1973; Birch, Brown, and Coleman 1979; W. Grigsby et al. 1980). If new construction continues to take place on the fringe far in advance of new household formation in the region, inner-city neighborhoods empty out and the rate of neighborhood decline in the city proceeds more rapidly (Bier 1991). If there is no demand in the weakest central-city neighborhoods, homes are lost through demolition or boarding-up—in either case, further blighting city neighborhoods. Meanwhile, poverty, racial discrimination, and the manipulation of development regulations discourage similar outward shifts by African Americans, Hispanics, and other minorities and concentrate them in the distressed neighborhoods of the central city. Thus a new regional highway affects transportation, land use, housing, population, and the vitality of urban neighborhoods across the entire metropolitan region.

The flow to the suburbs, which was a relative trickle before World War II, became a flood after the war and has accelerated further between 1980 and 1990. In 1950 central cities contained 57 percent of metropolitan-area residents and 70 percent of metropolitan-area jobs (Mieszkowski and Mills 1993). By 1990 central cities contained only 37 percent of all metropolitan residents and 45 percent of all metropolitan-area jobs. Manufacturing, once heavily concentrated in central cities, now finds the suburbs, where highways provide improved access and where land is available to build sprawling, single-story plants, a more attractive location. Between 1980 and 1990 the suburbs captured 120 percent of the net job growth in manufacturing; central cities consistently suffered losses in manufacturing employment (Hughes and Sternberg 1992).

Central cities have also lost their competitive advantage as locations for office space. In 1970 only 25 percent of the nation's office space was located outside central cities; by 1990, 57 percent was in the suburbs and commentators were writing about "edge cities" (Garreau 1991). Between 1980 and 1990, the rate of population growth in the suburbs was twice that in central cities, and two-thirds of all job growth during that decade was located in the suburbs (Hughes and Sternberg 1992).

In 1990 eight out of ten Americans lived in one of America's 330 metropolitan areas; between 1950 and 1990 the U.S. metropolitan population grew by 103.4 million to reach a total of 192.7 million while the country's nonmetropolitan population actually declined (Richmond 1994). In summary, population, private investment, jobs, and economic opportunity all have been migrating outward from the central city and into the metropolis, and the pace of this outmigration seems to be increasing.

CENTRAL-CITY/SUBURBAN DISPARITIES

As metropolitan growth takes place and expands, economic class and racial disparities widen between regional jurisdictions and central cities. Suburban jurisdictions, competing vigorously for new jobs, investment, and taxes, use tax-inducement tools to lure investment from central cities and legally prohibit lower-income families from moving into new-growth neighborhoods through the use of excessive building codes, exclusionary zoning, and other land-use regulations that make housing too costly for the poor. The central cities are left with disproportionate percentages of the poor, older neighborhoods, obsolete infrastructure, and a tax base that cannot support high-level public services. Central cities cannot levy taxes on suburban real estate. Outlying communities, however, with tax bases enriched by new industrial and commercial properties and the expensive homes of the affluent, can afford all the amenities, first-rate schools, and good public services.

Racial discrimination in urban housing markets further perpetuates disparities between central cities and mostly white suburbs. More than twenty-five years after passage of the 1968 Fair Housing Act, minority homeseekers routinely face discrimination about 50 percent of the time when they search for housing (Turner, Struyk, and Yinger 1991). Because of continued racial discrimination, American communities remain profoundly divided by race and ethnicity, with minorities living in neighborhoods that are predominantly minority and whites living in neighborhoods that are predominantly or exclusively white (Massey and Denton 1993). Because minorities are more likely to be poor than whites, the spatial concentration of minorities in inner-city neighborhoods concentrates poverty there and makes city governance more difficult and metropolitan solutions more intractable. These interrelationships of metropolitan growth and the realities of social and racial discrimination have produced the sharp contrasts that now exist between central cities and their suburbs. For example, in 1990 median income in central cities was almost 30 percent lower than in their suburbs, and the city poverty rate averaged 18 percent, compared with 8.1 percent in the suburbs. Disparities between cities and suburbs were greatest in the Northeast and Midwest, with New York City having three times the suburban poverty rate and Detroit having five times the poverty rate of its suburbs (HUD 1995).

CONSEQUENCES OF METROPOLITAN DISPARITIES

There are many consequences of this bifurcated and uneven metropolitan development pattern. A major consequence for poor urban neighborhoods and their people is the fact that they are becoming increasingly disconnected from the opportunities and general prosperity of their metropolitan regions (Massey and Denton 1993; Goldsmith and Blakely 1992; Downs 1994). America no longer defines itself as a "nation of cities" where immigrants of different cultures and languages gather together to be educated, urbanized, and employed in the larger economy. Instead, our national economy is increasingly being described as a system of metropolitan-centered regional economies that transcend city boundaries and even state lines (Peirce 1993). Within this metropolitan context, the central cities typically lag behind the economic performance of the region.

We have an obligation to improve the lives of these families, mostly minority, who have been "filtered" out of the suburbs and must cluster together in the oldest, most dilapidated neighborhoods of the central city. Here they suffer from the cumulative effects of persistent poverty, unemployment, crime, bad housing, poor health, and a host of other multilayered problems that make it difficult for them to improve their situation. The needs of this persistently poor population are immediate and urgent; if their isolation and distress are not addressed, social peace in America might be severely compromised.

Other serious consequences exist. Recent studies have suggested strong relationships between the overall health of metropolitan economies and city-suburban economic disparities (Ledebur and Barnes 1993; Savitch et al. 1993). Where city-suburban economic disparities are lowest, regional employment grows fastest. These studies suggest that lagging central cities act as a drag on the totality of regional economic growth. Smoothing the disparities could very well spur the pace of regional growth and development.

Inner-city decay and regional sprawl impose other major costs on society as a whole. Existing infrastructure in depopulated city neighborhoods becomes redundant and must be built anew in the region; downtown employees who might wish to move closer to their jobs fear the inner city and decline to consider close-in neighborhoods, compromising the city's redevelopment plans; labor is wasted when central-city residents cannot find work in firms that have moved to the suburbs; reliance on private transportation to connect increasingly spatially separated places of work and residence is wasteful, consumes green space, causes environmental pollution, and is very expensive. To underline this point, the United States spends 15 to 18 percent of its gross national product on transportation; Japan spends only 9 percent.

The fiscal bind of many central cities caused by having high fractions of low-income residents and low fractions of high-income residents results in curtailing police, fire, educational, and other public services, thus making problems of crime and antisocial behavior even worse. Fears of crime and violence provide many families with another reason to leave troubled city neighborhoods.

The poor performance of inner-city school systems significantly threatens the nation's economic future. We know that education is the key to success—personally and nationally—but educational achievement of public school students in our inner cities is well below that of their peers in more affluent communities. Inner-city schools educate about one-third of all American schoolchildren. If we are to compete effectively in world markets, we must improve the skill levels of these students. Yet concentrated poverty reduces the resources available for public education.

Changing these metropolitan growth dynamics and improving distressed central-city neighborhoods seem an overwhelmingly difficult task. The forces involved—federal and state transportation policies, pervasive poverty, mortgage-lending and other real estate practices, the desire of most American families for a single, detached home in new surroundings, white preferences for racially dominant neighborhoods, ingrained patterns of racial discrimination—seem to be of such scale and power as to be beyond shaping by any city or any neighborhood (Birch 1971).

Intervention for creating stable or revitalized urban neighborhoods requires an approach that challenges past trends and the notion of inevitability. Indeed several studies do suggest that purposeful action by neighborhood groups, government, local institutions, or business at the neighborhood level may be effective in stabilizing or reversing neighborhood decline (R. Smith 1993; Taub, Taylor, and Durham 1984; Cunningham and Kotler 1983). Even more encouraging is the success of community-based development corporations in rebuilding parts of disinvested neighborhood infrastructure. These emerging signs of neighborhood recovery are still tentative, but solid pockets of revitalization are appearing in older cities like Chicago (Ahne and Holli 1993), Newark (Sviridoff 1994), and the South Bronx (Horowitz 1994). It is possible that these early signs of neighborhood revitalization might be facilitated by a broader local, state, and federal strategy than now exists.

TOWARD A COMPREHENSIVE NEIGHBORHOOD REVITALIZATION STRATEGY

The best strategy to undertake in the revitalization of distressed urban neighborhoods is one that follows the recommendations of the National Advisory Commission on Civil Disorders (Kerner Commission) in its 1968 report: attempt both to enrich ghetto neighborhoods and seek more racial integration. This strategy rejects the choice between empowering poor people and revitalizing distressed places. Both types of assistance are necessary to improve city neighborhoods and connect poor people to housing, jobs, and opportunity wherever they exist in the region. Good services and housing in inner-city neighborhoods are crucial to the people who live there. Yet, we must look beyond the neighborhood and its problems for ultimate solutions.

Our past failures in neighborhood revitalization are due partially to a lack of metropolitan perspective. Every president since the 1950s has affirmed his support for urban neighborhoods. Such programs as Urban Renewal (1954), Community Action Program (1964), Model Cities (1966), Community Development Block Grants (1974), Neighborhood Self-Help Development Grants (1977), Urban Development Action Grants (1977), and Empowerment Zones (1994) in one way or another were created to provide support for urban neighborhoods. All have fallen short because they have not dealt with the fact that metropolitan problems are linked and that regional disparities are found in the primacy of the regional marketplace in defining people's worth and entitlements. Building a reform agenda for neighborhood revitalization must take these metropolitan factors into consideration.

A key first element in a comprehensive neighborhood revitalization strategy is a neighborhood advocacy organization or community development corporation. Cities should help fund and empower such neighborhood-based organizations. The goal is to upgrade neighborhoods while protecting the interests of low-income owners and renters. Neighborhood-based organizations provide the crucial interface between neighborhood needs, energy, and resources. Advocacy organizations focus on the basic needs of their neighborhoods and generate attention and increased investment. In the face of great obstacles, CDCs have developed an impressive record over the last decade.

Community-based initiatives are particularly important because they ensure that the community both initiates and supports programs for their neighborhoods. Chances for success improve dramatically when the community is a partner to development. Further, community-based organizations may be able to do more than simply develop housing and economic development projects. They may also be able to encourage community discipline, tap neighborhood spirit, and promote self-help, all in short supply in many troubled city neighborhoods.

Viable community-based organizations may also be the key to encouraging private neighborhood investment and maintaining support from key institutional actors whose decisions are vital to neighborhood revitalization. Such institutions as hospitals, universities, banks, and other commercial businesses can use their resources and institutional power to sway governmental decisions, bolster the real estate market, and create neighborhood confidence. Any city interested in the revitalization of its neighborhoods must engage these key institutions in support of its neighborhood-based organizations.

Cities must also encourage banks and other lenders to observe the letter and spirit of the Community Reinvestment Act of 1975 and the Home Mortgage Disclosure Act of 1976. Both acts represent the culmination of successful neighborhood advocacy, as Gregory Squires points out in the following chapter. Cities willing to use the leverage of the reinvestment act can expect significant results. In Cleveland, for example, the city's intervention in the merger of Society and Ameritrust banks in 1991 resulted in a $260 million lending commitment over five years for neighborhood housing and commercial development. Cities must also continue to support such vehicles as the Low Income Housing Tax Credit, which is a primary source of equity funds for housing development. A free flow of mortgage credit and equity financing can make an enormous difference for the better in disinvested neighborhoods.

The need for functioning, viable neighborhood-based organizations is particularly crucial in low-income neighborhoods with bad conditions and few neighborhood institutions. Strong neighborhood organizations can help rebuild neighborhood infrastructure and also improve services by pressuring city government to raise the level of service delivery and perhaps by delivering some services themselves. They also may be able to strengthen the social fabric of their communities by supporting mediating structures such as churches, credit unions, and PTAs. The purpose is to help low-income residents gain more control over their own lives, build self-worth, and have more influence over local affairs (Ahlbrandt and Cunningham 1979). For these reasons, cities, foundations, and other supportive institutions should devote significant resources to creating and empowering such organizations.

Some cautionary notes should be added. Although the work of neighborhood advocacy groups and CDCs is positive, it is often difficult to discern in their work a long-term, coherent, city-wide strategy. Many CDCs rehabilitate abandoned housing in their areas, unaware that, given a city's soft housing market, they may simply be shifting the abandonment problem to another neighborhood. As groups work on present problems and issues, they operate without nessarily having a larger, long-term perspective. CDCs assume that the problems of their neighborhoods can be resolved there, but this assumption is questionable given the interrelated nature of the metropolitan housing market. Each neighborhood group competes for services and resources with other neighborhood groups, assuming that all neighborhoods in the city can be revitalized equally. But the causes of neighborhood change are complex. Any city's resources are extremely limited, and neighborhoods have widely different strengths and weaknesses, making it unlikely that all distressed neighborhoods can be restored.

Therefore, cities cannot depend on neighborhood-based development alone. A more comprehensive, long-term strategy is needed, one that stresses city and neighborhood efforts but that involves regional, state, and federal responsibilities as well. This comprehensive strategy must be prepared by the city and should include ten-year projections of such variables as population, housing, income, employment, and so forth for each neighborhood, along with target accomplishments and review procedures. These analyses should guide over-all city investment strategies. Neighborhood groups cannot be expected to have such a long-range, broad strategy. Rather, they are partisans for their own turf. That makes them ideal organizations to pressure the city to improve services, pressure major institutions and businesses to support their neighborhood, and pressure property owners to maintain standards but not necessarily to take a longer view.

A second cautionary note has to do with race. Cities should make a special effort to control rapid neighborhood change based on race. Such change often involves panic selling and speculation and leaves both buyers and sellers with losses and grievances. Instead of accepting such change as inevitable, cities should seek to stabilize racially integrated neighborhoods. The goal is to maintain a level of white confidence so that the neighborhoods will remain integrated and in so doing, keep the market and property values strong. Shaker Heights, Ohio, has successfully used this strategy for many years as has Oak Park, Illinois (Keating 1994). It involves strong code inspection, strict regulation of the real estate market to avoid racial steering and blockbusting, counseling, and subsidies for families making integrative moves. Both the Shaker Heights and Oak Park examples suggest that racial (and some income) diversity can be sustainable if a strong, proper effort is made.

Part of a city's neighborhood revitalization strategy should include encouraging and cooperating with growth management schemes that may be undertaken by their suburbs. Some suburbs are interested in slowing or entirely blocking growth for environmental or other local reasons. In regions of vigorous population expansion, restricting suburban growth could restore strong demand for central-city neighborhood housing. This strategy could also work, but to a lesser extent, in slow-growth areas. For example, Cleveland's suburbs grew by 280,000 people in the 1960s. If half that gain had been redirected at city neighborhoods, they would have gained population instead of losing 125,000 residents.

Low-growth or no-growth cities anxious to revitalize their neighborhoods should add other metropolitan-wide dimensions to their strategy. The intent of these approaches is to encourage region-wide racial and economic integration. They could include:

- "fair share" housing policies (supported by planning and zoning) that will encourage the development of low- and moderate-income housing in all jurisdictions of the metropolitan area. Roisman and Botein (1993) suggest a variety of such "housing mobility" schemes;
- strict enforcement of fair employment and fair housing policies to ensure full access by minorities to the job and housing markets of the region;
- housing assistance policies, modeled on Chicago's Gautreaux program or Montgomery County, Maryland's program, to voluntarily scatter low-income families to small-scale housing developments and to rent-subsidized private rental housing throughout a diversified metropolitan housing market (Rosenbaum 1995);
- tax-sharing arrangements, such as those in Minneapolis–St. Paul, that will offset tax-base disparities between the central city and its suburbs.

STATE AND FEDERAL POLICIES

The federal government could help revitalize central-city neighborhoods by providing more favorable tax treatment for rehabilitation than for new construction and by providing enough housing-assistance subsidies to help low-income families improve in-place residences or relocate to suburban housing. It could also help enormously by accepting its responsibilities to act vigorously against racial discrimination in housing under Title VIII of the Civil Rights Act of 1968. In that regard, the government should move in three directions: first, by carrying out fair-housing audits and encouraging audits by state and local agencies; second, by making sure that discriminators pay a substantial price for their violations of the law; and third, by taking steps to improve the access by all people to information about available housing. There is ample evidence that control over this flow of information is a key tool used by persons who discriminate (Yinger 1987).

If these suggested metropolitan-wide programs worked, and minorities were distributed in some reasonable proportion throughout the entire region, there would be no serious racial disparities among neighborhood schools, nor would poor minorities be entrapped in backwater, central-city neighborhoods far from suburbanizing job opportunities. A metropolitan-wide program of racial integration would have other benefits as well. Urban neighborhoods that are all or mostly nonwhite are now seen as off-limits for white movers who might otherwise prefer to locate there. As neighborhoods change, losing businesses, investment, and jobs in the process, the boundaries of this area of exclusion come to embrace more and more of the city. In the process, the city's own ability to redevelop itself is severely compromised.

Finally, it should be emphasized that poverty is a fundamental root cause of neighborhood decline. The best neighborhood revitalization strategy, then, would simply be the elimination or substantial reduction of poverty. Federal programs directed toward the elimination of poverty are to be sought for many objectives other than neighborhood revitalization, but focusing on poverty would direct attention to the root causes of neighborhood decline and also highlight the urgent need for improvement of all types in the poorest urban neighborhoods.

Ending or substantially reducing poverty must include efforts to provide jobs for low-income city residents and to raise the real incomes of the central-city poor. In adopting the first of these objectives, it should be clear that the need is to create jobs for low-income city residents, not necessarily to create jobs in inner-city neighborhoods. Given the metropolitan nature of our economy, it is likely that the best employment opportunities for inner-city residents are in the suburbs. There are, after all, powerful economic reasons why the economy has decentralized to such an extent. Government policy should help connect the inner-city poor with employment opportunities wherever they occur in the region using information networks, child-care, and transportation support as appropriate. Most of these inner-city workers would probably continue to live in the inner city and bring money back to their city neighborhoods to spend on housing or in local retail stores, improving the overall neighborhood economy. But if city workers with suburban jobs want to move to the suburbs, we must be ready to translate the worker's economic achievements into real housing opportunities wherever they occur in the region. Minority inner-city workers must have the same degree of choice about where to live as white working-class Americans do.

So far as job-creating subsidies are concerned, capital subsidies may produce new buildings and investor profits in real estate, but they are not the answer to reducing unemployment in the ghetto. Labor subsidies would be much more efficient. Employers hiring a worker who had been certified unemployed for a given period of time would receive an hourly cash subsidy, with the amount decreasing over time as the worker's productivity increased with training and experience.

But full employment would do little to eliminate poverty among those millions of working American families whose full-time earnings are insufficient to lift them out of poverty. For those households, an expansion of the Earned Income Tax Credit (passed in 1993) would provide a pay raise for the working poor, making a $4.25-an-hour job pay the equivalent of $6.00 an hour. Also, an increase in the minimum wage as proposed by President Clinton in 1994 would be helpful. At $4.25 an hour, the present minimum wage has fallen far behind inflation. The $.90-an-hour increase that has been proposed will enable workers in low-paid jobs to better support themselves and their families.

Overall, our efforts in neighborhood rebuilding will be easier when we come to realize that we have been using central ideas such as competition, individual choice, local control, and community to divide our metropolitan regions rather than to build common ground. In the process, we have created problems that threaten our future and the long-range prosperity of the entire U.S. economy. It is time to build bridges and correct these problems.

14
Friend or Foe? The Federal Government and Community Reinvestment

Gregory D. Squires

Following decades of passivity and neglect in enforcing its fair-lending requirements, and often serving as a force for explicit racial discrimination in credit markets, the federal government has begun to alter its course. Primarily as a result of pressure from community-based organizations, federal financial regulatory agencies constitute a sleeping equal-opportunity giant that is beginning to wake up. Lenders themselves are starting to acknowledge that racial discrimination is a problem, and federal regulators have recently begun to take some tentative actions to alter lending behavior.

Fair access to credit, however, remains a highly contentious political struggle. Despite some recent victories that do suggest important changes in both lender and regulator activity, conflicts still remain and signs of a backlash have appeared. The trajectory of future developments is not at all clear. As one HUD official recently asked, "Are we going through a period of fair housing lite, or are we in the process of implementing real fair lending law enforcement?"

In this chapter the centrality of race and racism in credit markets within urban communities is briefly reviewed. Recent changes in the law, regulatory actions, and lending behavior itself are then discussed, focusing on the role of community organizations both in conjunction with and opposition to regulatory agencies and financial institutions. Tentative projections for future developments and outlines for actions that can have a favorable impact on those developments are then offered.

RACE AND RACISM IN URBAN CREDIT MARKETS

Race has long been an explicit and central factor in mortgage lending markets in urban America. Sixty years ago University of Chicago sociologist and federal housing policy adviser Homer Hoyt ranked fifteen racial and ethnic groups in terms of their impact on property values in a report he prepared for the Federal Housing Administration. Those having the most detrimental impact were Negroes and Mexicans (Hoyt 1933). Following the advice of its expert, in its 1938 underwriting manual the FHA concluded, "If a neighborhood is to retain stability, it is necessary that properties shall continue to be occupied by the same social and racial classes. A change in social or racial occupancy generally contributes to instability and a decline in values" (U.S. Federal Housing Administration 1938, par. 937).

The FHA was also a leading advocate of racially restrictive covenants that virtually guaranteed that properties would be occupied by the same classes over time. These covenants were enforceable in court until the U.S. Supreme Court ruled them unenforceable in the 1948 case *Shelley v. Kraemer.*

The FHA was a major source of home financing from its inception in 1930 through the 1950s, when it financed 60 percent of all home purchases, virtually all of which were in suburban communities (Lief and Goering 1987, 229). During the 1960s, the FHA reversed itself and flooded central cities with federally insured mortgages. Liberal loan terms and lower costs made the loans attractive to low-income buyers. Since the costs were paid up-front and were insured by the federal government, they were attractive to many lenders. Often working with local realtors, lenders would solicit home purchases from families who could not, in fact, afford the acquisition. Exploiting racial fears in many cases, blockbusting resulted in the swift racial transition of urban communities. Thousands of families shortly defaulted on the loans, contributing directly to the deterioration of once vibrant neighborhoods. The linchpin of such destruction was the availability of federally insured loans that guaranteed the profits of lenders and realtors but cost many families their homes and life savings. The operation of the dual housing finance system—conventional loans for white suburbanites and FHA loans for nonwhite inner city residents—cemented the division of American society into the predominantly white and affluent suburbs and largely poor nonwhite central cities forewarned by the Kerner Commission in 1968 (Bradford 1979; Bradford and Cincotta 1992).

The racist policies and practices of the federal government were matched by those of the private housing industry. In 1932 a leading real estate theoretician, Frederick Babcock, observed, "There is one difference in people, namely race, which can result in very rapid decline. Usually such declines can be partially avoided by segregation and this device has always been in common usage in the South where white and negro populations have been separated" (Babcock 1932, 91). The American Institute of Real Estate Appraisers used the following example to illustrate neighborhood analysis into the 1970s: "The neighborhood is entirely Caucasian. It appears that there is no adverse effect by minority groups" (Greene 1980, 9). Until 1950, the National Association of Realtors stated in its code of ethics that "a Realtor should never be instrumental in introducing into a neighborhood a character of property or occupancy, members of any race or nationality, or any individual whose presence will clearly be detrimental to property values in the neighborhood" (Judd 1984, 284). And in 1988 a sales manager for the American Family Insurance Company, in a tape-recorded statement, said, "I think you write too many blacks. . . . You gotta sell good, solid premium paying white people. . . . They own their homes, the white works. . . . Very honestly, black people will buy anything that looks good right now . . . but when it comes to pay for it next time . . . you're not going to get your money out of them." The explicit attention paid to race has been a key factor in accounting for the dual housing market and rigid patterns of racial segregation in urban areas throughout the United States (Jackson 1985; Massey and Denton 1993).

In the late 1960s the federal government began an about-face in its approach to the dual housing finance market and the dual housing market generally. With passage of the Federal Fair Housing Act in 1968 and the Equal Credit Opportunity Act in 1974, prohibiting discrimination in housing and housing finance markets; the Home Mortgage Disclosure Act of 1975, requiring disclosure of where mortgage loans were being made; and the Community Reinvestment Act of 1977, requiring depository institutions affirmatively to ascertain and be responsive to the credit needs of their entire service areas, the federal government began to act as a force to dismantle systems of discrimination.

Not surprisingly, enactment of these statutes has not eliminated discrimination in mortgage lending. Racial disparities have been documented by several academic researchers (Bradbury et al. 1989; Shlay et al. 1992), government agencies (Munnell et al. 1992; Canner and Smith 1992), journalists (Dedman 1989; Everett et al. 1988), community organizations (Woodstock Institute 1993; National Community Reinvestment Coalition 1994), and others (Carr and Megbolugbe 1993; Housing Policy Debates 1992).

Nationwide, black mortgage-loan applicants are rejected approximately twice as often as whites, with the Hispanic rejection rate falling between that of blacks and whites. The gap can be partially explained by differences in the socioeconomic status and, therefore, credit worthiness of these groups. But other factors, including discrimination, also contribute to the gap. The most comprehensive study of mortgage lending discrimination was conducted by the Boston Federal Reserve Bank (Munnell et al. 1992). In examining over 3,000 loan application files with 131 Boston area lenders, the researchers found that among black and white applicants with identical credit records, debt histories, income, and other financial characteristics, the black applicants were rejected 60 percent more often than the white applicants.

Among the discriminatory practices that contribute to the racial gap in mortgage lending is the differential "coaching" that black and white applicants receive. Marginal white applicants (e.g., those whose current debt-to-income ratios slightly exceed traditional guidelines) are more likely to be counseled during their application so that the final application can be approved, but black applicants will simply be rejected. White applicants, for example, may be advised to pay off or consolidate certain debts. Loan officers may also look more closely for compensating factors in the application of white borrowers or simply be more familiar with existing compensating factors of white applicants (Munnell et al. 1992; Hunter and Walker 1995). Concentration of bank offices in suburban communities, underwriting guidelines that have a disparate impact on minority applicants though no racial animus is intended (e.g., minimum loan amounts that exclude a disproportionately higher number of racial minorities than whites), and the relatively small number of black employees in lending institutions are some of the contributing factors (Squires 1992; Kim and Squires 1994).

The accumulation of research and attention paid to the issue of racially discriminatory lending by regulators, public officials, journalists, and lenders themselves has begun to alter lender and regulatory activity. The primary stimulus of such rethinking has been the efforts and effective organizing by community groups.

COMMUNITY ORGANIZING AND THE COMMUNITY REINVESTMENT ACT

Unable to obtain mortgage loans from area lenders, a group of homeowners in Chicago organized the West Side Coalition, a merging of community organizations. They used a variety of Alinsky-style tactics to get the attention of those financial institutions. They would drop pennies on the floor of banks and savings and loans during their busiest hours. On Saturdays they would open and close accounts for one dollar. Picket lines were organized and depositors agreed to close their accounts if lenders did not meet with leaders of their community organizations. In 1974, one year before HMDA and three years before CRA, the first CRA–type agreement was signed. The Bank of Chicago agreed to prioritize and target loans to residents of neighborhoods represented by the Organization of the Northeast (ONE). Three similar agreements were negotiated by ONE with three other lenders later that year (Pogge 1992).

The same community organizations played key roles in securing enactment of HMDA and CRA shortly after these victories. HMDA requires most federally regulated depository institutions publicly to report the number of loans, the type and purpose of those loans, and the dollar volume of its mortgage lending activity in urban areas by census tract. As amended in 1990, HMDA requires lenders to disclose the race, gender, and income of all applicants and the disposition of all applications. Under the CRA, federally regulated lenders "have a continuing and affirmative obligation to help meet the credit needs of the local communities in which they are chartered." Federal financial regulatory agencies (the four principal regulators are the Federal Reserve Board, the Office of the Comptroller of the Currency, the Federal Deposit Insurance Corporation, and the Office of Thrift Supervision) periodically evaluate lenders under their jurisdiction. Those evaluations and a final rating (outstanding, satisfactory, needs to improve, or substantial noncompliance) are to be kept on file and also made available to the public upon request. Regulators are required to take lenders' CRA performance into account when evaluating applications from those institutions they supervise whenever the lenders seek permission to open a new branch, merge or purchase another institution, increase their depository insurance, or to make almost any other significant change in their business practices.

The key provision of the CRA is that third parties—usually community organizations—can challenge such applications. The challenges often delay consideration of the application and therefore can be quite costly for the financial institution. Regulators rarely deny applications on CRA grounds, but often they take time to review the challenges and frequently ask the lender and the organization filing the challenge to attempt to seek a voluntary solution. The challenge process provided leverage that several groups have used to negotiate reinvestment or CRA agreements.

Community organizations, often in conjunction with supportive public officials, sympathetic reporters and academics, and friendly lenders, have used the opportunities created by the information made available through HMDA and the affirmative requirements established by the CRA. Chicago, again, led the way.

The Community Reinvestment Alliance, a coalition of over thirty community groups in Chicago, negotiated agreements totaling $173 million over five years beginning in 1984 with three of that city's major banks. In 1988 and 1989 the three banks announced extensions of these agreements for an additional $200 million over another five years. These commitments covered various types of financing, including home purchase and home improvement loans, mixed-use real estate and commercial loans, and home equity loans. And up to $3 million in direct grants was provided from the lenders' foundations for community groups involved in housing and business development.

In Atlanta, a Pulitzer Prize–winning series of reports by Bill Dedman (1989) led to a $65 million commitment by lenders in that city. Using research assistance from Calvin Bradford with Community Reinvestment Associates and Charles Finn with the Hubert H. Humphrey Institute at the University of Minnesota, Dedman documented that white areas received five times as many loans as black areas with comparable incomes. Dedman's subsequent research (1989) on the ratio of black-to-white mortgage-loan-application rejection rates had national policy implications. The Atlanta commitments included low-interest loans to low-income families for home purchases and improvements and the creation of a loan pool for working-class neighborhoods.

The city with the largest black/white ratio in rejection rates during the 1980s, as Dedman's research showed, was Milwaukee, Wisconsin, where blacks were rejected four times as often as whites. Immediately after the publication of Dedman's findings the mayor of Milwaukee and the governor of Wisconsin convened several meetings involving local lenders and regulators, civil rights and community groups, and others. Frustrated by the lack of progress in altering industry practices, an ad hoc coalition of labor unions and community groups was formed to pressure one large bank, leading to the successful negotiation of a reinvestment agreement. Buoyed by this experience, the Fair Lending Coalition was formed as a permanent organization. The coalition consists of several community organizations, civil rights groups, churches, and labor unions. With financial support from the City of Milwaukee, local foundations, and its members, the coalition, working with faculty and students at the University of Wisconsin–Milwaukee, began researching lending patterns and filing CRA challenges. To date, the coalition has negotiated agreements with ten lenders totaling over $100 million over five years. The agreements also call for new branch banks (three of which have opened), affirmative action commitments to create more employment opportunities for racial minorities with local financial institutions, and commitments to increase purchases from minority contractors.

Research noted earlier by the Boston Federal Reserve Bank led to similar outcomes. Six community groups formed the Community Investment Coalition, and with the strong backing of then mayor Raymond Flynn negotiated a five-year $400 million lending program with ten area banks. These commitments included financing for home purchases, with some loans at below-market rates, for inner-city residents; new branch banks; improved banking services, including the cashing of Social Security and welfare checks; additional automatic teller machines; and other reinvestment provisions (Squires 1992).

Similar stories have unfolded in at least thirty-one states involving over 100 community organizations and over 200 financial institutions. Over $60 billion has been committed for reinvestment in more than 300 agreements (National Community Reinvestment Coalition 1994; 1995). Although there are some common elements in most agreements (e.g., commitments to increase the number of dollars for housing and community development) each agreement is unique. A variety of features has been incorporated into these partnerships.

CRA agreements include commitments for home purchase and improvement for single-family and multifamily units. Some are at below-market rates, others waive various closing costs, some reduce points, and still others eliminate or reduce mortgage insurance requirements. Underwriting standards have been altered and made more flexible. Counseling, second reviews of rejected applications, and self-testing for discrimination are other elements of some agreements. Business loans are frequently incorporated, often targeting small businesses, minority- and women-owned businesses, and other commercial development projects. Participation in public and privately formed loan pools is featured in some agreements. Consumer and farm loans are required by others. Improved banking services are a feature of many programs. Improvements include new branch banks, free checking accounts, cashing of government checks, hiring bilingual staff, and other affirmative action to diversify lender work forces.

A variety of new marketing and educational programs are also frequently incorporated. Specific elements include advertising in minority media, calling programs to meet with local realtors in minority areas, seminars on homeownership, individual and family counseling, and various reporting programs to increase accountability. The CRA has proven to be an effective and flexible tool for reinvestment, particularly where there is an effective community-based organization to employ the law (National Community Reinvestment Coalition 1994).

FEDERAL INITIATIVES AND THE RESPONSE OF LENDING INSTITUTIONS

Organizing efforts by community-based groups have also led to more aggressive enforcement efforts by federal regulatory agencies and more creative voluntary responses from private lenders. As one bank official in Milwaukee acknowledged, "Community based organizations helped us understand how to market ourselves better and understand the market and programs that might have to be developed to meet the need in the inner city." He also admitted, however, "Without the law, the bank would never have done these things on its own" (Squires 1992, 1, 22).

Perhaps the most concrete evidence of the shifting role of the federal government is a series of settlements that the Department of Justice has entered into with six lenders. In 1992 the department settled the first pattern-and-practice lawsuit brought by the federal government against a mortgage lender. Following up on Bill Dedman's Atlanta research, the department launched an investigation of one of Atlanta's largest mortgage lenders, Decatur Federal Savings and Loan. Among the evidence obtained by Justice was the fact that between 1985 and 1990 over 97 percent of the lender's mortgage loans were made in predominantly white census tracts, and not one of the institution's forty-three branch offices was in black census tracts. Little marketing was done in minority areas, and few minorities were employed in professional positions. Black applicants were rejected more than four times as often as whites, and a multivariate analysis of more than 2,000 loan files found race to be a significant factor in determining whether or not to approve the loan after controlling on relevant socioeconomic characteristics. The settlement included $1 million for forty-eight plaintiffs and changes in the lender's underwriting practices, commitments to increase advertising in minority media and marketing efforts in minority communities, affirmative action commitments to increase minority employment, and changes in the compensation structure of loan officers to encourage more inner-city lending (*United States v. Decatur Federal Savings & Loan Association* C.A., no. 1:92-CV-2198 [N.D. Ga.] 1992).

In its lawsuit against Shawmut Mortgage Company in Boston the Justice Department charged that the company required black and Hispanic applicants to provide more information than whites, applied more stringent underwriting requirements to blacks and Hispanics by failing to consider compensating factors that were taken into consideration with white applicants, and failed to approve the applications of blacks and Hispanics that did not meet all the lender's underwriting standards but that were equal to or better than applications from whites that were approved. Justice also charged that the lender used several underwriting guidelines that exerted a disparate impact on black and Hispanic applicants, including failure to consider the stability of an applicant's income as opposed to employment stability, prior record of rent and utility payments, and nontraditional sources of cash for down payments. Terms of the settlement included the creation of a $960,000 compensation fund for individuals injured by the lender's previous practices; opening a new branch in the predominantly minority community of Roxbury; more advertising in minority communities; training of loan officers in the principles of fair lending; and expansion of its mortgage review board, which reevaluates qualifications of rejected minority applicants (*United States v. Shawmut Mortgage Company* C.A., no. 3:93-CV-2453 [D. Conn.] 1993).

The Department of Justice charged First National Bank of Vicksburg with charging higher interest rates and offering different terms and conditions to minority borrowers than were offered to whites. The bank agreed to develop new loan policies that would provide for nondiscriminatory loan terms, to implement a loan review process to ensure compliance with fair-lending requirements, to develop an educational program on fair lending for loan officers, to contract with a qualified organization to conduct paired testing of the bank in the future, and to deposit $750,000 into a trust account to be administered jointly with Justice for loans to parties aggrieved by the bank's past practice (*United States v. First National Bank of Vicksburg* C.A., no. 5:94-CV-6 [B] [N] [W.D. Miss.] 1994).

Blackpipe State Bank in South Dakota was charged with discriminating against American Indians by refusing to make loans on properties located on Indian reservations and in providing different terms and conditions on loans it did make for American Indians. The lender agreed to expand its service area to include reservations, train its loan officers in fair-lending practices, recruit Indian employees, market its loan products to American Indian communities, and provide $125,000 in compensation to victims of past practices (*United States v. Blackpipe State Bank* C.A., CV: 93-5115 [D. S.D.] 1994).

In its case against Chevy Chase Federal Savings Bank, the Justice Department did not find evidence of discriminatory treatment in the underwriting of applications from minority borrowers but charged the bank with discriminating in its marketing practices due to its failure to market its products in minority communities within the Washington, D.C., metropolitan area. Over 97 percent of the bank's loans were in white areas, in part because only four of its seventy-seven branches and eighteen mortgage offices were in predominantly black census tracts. Justice also charged the bank with failing to solicit loans in black neighborhoods, advertising primarily to white customers, and using a commission structure discouraging small loans, which adversely affects minority areas. The bank agreed to pay $11 million to redlined areas through a special loan program and to the opening of three branch banks and one mortgage office. Chevy Chase also agreed to advertise extensively and target sales calls in black areas, recruit black loan officers, and take steps to obtain a market share in black communities comparable to its share in white areas (*United States v. Chevy Chase Federal Savings Bank* et al., C.A., CV: 9-1-1824JG [D. D.C.] 1994).

In spring 1995 the Justice Department settled a case against the Northern Trust Company in Chicago, relying primarily on a review of loan files the department found showing that the bank provided white but not black or Hispanic applicants with an opportunity to explain adverse items on their credit reports. The bank also often helped white applicants find offsetting qualifications to compensate for those negative factors but did not provide the same assistance for blacks and Hispanics. As a result, sixty victims received $566,500 in damages, an additional $133,500 was placed in a fund to compensate additional victims who may be identified, and the bank agreed to take actions to ensure that all applicants have the opportunity to present their qualifications fully (*United States v. Northern Trust Company* C.A., no. 95C3239 [E.D. Ill.] 1995).

The Justice Department is not alone in its efforts to combat discrimination and redlining. In 1993 the Office of the Comptroller of the Currency announced that it would soon be using paired testing as part of its investigatory tools. HUD has also begun to use paired testing in its enforcement efforts.

The 1992 Federal Housing Enterprises Financial Safety and Soundness Act established specific numerical goals for the purchase of loans by the Federal National Mortgage Association (Fannie Mae) and the Federal Home Loan Mortgage Corporation (Freddie Mac) to finance mortgages for low- and moderate-income families and in central cities. These two private government-sponsored enterprises are major actors in the secondary mortgage market, which purchases loans from loan originators, and in doing so they increase the pool of funds available for mortgage loans. Under the act, the 1994 targets called for 30 percent of the dwellings financed by loans purchased by these two agencies to be located in central cities and 30 percent to be for low- and moderate-income families.

In January 1994 President Clinton issued Executive Order 12892 calling for all relevant federal agencies to develop rules ensuring that their programs will be administered in a manner that affirmatively furthers fair housing. Among the specific mandates of the order is a directive to HUD to promulgate detailed regulations describing the nature and scope of lending conduct that violates the Federal Fair Housing Act. Although discriminatory lending practices have been explicitly prohibited since the act was passed in 1968, HUD (the agency charged with primary responsibility for enforcement and the only agency with authority to issue clarifying regulations) had never previously promulgated such rules.

An Interagency Task Force on Lending Discrimination was also created in 1994. The task force consisted of eleven agencies, including the Department of Justice, HUD, Treasury, the Federal Reserve Board, Comptroller of the Currency, Office of Thrift Supervision, Federal Deposit Insurance Corporation, Federal Housing Finance Board, Federal Trade Commission, National Credit Union Administration, and Office of Federal Housing Oversight. The task force issued a Policy Statement on Discrimination (1994) to provide guidance for lenders, consumers, and others on the types of practices that would constitute illegal lending discrimination. The statement does not supplant the detailed regulations of each regulatory agency, but it represents an initial step to provide a more coordinated response to the problem of discrimination. Perhaps its most significant component is the conclusion that unlawful discrimination can occur as a result of disparate impact as well as by intentional discrimination or disparate treatment. Under the disparate-impact standard, particular policies or practices that are applied uniformly across all applicants and are neutral on their face may exclude a disproportionate share of protected class members and, therefore, may constitute unlawful discrimination. Where such a practice can be justified as a business necessity and where no less discriminatory alternative is available that would serve that business purpose, there would be no violation. But, as the Chevy Chase case cited indicates, intentional discrimination against black or Hispanic applicants, or individual members of any protected class, may not be necessary to establish the presence of unlawful discrimination and to trigger remedial and affirmative actions by lending institutions.

Several voluntary initiatives have followed from the pressure generated by community groups and law enforcement authorities. The word "voluntary," of course, must be used advisedly in this context. But for whatever reason, several lenders have initiated efforts, sometimes in collaboration with community organizations and regulators and often on their own, to increase their presence in low-income areas and minority communities.

A recent survey of 130 lenders by the Consumer Bankers Association indicates how widely at least certain changes have been institutionalized (Harney 1994). Of the lenders surveyed, 96 percent had lowered their down payment requirements for moderate-income buyers, with the average down payment on "affordable housing" being just 4.2 percent. Over 93 percent reported they had developed more flexible standards for their front-end ratio (monthly housing payment compared to monthly income) and back-end ratio (total monthly debts compared to income). Industry standard ratios are approximately 28 percent and 36 percent; for moderate-income buyers these ratios average 33 percent and 39 percent among those reporting more flexible standards.

Lenders are also using new approaches for evaluating credit and work histories. More than 94 percent of the respondents to the survey report that they now take into consideration rent and utility payments in addition to conventional credit reports. Almost 80 percent reported they now look beyond length of employment with current employer and consider such factors as length of time employed generally and income stream over time.

HUD and the Mortgage Bankers of America (MBA) announced a collaborative effort to stimulate more lending activity in minority areas. In a Fair Lending–Best Practices Master Agreement (1994), HUD and the MBA set out a series of Best Practices that they will encourage mortgage lenders to pledge to follow. Indeed, the MBA will encourage its members to sign an agreement to pursue these policies and objectives. The initiative is strictly voluntary and has no force of law.

Under the agreement the MBA will assist its members in conducting self-testing. The association will also foster closer working relationships between its members and real estate agents, developers, and others active in minority communities. It will develop educational and other outreach programs to increase minority employment in the industry. It will also foster education and training programs for consumers and current loan officers. And the association will assist in the development of more flexible underwriting standard and market-analysis tools for lenders.

Individual lenders will be asked to sign a pledge to pursue Best Practices to improve their performance in minority and low-income neighborhoods. Efforts include setting goals to increase lending activity in such areas, promotion of more flexible underwriting guidelines, establishment of second-review programs to reconsider rejected loan applications to ensure compliance with fair-lending principles, self-monitoring efforts to assess market share in previously underserved areas, establishing outreach programs to work with local business and community groups, and minority recruitment and training efforts to increase minority employment. Performance targets will be established to permit evaluation of these efforts in the future.

Unquestionably, there are a variety of motives that stimulate such "voluntary" actions. As James McLaughlin, a lobbyist for the American Bankers Association, commented, "It's pretty clear the mortgage bankers were hoping to fend off CRA–type regulation" (Knight 1994). (Independent mortgage bankers not tied to federally regulated depository institutions are not covered by the CRA.) Still, such efforts would not have been contemplated just a few years ago.

COMMUNITY REINVESTMENT AND FAIR LENDING:
AN ONGOING STRUGGLE

Despite the progress that has been made, conflict persists. Community groups are still challenging lenders under the CRA and criticizing regulators for lax enforcement efforts. Lenders openly attack what they view as overzealous efforts by regulatory agencies. The agencies themselves are split on key issues. Real changes have taken place within the past few years that have resulted in concrete benefits for previously underserved communities; however, there is evidence of an emerging backlash.

In 1993 President Clinton called for new regulations under the CRA that would focus enforcement efforts more on performance and less on procedures. After two rounds of proposed rules and highly contentious discussion (over 6,700 comments were received by regulators in response to the first proposed rule and more than 7,200 were received in response to the second), the end result is a highly complex and ambiguous set of guidelines. Financial institutions will be evaluated primarily in terms of their performance in three areas: lending, investment, and banking services. But specific rules are few and the expectations for lenders remain vague.

Regulatory agencies have broad discretion in evaluating those institutions they supervise, and it is likely that the new rules will be perceived by many community groups and lenders as providing little clarification regarding the requirements of the law.

Another point of contention is the mix of institutions that is covered by the CRA. Currently, independent mortgage banks are not covered. Representatives of commercial banks and thrift institutions that are covered claim that the mortgage banks should be covered by the CRA to create a level playing field. In 1995 over half of all mortgage loans were originated by financial institutions that are not subject to CRA rules, and their share of the market is increasing (Fiechter 1994, 7).

Despite efforts to foster greater coordination of federal regulatory activity, schisms persist among the agencies. In fall 1994 Jonathan L. Fiechter, acting director of the Office of Thrift Supervision, publicly criticized the Clinton administration's approach to fair lending. He expressed particular concern with the Chevy Chase settlement, which he said "represents an application of the law that is untested in the courts. . . . The OTS has never criticized an institution for failing to open a branch somewhere" (Glater 1994a).

The Federal Reserve Board has come under particularly strong criticism for lax fair-lending enforcement (Thomas 1993). Most recently, the Fed approved an application for an acquisition by Barnett Banks of Jacksonville, Florida, despite letters from the Justice Department that the bank was under investigation for lending discrimination. John Taylor, executive director of the National Community Reinvestment Coalition, responded: "The message this sends out is: 'Even if the highest law enforcement agency in the country thinks that you're practicing discrimination, we're going to allow you to do business as usual and even expand.' That's a bad message to send" (Glater 1994b).

These differences are unlikely to be resolved amicably in the near future. Following the Chevy Chase settlement, the Savings and Community Bankers of America—a trade association representing thrifts and banks—created a $100,000 war chest to fight at least some fair-lending initiatives. The funds will be used to defend selected institutions and may also be used to support research, public relations campaigns, or a friend-of-the-court brief as part of an advocacy campaign (Meredith 1994).

If changes are in the wind, it is not always clear which way that wind is blowing. As Edward L. Yingling, chief lobbyist for the American Bankers Association, observed, "We've gone from a decade in which the consumer activists were really able to push their legislative agenda to a point where they not only can't push forward but we can begin pushing back" (Garsson and de Senerpont Domis, 1994).

Despite these recent skirmishes, clearly significant advances have been made in addressing the problems of redlining and discrimination in mortgage lending. Explicit use of race in the appraisal of properties and evaluation of borrowers are no longer the norm. At the same time, lenders and regulators generally acknowledge that problems of discrimination and credit availability in low-income communities persist and that they have an obligation to respond to these problems. It is equally evident that further progress will be realized only if there is ongoing outside scrutiny and pressure on these institutions to perform. One constant, which has been demonstrated over decades and will persist into the future, is the essential role of effectively organized community-based organizations in the nation's urban neighborhoods.

15
Neighborhood Revitalization: Future Prospects

Norman Krumholz and Philip Star

The future of urban neighborhoods is in doubt. Although it is difficult to postulate a city without neighborhoods, it is certainly feasible to imagine the continuation of the decline of urban neighborhoods to the extent that they no longer fulfill their historic role and are little more than places that people who have no other resources are forced to occupy. Some of the worst inner-city ghetto public housing projects in urban America are certainly proof that deterioration of buildings and spirit can fall to such levels. Is there reason to believe that such decline might happen or that it might be accepted by our society?

The writers of this book who chronicle the success of community organizing and community development corporations, along with the national political movement that seeks to devolve decisionmaking to the state and the local community, provide some strong evidence that such pessimism is not in order. However, the objective facts must give us pause. Over the past thirty years, our cities generally have become poorer and are struggling financially, poverty has increased and become more concentrated, population has decreased and employment opportunities have either decreased or are available in the service sector at significantly lower wage rates. These trends have occurred during a period of innovation in community development and the rise of significant public/private partnerships to address urban problems.

There is little doubt that by virtually any measure, the condition of urban America, at least in its older cities and their neighborhoods, has worsened significantly in recent years. Disinvestment persists and jobs, especially manufacturing jobs, continue to leave these neighborhoods, while unemployment and poverty, especially affecting racial and ethnic minorities, keep rising sharply.

There is also little doubt that local political and civic leadership generally has responded to the rising tide of neighborhood disinvestment and poverty by downplaying it and emphasizing their "successes" in building new downtown projects. While troubled neighborhoods and their residents languished, mayors and civic elites in the 1980s addressed most of their attention to building new hotels, sports arenas and stadiums, and convention centers—embellishing their cities' image as they prepared for a tourist-driven economy in the future (Frieden and Sagalyn 1989).

Unfortunately, for many large cities, neighborhoods now fall into one of four categories: (1) nonviable—areas that are no longer viable because of extensive and concentrated poverty, few services, and little hope; (2) rapid decline—neighborhoods that are quickly worsening and moving to the first category; (3) slow decline—neighborhoods that are experiencing incipient deterioration and have fought to avoid more rapid decline; and (4) stable and viable. It is mostly those cities that have grown along with the expansion outward through annexation or have experienced significant gentrification that can point with pride to improving neighborhoods.

There have of course been victories and accomplishments. Undoubtedly, without community organizing, the work of CDCs, and locally initiated revitalization efforts supported through federal funding, our cities would be even less viable. A strong sense of neighborhood and community still prevails in many of the second and third categories in our cities, but the stresses and strains continue to build that have brought about the drastic decline of many of our older city neighborhoods. In any statistical description of this decline that looks at poverty rates, unemployment, increased crime and drug use, and infant mortality, our cities appear to present living conditions that seem to be intolerable. Yet the residents in these neighborhood areas do survive, do provide support networks, do find community, and have found ways in some places to rebuild and improve their living environment. Tragically, even for the most positive examples of change that have been documented, and for urban areas generally, the neighborhoods are much worse to live in today than they were in the past.

This pattern is reflected in polls showing that most Americans do not want to live in cities. Less clear is whether the decline of our urban neighborhoods is inevitable as part of the process of urbanization or whether we have established significant experience and models that can provide the blueprint for revitalization and the national will to address neighborhood needs. In reality, residents in these areas, no matter how well organized, will not have much say in what happens to their neighborhood. Urban neighborhoods are at the mercy of the national debate on the role of the federal government, fundamental economic trends in our economy, and the shift to a majority suburban electorate brought about by the forces of urban sprawl. Moreover, central cities with large minority populations do not claim sympathetic attention from an America that has not successfully dealt with segregated public schools, housing patterns, and racist attitudes.

The present national debate over the role of the federal government in terms of solving local problems like urban blight has been joined in one way by the

Contract with America, passed in the U.S. House of Representatives in 1995 by the newly elected Republican majority. Proponents of the Contract interpreted the electoral results as a call by the American people to get government off their backs and decrease federal spending. In response, the House passed a budget with $1.4 trillion in cuts, including major slashes in housing and community development. The implications for urban neighborhoods are significant. The Clinton administration has offered only minimal assistance to central cities, including funding for the Empowerment and Enterprise Zone program, and has not articulated a clear urban policy.

It must first be noted that this conservative Congress was elected mostly by suburban voters. There are presently more suburban registered voters than there are registered voters residing in American cities, and the gap is widening. Given the numbers, it will be difficult for large cities to exert their historical political power on the state or national level. Suburbanites generally have higher incomes than central-city residents and little political will to pass tax increases that shift resources back to the central cities.

At this writing, it is impossible to know the full extent of federal deficit reduction efforts. The early proposals suggest that many of the programs that have been available to assist community development activities in cities, such as the Community Development Block Grant program, will be significantly decreased to aid deficit reduction. Progress that has been made so far in our cities has been accomplished through a combination of renewed local activity and local government response supported by state and federal funding. The further loss of federal funding will cripple many of the new initiatives. Ironically, when communities have finally begun to find ways to plan their own future through community-based and locally generated initiatives, the lack of federal support for their efforts may undo what has been achieved.

The impact of federal funding cannot be overemphasized. The success of community efforts is often cited as evidence that local communities know their own needs and can act themselves without excessive intervention by the federal government. The success that has been achieved, however, in most cases results from significant federal support that is used locally to address identified neighborhood needs. Between 1985 and 1995, the CDC movement has produced 175,000 housing units that are community-generated and controlled. Yet in one year before the Nixon moratorium on federal subsidized housing construction, the federal government allocated funds for the development of 570,000 new and substantially rehabilitated housing units. In 1995 federal funding was appropriated for fewer than 20,000 new and rehabilitated units a year, and almost all low-income units are produced with federal assistance in the form of Low Income Housing Tax Credits and through CDBGs. Over the twelve years of the Reagan-Bush administrations, over 80 percent of the HUD budget was cut. Further cuts proposed in 1995 will have strikingly similar results.

FACTORS IN HOUSING

Providing housing is an important part of the process of reclaiming neighbor-hoods, and federal support is one of the key factors in a community's ability to rebuild. The lack of direct federal participation in the production of affordable housing does not signal a complete retreat from the housing field; rather, it exem-plifies the shift of resources from cities (with shrinking economic bases) to the suburbs.

The federal government is involved in housing in a major way through the encouragement of homeownership via the tax system, which allows the deduc-tion of mortgage interest for homeowners who itemize deductions on their income tax returns. The greater the mortgage, the greater the interest deduc-tion. Thus, middle-income homeowners with household incomes from $20,000 to $40,000 a year received a $6.2 billion subsidy, but only one in three received any benefit (income figures adjusted to 1992 dollars based on a 1989 American Housing Survey). However, for homeowners with incomes above $90,000, the federal subsidy was $25.4 billion, and 83 percent of these owners were able to take advantage of the subsidy. It is interesting to note that home-owners with incomes above $65,000 received over $41 billion in subsidies, but that renters with incomes below $20,000 received direct subsidies of only $13.6 billion. In fact, of the lowest-income renters (incomes below $10,000), only one out of three received any type of subsidy. The gap in subsidies for the very low-income residents who live in our nation's cities and the upper middle class who live in our suburbs has been widening over the past ten years.

This sort of tax break is just one example of the increasing disinvestment in our city neighborhoods and the type of policy options that favor suburban development. Present efforts to attract the middle class to our cities rely upon favorable tax treatment for higher-income homeowners. Yet the average city dweller in the income range of $20,000 to $40,000 gains little assistance from the federal government on this front. With the more expensive housing stock and greater tax benefits available in the suburbs, there is an ever-increasing pull on people to seek homeownership in the suburbs. Nevertheless, without subsidy programs such as CDBGs, the cities will not be able to produce hous-ing to attract homeowners and compete with suburban development.

In a period of concern for deficit reduction, our approach to housing subsidy policy and its impact on cities raises some serious policy issues. Why do we favor homeownership? It is assumed that homeownership provides stability, security, an improved quality of life, and a stake in the community. However, most low-income families are renters, and the majority of housing units in most cities are rental properties. Public policy that emphasizes homeownership by its very nature overlooks the needs of a majority of city dwellers. Present policy reinforces a notion of neighborhood and housing as a place to invest, not as a place to live and find community. Climbing the ownership ladder moves people out of cities, but incentives to encourage people to stay are needed, along with attempts to address problems that renters face. The Mutual Housing Associations described by Rachel Bratt and the Low-Income Housing Coalitions described by Edward Goetz in Part Three serve as examples of solutions to deal with this imbalance.

The lack of equity and the imbalance in the housing subsidy picture is also mirrored in the way highway and infrastructure funds are allocated, in tax incentives that encourage employers to move to the suburbs, and in utility rates that subsidize outward expansion. Urban sprawl is a relentless process that continues to erode our cities and their neighborhoods. Originally considered a process of filtering that allowed people the possibility to improve their surroundings and open up opportunities for the next wave of residents, the process has taken on a life of its own. In many communities characterized by low growth, urban sprawl has eroded the basic structure and viability of neighborhoods.

The latest threat to urban neighborhoods is the cost of reusing land. Monumental efforts have been made since the 1970s to provide available financing through the Community Reinvestment Act to fund new development and to assemble land through tax foreclosures and land-banking. However, although land acquisition presents great opportunities for competition with the suburbs, it often can create a further challenge for the urban neighborhood. Often the land is contaminated or has had previous structures that have been buried on the site. The additional cost of rehabilitating it must be absorbed by the community, a cost not present in the development of farmlands. Inner-city land, or "brownfields," may present the greatest challenge to the rebuilding of our urban neighborhoods if the federal government no longer is an available partner. The costs of environmental clean-up are often beyond the reach of local resources and cannot be passed on to new owners if the site is to be competitive.

Moreover, in addition to the pressures of suburban development, dwindling federal resources, and mounting problems with schools and crime, inner-city neighborhoods may face the biggest challenge yet from advances in technology and the information superhighway. Integral to the life of the city in the past was the walking community. The advent of the streetcar reshaped the American city, and the development of the automobile made the suburb possible. The computer challenges our long-held conception that community has a spatial component. We know that many people now find community in ways that are not related to a geographic place or to a family network.

Recently, the importance of community has been raised and reviewed in many different forums. One philosophical approach has been that of the communitarians, who look to the need to reassert community over individualism. Their view is that individual rights have been given an unnatural position over individual responsibilities and that in order for our society to survive we need to readjust the imbalance. Those people involved in community-building and urban development must struggle with these same issues. In our efforts to rebuild urban neighborhoods, issues concerning the value structure are implicit. The communitarians suggest that we need to be clear in our understanding and in our actions that the replication of the past may not be sufficient grounding for the community of the future.

COMMUNITY-BUILDING

A current trend is the effort to move neighborhood development to the level of community-building. This approach suggests that although individual efforts within neighborhoods have had some positive impact, ultimately they are limited since they provide only for a piecemeal approach. The community-building movement is based on a holistic approach that suggests all efforts must be integrated into a plan that has been developed by all the stakeholders in the neighborhood.

The community-building approach has had a variety of sponsors and forms. The Ford Foundation, working with local community foundations in Boston, Cleveland, Denver, Oakland, San Antonio, and Washington, D.C., has sponsored research on poverty that has evolved into five local community-building projects. The Enterprise Foundation, in addition to funding housing development for low-income families, has become a sponsor with the City of Baltimore in a neighborhoodwide community-building initiative in the Sandtown-Winchester area. The Annie E. Casey Foundation's New Futures program is operating in five cities: Bridgeport, Dayton, Little Rock, Pittsburgh, and Savannah. Each New Futures project serves as a focal point for local decisionmaking about at-risk youth and as a mechanism for improving the performance of youth-serving institutions.

Other initiatives have gone beyond individual neighborhoods to focus attention on revitalization of the entire community. The Atlanta Project and Healthy Boston are just two examples of such projects identified by the National Civic League. These projects stress a collaborative leadership model with broad-based community involvement in setting comprehensive neighborhood goals and plans for realizing them. As Susan Fainstein and Clifford Hirst point out in Chapter 7 in regard to the Minneapolis Neighborhood Revitalization Program, there is often a significant difference between the concept of neighborhood planning and the ability to provide a process that guarantees that the entire community is represented and that revitalization can be achieved. Although the ideal of a community's participation in defining its own future is often articulated as an important tenet of democracy, local politics and political realities tend to undercut effective participation. Even when local political leadership is supportive, the external forces affecting the neighborhood can undermine local citizen efforts. However, as we have seen in Minneapolis and Los Angeles, citizen participation through neighborhood planning provides a positive model that can be built upon to achieve a mechanism that does help to rebuild community and avoid issues that divide rather than unite. Outward sprawl and economic realignment are simply forces far beyond the control of neighborhood organizations or local planning efforts.

Even with the impressive results of some CDCs and neighborhood revitalization strategies, given the fact that urban neighborhoods still serve an important function for new immigrants to our country and as a safety net for people in poverty, there is considerable concern for the future of neighborhoods. If only the present efforts are maintained it is fair to conclude that some urban neighborhoods will see a revival of the market and some improvement. Yet there is little to suggest that the downward trend of the past several decades in our urban areas, in terms of poverty, unemployment, crime, and increasing infant mortality, will change.

Moreover, there is reason to speculate that the downward trend will actually accelerate as more and more strands of the safety net are cut on the national level. Just as there is the emerging recognition that neighborhood revitalization must be comprehensive, with various activities building incrementally, the opposite appears to happen. As supports are removed, there is a multiplier effect; the speed of decline is intensified and the downward spiral increased. Fragile communities that have begun to experience some sense of hope and change can easily be shattered. Significant investments in time, resources, and planning can easily be undercut if efforts are just continued but not enhanced. The present rate of investment and resources will provide only marginal change. A reduction of resources may challenge our ability to maintain any viable inner-city neighborhoods, thus beginning the cycle of decline in the inner-ring suburbs. This need not happen. The importance of community and the historical value of settlement in neighborhoods is clear. To decide wisely how we allocate our resources is the challenge for the future.

HOPE FOR THE FUTURE

There are solid reasons to hope that most older urban neighborhoods can still be revitalized. Indeed, in 1995 the map of urban America was dotted with neighborhoods that had been declining only a short time earlier but that are now enjoying a wave of new investment. These neighborhoods have been described by Richard Nathan (1992) as "zones of emergence." According to Nathan, these emerging neighborhoods are areas that are increasingly occupied by minority low-wage earners who are joining an expanding minority middle class. In the process, they are moving up from slum and persistently poor neighborhoods into the economic mainstream, where many are becoming homeowners. Homeowners have deep concerns about community safety, good public services, and general neighborhood stability, and such concerns may help improve city services and revitalize neighborhoods. Nathan has identified such zones of minority middle-class emergence in the New York boroughs of Queens and Brooklyn as well as in Cleveland, Indianapolis, St. Louis, Columbus, and Kansas City.

SOURCES OF NEIGHBORHOOD VITALITY

Besides a growing minority middle class, four other promising sources of urban neighborhood vitality have been mentioned in the preceding chapters: (1) the Community Development Corporations, which emerged in the 1980s as important producers of low- to moderate-income housing and other neighborhood infrastructure; (2) the elaborate network of intermediaries that help support the CDCs; (3) the federal Empowerment Zone program; and (4) the possible return of the middle class to city neighborhoods.

Community Development Corporations

The origins, history, and accomplishments of the CDCs have already been well-documented in this book. Many other studies have also documented the large number of new and rehabilitated affordable housing units built by the CDCs, the amount of commercial square footage they have under management, and the housing repairs and energy conservation retrofits they have accomplished (NCCED 1989).

As important as the actual production of housing units and commercial space is, the much larger mission of the CDCs is the reconstruction of the social fabric of devastated neighborhoods. As the CDCs have flourished, whole new groups of neighborhood leaders have been educated about housing and the potentialities of community organizing and leadership. The hope and promise of this approach to neighborhood development are that by building the capacities and power of low-income and working-class people and by developing their community leadership and institutional capacity, they will be in a position not only to maintain and stabilize their neighborhoods but also to demand even more far-reaching economic and political changes in the future. It was, after all, neighborhood advocacy and organization that inspired the Community Reinvestment Act and the Home Mortgage Disclosure Act of the 1970s and the Low Income Housing Tax Credit of 1986.

There are signs that the CDCs understand well the need to maintain the link between community organization, social advocacy, and their own development work. For example, in February 1992 a coalition of CDCs in the South Central neighborhood of Los Angeles applied for a charter to establish a credit union. It was rejected; one reason given was that South Central did not constitute a community because of to its "size and geographic configuration." After the civil disturbance, the application was resubmitted with a map showing that the South

Central area had distinct borders for imposing the curfew during the riots. The charter was immediately granted, and the South Central People's Federal Credit Union is now doing business (Johnson et al. 1994).

Another example of skilled advocacy has to do with the New Community Corporation in Newark. In 1989 NCC wanted to construct a 102-unit homeless shelter. Obstacles to the project were presented by HUD, which held the title to the land and claimed it would take six months to review the proposal, and by the City of Newark, which was reluctant to issue an occupancy permit because of disagreement over previous tax policies. The day following its meeting with HUD and the city, NCC broke ground for the project anyway. NCC's coordinator said, "We built the building and sent HUD a picture and they . . . were extremely upset. We got [HUD Secretary] Kemp to call Newark's HUD office and tell them to wake up and smell the coffee, that helping the homeless is what their mission is all about. They resolved the title situation within an hour." To force the city's hand, NCC contacted a local TV station and assembled families who would be homeless at Christmas. "A reporter confronted the mayor and asked: 'Do you want to be Scrooge or Santa Claus?' Ten minutes later, NCC had its certificate of occupancy" (Lewis 1993).

There is reason to believe that CDCs may be able to maintain or increase their political support, funding base, and overall achievements. However, it hinges on the CDCs' ability to expand their political voice through coalitions built with minorities, liberals, labor unions and the like, on continuing their efforts to resolve disorganization and chaos, and on garnering additional support from corporations for their self-help approach to community revitalization.

Intermediaries

Intermediaries have been essential to the success of the CDCs. Because of their crucial function, it is worth providing some amplification of earlier discussions on intermediaries in the chapters by Edward Goetz and Avis Vidal. To revitalize their deprived and disinvested communities, CDCs need capital, technical support, and access to various social subsidies. Yet local governments are often reluctant supporters of community-based development since dealing with neighborhood groups may be difficult and politically embarrassing. For their part, banks, developers, and for-profit investors are also nervous about investing in capital projects in neighborhoods that they perceive as high-risk. And few people in the conventional business world understand the complex difficulties that confront CDCs on a daily basis.

To help bridge this gap in understanding and to obtain the resources needed to function, CDCs work with numerous intermediaries, a sector that includes hundreds of organizations. They range from multimillion-dollar foundations such as the Ford, Joyce, MacArthur, and Rockefeller foundations that may fund CDCs directly and that also fund other supporting organizations, such as the Local Initiative Support Corporation and James Rouse's Enterprise Foundation, to one-person technical assistance agencies that may teach CDCs how to syndicate tax credits or manage apartments. These intermediaries share the concern of the CDCs for improving the lot of the urban poor and revitalizing their neighborhoods. Their funding and technical assistance is provided in support of these objectives.

Intermediaries cluster into two broad groupings. One grouping consists of organizations that provide information to CDCs and work to reshape the political agenda to encourage others to provide support. Two examples (of many in this category), on the national level are the Center for Community Change and the National Congress for Community Economic Development. Locally, citywide organizations that provide technical assistance on projects exist in many large cities, and urban universities provide outreach and technical support. The second set of intermediaries provides direct financial support, equity investments, and political assistance when necessary. It consists of socially benevolent foundations and housing partnerships. Also included are banks that seek to satisfy the requirements of the Community Reinvestment Act and federal banking enterprises such as Fannie Mae and Freddie Mac. These institutions grant or lend money, work to give shape to the development agenda, and are also frequently influential in the realm of providing essential political support.

The largest of the intermediaries in 1995 was the Local Initiatives Support Corporation, set up by the Ford Foundation in 1979 on the theory that organizing and protest were not enough to revitalize a deprived community and that visible brick and mortar projects were also essential. LISC was established to provide the financial wherewithal to help CDCs bring about the physical change needed for social uplift. Not only does LISC provide funds to support affordable housing and commercial projects in disinvested neighborhoods, but it also encourages other private-sector sources to invest in similar projects. Further, LISC acts as a leading lobby in Washington to pressure for increased support for housing programs and to advocate changes in the tax code to help the nonprofit development industry. By 1994 LISC had raised more than $880 million from 1,100 private-sector sources to support 875 CDCs. LISC and its constituent organizations have leveraged another $1.9 billion and built or rehabilitated 44,000 affordable homes in some of the nation's most distressed neighborhoods (Sviridoff 1994).

The political and institutional support and funding of the intermediaries are key to CDC success. According to one knowledgeable commentator: "The rise of the national, state, and local intermediaries is the single most important story of the non-profit development sector in the 1980s. Arguably, without this source of support for grassroots development activity, state and local governments would have displayed far less responsiveness to non-profit developer needs over the decade. . . . National intermediaries [such as LISC, the Enterprise Foundation, the Neighborhood Reinvestment Corporation, and so on] have been the single most important stimulus to local creation of housing partnerships and other local intermediaries" (C. Walker 1993).

Empowerment Zones

In December 1994 the Clinton administration announced the winners among the cities that had applied for Empowerment Zone funding, a $3.5 billion urban revitalization program. Six cities (Atlanta, Baltimore, Chicago, Detroit, New York, and Philadelphia-Camden) each were to receive $100 million in block grant funds and $150 million in federal tax credits to implement their plans to revitalize their most distressed neighborhoods. Los Angeles and Cleveland were designated as Supplementary EZs with slightly lower fund allocations and another sixty-nine cities received much smaller block grants ($3 million each) to plan for future revitalization projects.

The EZ program includes many parallels to the 1966 Model Cities program, which was an important part of President Johnson's War on Poverty. Like EZ, the Model Cities emphasized concentration of resources on distressed target neighborhoods, coordination among existing efforts, participation and empowerment of community residents, and a comprehensive strategy that went beyond bricks and mortar to include investments in education, job training, and employment. Given the similarities between the generally disappointing results of the Model Cities program and EZ, why should the latter be regarded more hopefully?

Although the EZ initiative can be traced to previous failed federal efforts like Model Cities, it seems that this time the federal government is following rather than leading in its attempts to revitalize distressed neighborhoods. Model Cities was in part designed to organize and provide neighborhood infrastructure if none existed at that time, but EZs are building on strong initiatives that already exist in most cities. Local networks of CDCs and their local and national intermediaries have been hard at work since 1975, gaining expertise and political support in the process and delivering essential improvements in neighborhoods of persistent poverty and decline. These local efforts already include extensive collaboration and support involving key sectors of the community, comprehensive approaches to neighborhood development that often include human development as well as housing, and a commitment in the community to "empower" neighborhood residents and businesspeople. Moreover, large community development initiatives similar to EZs are already under way in many cities. Most visible of these is the Atlanta Project, the Enterprise Foundation's Sandtown-Winchester project in Baltimore, the Surdna Foundation's Comprehensive Community Revitalization program in New York's South Bronx, and the Casey Foundation's New Futures initiative in four other cities. Given this existing structure and experience, it is not unreasonable to hope that the EZ program will build successfully on these existing initiatives.

The Middle Class

The final hope for the revitalization of older urban neighborhoods is the possible return of sizable sections of the middle class from the suburbs. The middle class is still leaving the city, but their relative economic position has been weakening in the last two decades because of the stagnation of their income. The mean real-cash income of the middle quintile of all families has actually fallen from $25,909 in 1973 to just $25,823 in 1989 (measured in 1989 dollars). These virtually flat incomes suggest that middle-income families may be hard-pressed to pay for the ever-increasing costs of homeownership in the suburbs. In contrast to housing values in the suburbs, housing in most city neighborhoods is a substantial bargain. Transportation may be seen as a bargain as well. In a suburban situation with a couple working, the ownership and expense of two cars is almost inevitable. Central-city neighborhoods with effective public transportation systems offer the potential of substantial transportation savings. Whether a large-scale, back-to-the-city movement actually will materialize is an unknown.

Obviously, continued support for urban CDCs from their intermediaries and the federal government is essential. These costs show up in the federal budget as the CDBG, the Home Ownership Made Easy program, the EZs, the Low Income Housing Tax Credit, and other subsidy programs. In its zeal to balance the budget, Congress may be tempted to cut or eliminate such programs. But if lawmakers properly understand the past accomplishments and future promise of the CDCs, they will continue to provide support to those organizations that have proven their ability to spend public money in an enormously productive way.

POLICIES FOR CHANGE

Lawmakers on both the state and national level could also review present policies that support urban sprawl and look at legislative alternatives that would support neighborhood revitalization and limit further expansion. The following list of initiatives or policy recommendations have been proposed to respond to the disinvestment and destabilization of our nation's urban neighborhoods. The list is not comprehensive, nor do we suggest that any one of these policies is the answer to our urban dilemma. Rather, the proposals are provided to indicate that there are other public policies and approaches that, if considered, would ensure a very different future for urban neighborhoods.

1. Increase federal resources for cities. The Milton S. Eisenhower Foundation on the twenty-fifth anniversary of the Kerner Commission Report issued a 1993 report, *Investing in Children and Youth, Reconstructing Our Cities: Doing What Works to Reverse the Betrayal of American Democracy.* Its authors argue that many of the federal efforts to eliminate poverty, such as Head Start, have had great success. The answer to urban problems is "to mount programs on a scale equal to the dimension of the problems." The report documents successful programs and suggests increased rather than decreased federal funding.

2. Limit urban sprawl. Portland, Oregon, has enacted growth limits based on state enabling legislation. A line has been drawn around the city restricting the expansion of sewers or water lines to any outlying areas. New, denser developments have occurred within the boundaries thus established.

3. Limit suburban residential growth in order to stimulate inner-city housing demand.

   a. Limit new sewer and water systems.

   b. Change the tax code to allow favored capital gains treatment for purchasing a less expensive home.

   c. Cap the deduction for mortgage interest for area median homes to decrease outward expansion and to provide tax incentives for purchasing homes within central-city neighborhoods.

   d. Establish yearly maximum permits for new housing in the entire metropolitan area.

   e. Enforce environmental protection regulations on air and water pollution to prohibit or limit growth in environmentally fragile portions of the metropolitan area.

   f. Create green belts for open space and recreation by purchasing all available vacant suburban land.

   g. Purchase development rights to agricultural land to keep it agricultural.

   h. Create a federal or state building-permit tax charged against every new suburban housing unit within those metropolitan areas with significant central-city housing surpluses.

   i. Shift the financing of new infrastructure that makes suburban development possible (such as roads, streets, sewer and water systems, street lights, and schools) from general property taxes to building permit fees.

   j. Require that utilities charge the actual cost of new service to areas of expansion instead of incorporating it into the rate base, which means central-city residents pay for new suburban developments.

   k. Require local governments to develop future land-use plans that must be approved by the largest municipality to address the issues of urban sprawl.

4. Require every suburban housing developer or other developer to prepare and file detailed environmental- and urban-impact statements concerning the effects of any proposed project before it could be built.

5. Finance environmental clean-up of urban land to make it competitive for reuse to compete with suburban greenfields.

6. Increase the use of the National Highway Trust Fund to address inner-city transportation needs rather than suburban interstate highway needs.

7. Strengthen Community Reinvestment Act provisions to require disclosure of business lending and to increase incentives for meeting community credit needs.

8. Provide for tax sharing between central cities and their suburbs, a system used, for example, in the Minneapolis–St. Paul region. Although it would require state enabling legislation, such a system would provide cities increased resources to maintain neighborhoods.

9. Merge cities with their surrounding suburban areas through regional government to address issues of public education, tax resources, and interdependence. David Rusk (1993) argues that "elastic" cities, those that have grown in size and

annexed the new suburbs, have reduced poverty and increased economic development more than cities that have remained inelastic and are limited by lack of annexation power.

10. Effectively enforce existing fair-housing laws to provide housing opportunities to all residents throughout metropolitan areas.

11. Recognize other forms of property ownership within the tax code to increase the equity that residents of urban neighborhoods have in their property.

12. Reform welfare to support family formation and economic security through employment (an issue that is part of the on-going national debate on welfare reform).

Many urban neighborhoods today are in great distress. In the past they have served a vital role in providing immigrants their start in this land and have provided community and support for generations of families. The forces of suburbanization, urban sprawl, and changing employment patterns have destabilized many traditional neighborhoods in our inner cities. The future of our cities is directly tied to the future of their neighborhoods. That neighborhoods have served and continue to serve vital functions is not in doubt. Two other issues are more problematic: Can cities survive if neighborhoods continue to decline? and Will the city as we know it today continue to be the economic focus of our society?

On both the local and national levels, there is an exciting effort within most cities and many neighborhoods to revitalize our traditional neighborhoods. Over the past few decades there has been significant support for and recognition of the importance of these revitalization efforts. Moreover, we have learned that there is not a simple formula for revitalization. There is, however, a need for locally based efforts supported by national resources. If we continue to recognize and value the importance of our city neighborhoods, with appropriate policy adjustments that balance the incentives for urban development, there is clear evidence that neighborhoods can be revitalized and continue to offer support, security, and community to their residents.

References and Selected
Bibliography

Abrams, Charles, with the assistance of Robert Kolodny. *The Language of Cities: A Glossary of Terms.* New York: Viking Press, 1971.

Ahlbrandt, Roger S., and James V. Cunningham. *A New Public Policy for Neighborhood Preservation.* New York: Praeger, 1979.

Ahne, J., and Melvin G. Holli. "Chicago's Seoul-Mates: Korean Immigrants Thrive as a New Merchant Class." *Chicago Enterprise* 8:3 (1993): 16–21.

Appelbaum, Richard, Peter Dreier, and John Gilderbloom. "Scapegoating Rent Control: Masking the Causes of Homelessness." *Journal of the American Planning Association* 57:2 (Spring 1991): 153–64.

Applebome, Peter. "Changing Texas Politics at Its Roots." *New York Times,* May 31, 1988.

Babcock, Frederick. *The Valuation of Real Estate.* New York: McGraw-Hill, 1932.

Baer, William, and C. Williamson. "The Filtering of Households and Housing Units." *Journal of Planning Literature* 3 (1988): 127–52.

Bahá, 'Abdu'l. *The Promulgation of Universal Peace.* Quoted in *The Power of Unity: Beyond Prejudice and Racism,* comp. Bonnie Taylor. Wilmette, IL: Bahá'í Publishing Trust, 1986.

Bahá'u'lláh. *Writings of Bahá'u'lláh.* New Delhi: Bahá'í Publishing Trust, 1986.

Banerjee, Tridib, and William C. Baer. *Beyond the Neighborhood Unit: Residential Environments and Public Policy.* New York: Plenum Press, 1984.

Barber, Benjamin R. *Strong Democracy: Participatory Politics for a New Age.* Berkeley: University of California Press, 1984.

Barton, Allen H., et al. *Decentralizing City Government: An Evaluation of the New York City District Manager Experiment.* Lexington, MA: Lexington Books, 1977.

Barton, Josef. *Peasants and Strangers: Italians, Rumanians, and Slovaks in an American City, 1890–1950.* Cambridge: Harvard University Press, 1975.

Bennett, Larry. *Fragments of Cities: The New American Downtowns and Neighborhoods.* Columbus: Ohio State University Press, 1990.

———. "Harold Washington and the Black Urban Regime." *Urban Affairs Quarterly* 28:3 (March 1993): 423–40.

Bennett, Lerone, Jr. *Before the Mayflower: A History of Black America.* New York: Penguin Books, 1987.

Berenyi, Eileen Brettler. *Locally Funded Housing Programs in the United States: A Survey of the 51 Most Populated Cities.* New York: Community Development Research Center, 1989.

Bernstein, Kenneth. "Rebuilding L.A. After the Riots: What's Been Done So Far?" *Planning Report* 7:9 (June 1992).

Berry, Jeffrey M., Kent E. Portney, and Ken Thomson. *The Rebirth of Urban Democracy.* Washington, DC: Brookings Institution, 1993.

Bier, Thomas E. "Public Policy Against Itself." In *Cleveland Development: A Dissenting View,* ed. Alvin Schorr, 43–52. Cleveland: David Press, 1991.

Birch, David L. "Toward a Stage Theory of Urban Growth." *Journal of the American Institute of Planners* 37 (March 1971): 78–87.

Birch, David L., and Edwin S. Mills. *The Community Analysis Model.* Washington, DC: HUD, 1979.

Bird, Brian. "Reclaiming the Urban War Zones." *Christianity Today* 34:1 (15 January 1990): 16–20.

Bobo, Lawrence, Camille L. Zubrinsky, James H. Johnson, Jr., and Melvin L. Oliver. "Public Opinion Before and After a Spring of Discontent." In *The Los Angeles Riots: Lessons for the Future,* ed. Narj Bakdassare, 103–33. Boulder, CO: Westview Press, 1994.

Boggs, Grace Lee, and James Boggs. "Prologue." In *Detroit Lives,* comp. and ed. Robert H. Mast, pp. 8–21. Detroit: Wayne State University Press, 1994.

Boston Redevelopment Authority. "Boston's Economic History" (draft). 26 January 1995.

———. *City of Boston: 1990 Census of Population and Housing.* Boston, March 1993.

———. *Diversity and Change in Boston's Neighborhoods: A Comparison of Demographic, Social, and Economic Characteristics of Population and Housing, 1970–1980.* Boston, October 1985.

Boston Urban Study Group. *Who Rules Boston? A Citizen's Guide.* Boston, 1984.

Boyte, Harry. *Commonwealth: A Return to Citizen Politics.* New York: Free Press, 1989.

Bradbury, Katherine L., Karl E. Case, and Constance R. Dunham. "Geographic Patterns of Mortgage Lending in Boston, 1982–1987." *New England Economic Review* (September/ October 1989): 3–30.

Bradford, Calvin. "Financing Home Ownership—The Federal Role in Neighborhood Decline." *Urban Affairs Quarterly* 14:3 (1979): 313–35.

Bradford, Calvin, and Gale Cincotta. "The Legacy, the Promise, and the Unfinished Agenda." In *From Redlining to Reinvestment: Community Responses to Urban Disinvestment,* ed. Gregory D. Squires, 228–86. Philadelphia: Temple University Press, 1992.

Bratt, Rachel G. "Community-based Housing: Strengths of the Strategy amid Dilemmas That Won't Go Away." In *The Affordable City: Toward a Third Sector Housing Policy,* ed. John Emmeus Davis, 122–44. Philadelphia: Temple University Press, 1994.

———. "Community-based Housing: Strengths of the Strategy amid Dilemmas That Won't Go Away." In *Neighborhood Policy and Programmes,* ed. Naomi Carmon, 181–200. New York: St. Martin's Press, 1990.

———. *Neighborhood Reinvestment Corporation-Sponsored Mutual Housing Associations: Experiences in Baltimore and New York.* Washington, DC: Neighborhood Reinvestment Corporation, 1990.

———. *Rebuilding a Low-Income Housing Policy.* Philadelphia: Temple University Press, 1989.

Bratt, Rachel G., Langley C. Keyes, Alex Schwartz, and Avis C. Vidal. *Confronting the Management Challenge: Affordable Housing in the Nonprofit Sector.* New York: Community Development Research Center, New School for Social Research, 1994.

Brehm, Robert. "The City and the Neighborhoods: Was It Really a Two-Way Street?" In *Harold Washington and the Neighborhoods,* ed. Pierre Clavel and Wim Wiewel, 238–69. New Brunswick, NJ: Rutgers University Press, 1991.

Brown, Jeffrey. "Boston." In *Cities Reborn,* ed. Rachel Leavitt, 14–53. Washington, DC: Urban Land Institute, 1987.

Brownstein, Ronald. "L.A. Left out of Urban Aid Program, U.S. Officials Say." *Los Angeles Times,* December 20, 1994.

Canner, Glenn B., and Dolores S. Smith. "Expanded HMDA Data on Residential Lending: One Year Later." *Federal Reserve Bulletin* (November 1992): 801–24.

Carr, James H., and Isaac F. Megbolugbe. "The Federal Reserve Bank of Boston Study on Mortgage Lending Revisited." Office of Housing Research, Federal National Mortgage Association, 1993.

Castells, Manuel. *The City and the Grassroots: A Cross-Cultural Theory of Urban Social Movements.* Berkeley: University of California Press, 1983.

Ceasar, Pearl, ed. "Texas IAF Network: Vision, Values, and Action." Brochure. Texas IAF Network, 1990.

Chargot, Patricia. "Focus:HOPE." *Detroit Free Press,* 7 July 1992.

Cisneros, Henry G., ed. *Interwoven Destinies: Cities and the Nation.* New York: W. W. Norton, 1993.

Citizens Housing and Planning Association. *Boston's Development and Housing: A Reorganization Proposal.* Boston, 1983.

Clavel, Pierre. *The Progressive City.* New Brunswick, NJ: Rutgers University Press, 1986.

Clavel, Pierre, and Wim Wiewel, eds. *Harold Washington and the Neighborhoods: Progressive City Government in Chicago.* New Brunswick, NJ: Rutgers University Press, 1991.

Clay, Phillip L. "Housing in Boston: A Five Year Restrospective." Boston: McCormack Institute of Public Affairs, University of Massachusetts, 1988.

———. *Neighborhood Renewal: Middle-Class Resettlement and Incumbent Upgrading in American Neighborhoods.* Lexington, MA: Lexington Books, 1979.

Clemetson, Robert A., and Roger Coates. *Restoring Broken Places and Rebuilding Communities: A Casebook on African-American Church Involvement in Community Economic Development.* Washington, DC: National Congress for Community Economic Development, African-American Church Project, n.d.

Cleveland Urban League. "The Negro in Cleveland, 1950–1963." Cleveland, n.d. Manuscript at the Cleveland Public Library.

Coalition of Neighborhood Developers. *From the Ground Up: Neighbors Planning Neighborhoods.* Los Angeles: CND and the Southern California Gas Company, April 1994.

———. *Housing LA* (newsletters). Los Angeles, 1989.

Cochrun, Steven. "Understanding and Enhancing Neighborhood Sense of Community." *Journal of Planning Literature* 9 (1 August 1994): 92–99.

Collins, Chuck, and Kirby White. "Boston in the 1980s: Toward a Social Housing Policy." In *The Affordable City,* ed. John E. Davis, 201–25. Philadelphia: Temple University Press, 1994.

Community & Human Resources, Inc. "Neighborhoods Planning Their Neighborhoods: The Lincoln Heights Cluster Planning Council." Report prepared for the Los Angeles Coalition of Neighborhood Developers, 1994.

Connerly, Charles. "A Survey Assessment of Housing Trust Funds in the United States." *Journal of the American Planning Association* 59:3 (1993): 306–19.

Council for Community-Based Development. *Expanding Horizons III: A Research Report on Corporate and Foundation Grant Support of Community-Based Development.* Washington, DC, 1993.

Cummings, Scott, ed. *Business Elites and Urban Development.* Albany: State University of New York Press, 1988.

Cunningham, James V., and Milton Kotler. *Building Neighborhood Organizations.* South Bend, IN: University of Notre Dame Press, 1983.

Dahl, Robert. *After the Revolution? Authority in a Good Society.* New Haven: Yale University Press, 1970.

David, Mike. *City of Quartz*. New York: Vintage, 1992.

Davis, John Emmeus. *Contested Ground: Collective Action and the Urban Neighborhood*. Ithaca, NY: Cornell University Press, 1991.

Dedman, Bill. "Blacks Turned Down for Home Loans from S&Ls Twice as Often as Whites." *Atlanta Journal/Constitution*, 22 January 1989.

————. "The Color of Money." *Atlanta Journal/Constitution*, May 1968.

DeLeon, Richard. *Left Coast City: Progressive Politics in San Francisco, 1975–1991*, Lawrence: University Press of Kansas, 1992.

Denton, Nancy, and Douglas Massey. "Patterns of Neighborhood Transition in a Multiethnic World: U.S. Metropolitan Areas, 1970–1980." *Demography* 28:1 (1991): 41–63.

DeParle, Jason. "How Jack Kemp Lost the War on Poverty: Blame Dick Darman. Or George Bush. Or Jack Kemp." *New York Times Magazine*, 28 February 1993.

De Witt, Karen. "Gay Presence Leading a Revival of Many Urban Neighborhoods." *New York Times*, 5 September 1994.

Didion, Joan. *Miami*. New York: Simon and Schuster, 1987.

Downs, Anthony. *Neighborhoods and Urban Development*. Washington, DC: Brookings Institution, 1981.

————. *New Visions for Metropolitan America*. Washington, DC: Brookings Institution, 1994.

————. *Opening Up the Suburbs*. New Haven: Yale University Press, 1973.

Dreier, Peter. "America's Urban Crisis: Symptoms, Causes, Solutions." *North Carolina Law Review* 71:5 (June 1993).

————. "Ray Flynn's Legacy: American Cities and the Progressive Agenda." *National Civic Review* (Fall 1993): 380–403.

————. "Redlining Cities: How Banks Color Community Development." *Challenge: The Magazine of Economic Affairs* 34:6 (November/December 1991): 15–23.

————. "The Vault Comes out of the Darkness." *Boston Business Journal*, 10 October 1983.

Dreier, Peter, and Bruce Ehrlich. "Downtown Development and Urban Reform: The Politics of Boston's Linkage Policy." *Urban Affairs Quarterly* 26:3 (March 1991): 354–75.

Dreier, Peter, and W. Dennis Keating. "The Limits of Localism: Progressive Municipal Housing Policies in Boston." *Urban Affairs Quarterly* 26:2 (December 1990): 191–216.

Du, Xu. "Residential Mobility in the United States." *Housing Economics* 38:9 (1990): 12–14.

Ducharme, Donna. "Planned Manufacturing Districts: How a Community Initiative Became a City Policy." In *Harold Washington and the Neighborhoods*, ed. Pierre Clavel and Wim Wiewel, 221–37. New Brunswick, NJ: Rutgers University Press, 1991.

Enterprise Foundation. *Many Roads Home: The Enterprise Foundation 1993 Annual Report*. Columbia, MD, 1994.

Epstein, Barbara. "Rethinking Social Movement Theory." *Socialist Review* 90 (January–March 1990): 35–66.

Estrada, Leobardo, and Sylvia Sensiper. "Mending the Politics of Division in Post-Rebellion L.A." In *South-Central Los Angeles: Anatomy of an Urban Crisis*, ed. Allen J. Scott and E. Richard Brown, 123–38. Los Angeles: Lewis Center for Regional Policy Studies, UCLA, June 1993.

Etzioni, Amitai. "Too Many Rights, Too Few Responsibilities." *Society* 48:4 (July/August 1991): 173–80.

Euchner, Charles C. *Playing the Field: Why Sports Teams Move and Cities Fight to Keep Them*. Baltimore: Johns Hopkins University Press, 1993.

Everett, David, John Gallagher, and Teresa Blossom. "The Race for Money." *Detroit Free Press*, 24–27 July 1988.

Fainstein, Susan S. "Neighborhood Planning: Limits and Potentials." In *Neighborhood Policy and Programmes: Past and Present*, ed. Naomi Carmon, 223–37. New York: St. Martin's Press, 1990.

Fainstein, Susan S., et al., eds. *Restructuring the City: The Political Economy of Urban Redevelopment*. Rev. ed. New York: Longman, 1986.

Fainstein, Susan S., and Norman I. Fainstein. "Economic Restructuring and the Rise of Urban Social Movements." *Urban Affairs Quarterly* 21:2 (1985): 187–206.

———. "Regime Strategies, Communal Resistance, and Economic Forces." In *Restructuring the City*, rev. ed. S. S. Fainstein et al., 245–82. New York: Longman, 1986.

Fainstein, Susan S., Norman J. Glickman, Clare Gravon, and Clifford Hirst. *An Interim Evaluation of the Minneapolis Neighborhood Revitalization Program*. New Brunswick, NJ: Center for Urban Policy Research, Rutgers University, 1993.

Fainstein, Susan S., Norman J. Glickman, Clare Gravon, Briavel Holcomb, and Grant Saff. *A Preliminary Evaluation of the Minneapolis Neighborhood Revitalization Program*. New Brunswick, NJ: Center for Urban Policy Research, Rutgers University, 1992.

Fainstein, Susan S., Clifford Hirst, and Judith Tennebaum. *An Evaluation of the Minneapolis Neighborhood Revitalization Program: Final Report of the Center for Urban Policy Research*. New Brunswick, NJ: Center for Urban Policy Research, Rutgers University, 1995.

Feldman, Paul. "Vacant Lots a Stark Tribute to 2nd Anniversary of Riots." *Los Angeles Times*, 22 April 1994.

Ferman, Barbara. *Governing the Ungovernable City: Political Skill, Leadership, and the Modern Mayor*. Philadelphia: Temple University Press, 1985.

Fiechter, Jonathan L. Remarks by Jonathan L. Fiechter, acting director, Office of Thrift Supervision, Before the Michigan League of Savings Institutions, 19 July 1994.

Fisher, Robert. *Let the People Decide: Neighborhood Organizing in America*. 2d ed., rev. Boston: Twayne, 1994.

Fisher, Robert, and Joseph Kling, eds. *Mobilizing the Community: Local Politics in the Era of the Global City*. Newbury Park, CA: Sage, 1993.

Foner, Nancy, ed. *New Immigrants in New York*. New York: Columbia University Press, 1987.

Formisano, Ralph. *Boston Against Busing: Race, Class, and Ethnicity in the 1960s and 1970s*. Chapel Hill: University of North Carolina Press, 1991.

Fox, Kenneth. *Metropolitan America: Urban Life and Urban Policy in the United States, 1940–1980*. Jackson: University Press of Mississippi, 1986.

Freedman, Samuel G. *Upon This Rock: The Miracles of a Black Church*. New York: Harper- Collins, 1993.

Frieden, Bernard J., and Marshall Kaplan. *The Politics of Neglect: Urban Aid from Model Cities to Revenue Sharing*. Cambridge, MA: MIT Press, 1975.

Frieden, Bernard J., and Lynne Sagalyn. *Downtown, Inc.: How America Rebuilds Cities*. Cambridge, MA: MIT Press, 1989.

Gale, Dennis E. "Conceptual Issues in Neighborhood Decline and Revitalization." In *Neighbourhood Policy and Programmes*, ed. Naomi Carmon. New York: St. Martin's Press, 1989.

Galford, Josef. "The Foreign Born and Urban Growth in Cleveland, 1850–1950." Typescript at Western Reserve Historical Society, n.d. Derived from "The Foreign Born and Urban Growth in the Great Lakes, 1850–1950: A Study of Chicago, Cleveland, Detroit, and Milwaukee." Ph.D. dissertation, New York University, 1958.

Gans, Herbert J. *The Urban Villagers: Group and Class in the Life of Italian-Americans*. New York: Free Press, 1962.

Ganz, Alex. "Where Has the Urban Crisis Gone: How Boston and Other Large Cities Have Stemmed Economic Decline." *Urban Affairs Quarterly* 20 (June 1985): 449–68.

Garner, Mark. "Housing the Downtown Worker: Housing Development, New Neighborhood Creation, and the Downtown Growth Coalition in Minneapolis." Unpublished manuscript.

Garreau, Joel. *Edge City: Life on the New Frontier.* New York: Doubleday, 1991.

Garsson, Robert M., and Olaf de Senerpont Domis. "GOP Win Looks Good for Banks." *American Banker,* 10 November 1994.

Gartland, Barbara. "The Decline in Cleveland's Roman Catholic Nationality Parishes." M.A. thesis, Cleveland State University, 1973.

Gelfand, Mark I. *A Nation of Cities: The Federal Government and Urban America, 1933–1965.* New York: Oxford University Press, 1975.

Gills, Doug. "Chicago Politics and Community Development: A Social Movement Perspective." In *Harold Washington and the Neighborhoods,* ed. Pierre Clavel and Wim Wiewel, 34–63. New Brunswick, NJ: Rutgers University Press, 1991.

Giloth, Robert. "Making Policy with Communities: The Research and Development Division of the Department of Economic Development." In *Harold Washington and the Neighborhoods,* ed. Pierre Clavel and Wim Wiewel, 100–120. New Brunswick, NJ: Rutgers University Press, 1991.

Giloth, Robert, and John Betancur. "Where Downtown Meets Neighborhood: Industrial Displacement in Chicago, 1978–1987." *Journal of the American Planning Association* 54 (1988): 279–90.

Giloth, Robert, and Susan Rosenblum. "How to Fight Plant Closings." *Social Policy* 17:3 (Winter 1987): 20–26.

Glater, Jonathan D. "Critics Say Fed Is Lax On Fair-Lending Laws." *Washington Post,* 1 November 1994.

———. "Regulator Questions Tactics on Loan Bias." *Washington Post,* 19 October 1994.

Godfrey, Brian J. *Neighborhoods in Transition: The Making of San Francisco's Ethnic and Nonconformist Communities.* Berkeley: University of California Press, 1988.

Goering, John M. "The National Neighborhood Movement: A Preliminary Analysis and Critique." *Journal of the American Planning Association* 46:4 (October 1979): 506–14.

———. "Neighborhood Tipping and Racial Discrimination: A Review of the Social Science Evidence." *Journal of the American Institute of Planners* 44 (1978): 68–78.

Goetz, Edward G. "Expanding Possibilities in Local Development Policy: An Examination of U.S. Cities." *Political Research Quarterly* 47:1 (1994): 85–109.

———. "Promoting Low Income Housing Through Innovations in Land Use Regulations." *Journal of Urban Affairs* 13:3 (1991): 337–51.

———. *Shelter Burden: Local Politics and Progressive Housing Policy.* Philadelphia: Temple University Press, 1993.

Goetz, Edward G., and Mara Sidney. "Revenge of the Property Owners: Community Development and the Politics of Property." *Journal of Urban Affairs* 16:4 (1994): 319–34.

Goetze, Rolf. *Income, Employment, and Housing Changes Revealed by the 1990 U.S. Census.* Boston: Boston Redevelopment Authority, July 1992.

———. *Population and Housing Composition by 69 Neighborhoods and 16 Planning Districts: 1990 Counts, Distributions, and Ratios.* Boston: Boston Redevelopment Authority, February 1995.

Goetze, Rolf, and Kent Colton. *Understanding Neighborhood Change: The Role of Expectations in Urban Revitalization.* Cambridge, MA: Ballinger, 1979.

Goldsmith, William W., and Edward J. Blakely. *Separate Societies: Poverty and Inequality in U.S. Cities.* Philadelphia: Temple University Press, 1992.

Goode, Judith, and Jo Anne Schneider. *Reshaping Ethics and Racial Relations in Philadelphia: Immigrants in a Divided City.* Philadelphia: Temple University Press, 1994.

Greene, Zina G. *Lender's Guide to Fair Mortgage Policies.* Washington, DC: Potomac Institute, 1980.

Greer, Scott. *Urban Renewal and American Cities: The Dilemma of Democratic Intervention.* Indianapolis: Bobbs-Merrill, 1965.

Grenier, Guillermo J., and Alex Stepick III, eds. *Miami Now! Immigration, Ethnicity, and Social Change.* Gainesville: University Press of Florida, 1992.

Grigsby, J. Eugene, III, Kimberly Jackson, and Elaine Lister. "Economic Development in Los Angeles." Report of the Planning Group, Los Angeles, 1989.

Grigsby, William G., M. Barantz, Duncan Maclennan, and George C. Galster. *Dynamics of Neighborhood Change and Decline.* Research Report, Series no. 4. Philadelphia: Department of City and Regional Planning, University of Pennsylvania, 1980.

Haar, Charles M. *Between the Idea and the Reality: A Study in the Origin, Fate, and Legacy of the Model Cities Program.* Boston: Little, Brown, 1975.

Haas, Gilda, and Allan Heskin. "Community Struggles in Los Angeles." *International Journal of Urban and Regional Research* 5 (1981): 546–64.

Haley, Alex. *The Autobiography of Malcolm X.* New York: Ballentine Books, 1973.

Hallman, Howard W. *Neighborhoods: Their Place in Urban Life.* Beverly Hills, CA: Sage Publications, 1984.

Halprin, Robert. *Rebuilding the Inner City.* New York: Columbia University Press, 1995.

Harney, Kenneth R. "Lenders Bending Over Backward to Make It Easier to Buy a Home." *Washington Post,* 1 October 1994.

Harrison, Bennett, and Barry Bluestone. *The Great U-Turn: Corporate Restructuring and the Polarizing of America.* New York: Basic Books, 1988.

Hartman, Chester. *Yerba Buena: Land Grab and Community Resistance in San Francisco.* San Francisco: Glide Publications, 1974.

Hartman, Chester, W. Dennis Keating, and Richard LeGates. *Displacement: How to Fight It.* Berkeley, CA: Legal Services Anti-Displacement Project, 1982.

Hays, Allen R. *The Federal Government and Urban Housing: Ideology and Change in Public Policy.* Albany: State University of New York Press, 1985.

Hebert, Scott, Kathleen Heintz, Chris Baron, Nancy Kay, and James E. Wallace. *Nonprofit Housing: Costs and Funding, Final Report, Volume I.* Washington, DC: HUD, November 1993.

Heckscher, August. "The Neighborhood." In *Housing: Symbol, Structure, Site,* ed. Lisa Taylor, 62–63. Washington, DC: Smithsonian Institution, 1990.

Henderson, Angelo, and Janice Hays. "Who Speaks for Black America? Church a Force in Rebuilding Souls . . . and Cities." *Detroit News and Free Press,* 9 August 1992.

Henderson, Audrey. "Draft Planning Document." N.p., n.d.

Henig, Jeffrey R. *Neighborhood Mobilization: Redevelopment and Response.* New Brunswick, NJ: Rutgers University Press, 1982.

Heskin, Allan David. *The Struggle for Community.* Boulder, CO: Westview Press, 1991.

Hoch, Charles, and Robert A. Slayton. *New Homeless and Old: Community and the Skid Row Hotel.* Philadelphia: Temple University Press, 1989.

Hoffman, Napthali. "The Economic Development of Cleveland, 1825–1910." Ph.D. dissertation, Case Western Reserve University, 1980.

Hollander, Elizabeth. "The Department of Planning Under Harold Washington." In *Harold Washington and the Neighborhoods,* ed. Pierre Clavel and Wim Wiewel, 121–45. New Brunswick, NJ: Rutgers University Press, 1991.

Hoover/Adams–Maple/Adams Neighborhood, South Central Los Angeles. *Proposals for Change.* Report prepared for the Coalition of Neighborhood Developers, South Central Los Angeles, June 1993.

Horowitz, Craig. "A South Bronx Renaissance." *New York Magazine,* 21 November 1984.

Housing Policy Debates. Special issue, *Discrimination in the Housing and Mortgage Markets* 3:2 (1992): i–745.

Hoyt, Homer. *One Hundred Years of Land Values in Chicago.* Chicago: University of Chicago Press, 1933.

Hughes, Mack A., and Julie Sternberg. *The New Metropolitan Reality: Antipoverty Strategy Where the Rubber Meets the Road.* Washington, DC: Urban Institute, 1992.

Hult, Karen. "Citizen Participation in Minneapolis." *CURA Reporter* (University of Minnesota Center for Urban and Regional Affairs) 14:5 (1984): 1–6.

————. *Institutionalizing Citizen Participation: Challenges and Opportunities.* Minneapolis: Center for Urban and Regional Affairs, 1984.

Hunter, William C., and Mary Beth Walker. "The Cultural Affinity Hypothesis and Mortgage Lending Decisions." Working Paper Series, Federal Reserve Bank of Chicago, July 1995.

Jackson, Kenneth T. *Crabgrass Frontier: The Suburbanization of the United States.* New York: Oxford University Press, 1985.

Jacobs, Jane. *The Death and Life of Great American Cities.* New York: Vintage Books, 1961.

Jennings, James, and Mel King, eds. *From Access to Power: Black Politics in Boston.* Cambridge, MA: Schenkman, 1986.

Johnson, James H., Jr., Walter C. Farrell, Jr., and Maria Rosano-Jackson. "Los Angeles One Year Later: A Prospective Assessment of Response to the 1992 Civil Unrest." *Economic Development Quarterly* 8:1 (February 1994): 19–27.

Johnson, James H., Jr., Cloyzelle K. Jones, Walter C. Farrell, Jr., and Melvin L. Oliver. "The Los Angeles Rebellion: A Retrospective View." *Economic Development Quarterly* 6 (November 1992): 356–72.

Jones, Bryan, and Lynn Bachelor. *The Sustaining Hand: Community Leadership and Corporate Power.* Lawrence: University Press of Kansas, 1986.

Jones, Lawrence N. "Urban Black Churches: Conservators of Value and Sustainers of Community." *Journal of Religious Thought* 39:2 (Fall–Winter 1982–1983): 41–50.

Judd, Dennis R. *The Politics of American Cities: Private Power and Public Policy.* Boston: Little, Brown, 1984.

Judd, Dennis R., and Michael Parkinson, eds. *Leadership and Urban Regeneration.* Newbury Park, CA: Sage Publications, 1990.

Kaiser Commission: President's Committee on Urban Housing. *A Decent Home.* Washington, DC, 1968.

Kasarda, John D. "Cities as Places Where People Live and Work: Urban Change and Neighborhood Distress." In *Interwoven Destinies: Cities and the Nation,* ed. Henry G. Cisneros. New York: Norton, 1993.

Katz, Jeffrey L. "Neighborhood Groups Buy In." *Governing* (November 1990).

Keating, W. Dennis. *The Suburban Racial Dilemma: Housing and Neighborhoods.* Philadelphia: Temple University Press, 1994.

Keating, W. Dennis, Keith P. Rasey, and Norman Krumholz. "Community Development Corporations in the United States: Their Role in Housing and Urban Redevelopment." In *Government and Housing: Developments in Seven Countries,* ed. Willem van Vliet and Jan van Weesep. Newbury Park, CA: Sage Publications, 1990.

Keller, Suzanne. *The Urban Neighborhood: A Sociological Perspective.* New York: Random House, 1968.

Kennedy, Lawrence. *Planning the City upon a Hill: Boston Since 1630.* Amherst: University of Massachusetts Press, 1992.

Kerner Commission. National Advisory Commission on Civil Disorders. *Report.* Washington, DC, 1968.

Kim, Sunwoong, and Gregory D. Squires. "Lender Characteristics and Racial Disparities in Mortgage Lending." *Journal of Housing Research* 6:1 (1994): 99–113.

Knight, Jerry. "Lenders Agree to Anti-Bias Pledge." *Washington Post*, 13 September 1994.

Kotler, Milton. *Neighborhood Government: The Local Foundations of Political Life*. Indianapolis: Bobbs-Merrill, 1969.

Kretzmann, John. "Affirmative Information Policy: Opening up a Closed City." In *Harold Washington and the Neighborhoods*, ed. Pierre Clavel and Wim Wiewel, 199–220. New Brunswick, NJ: Rutgers University Press, 1991.

Kriplen, Nancy. "Program Benefits Multiply: Building Community Beyond 'Bricks and Sticks.'" In *Progressions: A Lilly Endowment Occasional Report*, February 1995.

Krumholz, Norman. "Neighborhood Housing in Cleveland: Successes and Issues." In *Affordable Housing and Urban Development in the U.S.: Learning from Failure and Success*, ed. Willem van Vliet. Forthcoming.

Krumholz, Norman, and Pierre Clavel. *Reinventing Cities: Equity Planners Tell Their Stories*. Philadelphia: Temple University Press, 1994.

Krumholz, Norman, and John Forester. *Making Equity Planning Work*. Philadelphia: Temple University Press, 1990.

Kusmer, Kenneth. *A Ghetto Takes Shape: Black Cleveland, 1870–1930*. Urbana: University of Illinois Press, 1976.

Lampe, David, ed. "The Role of Gentrification in Central City Revitalization." *National Civic Review* 82:4 (Fall 1993): 363–70.

Lauria, Mickey. "Community Controlled Redevelopment: South Minneapolis." Ph.D. dissertation, University of Minnesota, 1980.

Leahy, Peter, and David Snow. "A Neighborhood in Transition: Hough, Cleveland." In *A Guide to Studying Neighborhoods and Resources on Cleveland*, ed. Edward Miggins, 101–8. Cleveland: Cleveland Public Library, 1984.

Leavitt, Jacqueline. "Los Angeles: The Community View." *City Limits* 17:7 (August/September 1992): 14–15.

———. *Residents Organizing and Planning Their Future*. Presented by Proyecto Pastoral in collaboration with the Boyle Heights Cluster of the Coalition of Neighborhood Developers. Report prepared for the Los Angeles Coalition of Neighborhood Developers, 1994.

Leavitt, Jacqueline, and Allan Heskin. "Housing and Community." In *South-Central Los Angeles: Anatomy of an Urban Crisis*, 21–42, N.p., 1993.

Leavitt, Jacqueline, and Susan Saegert. *From Abandonment to Hope: Community Households in Harlem*. New York: Columbia University Press, 1990.

Ledebur, Larry, and William Barnes. *All in It Together: Cities, Suburbs, and Local Economic Regions*. Washington, DC: National League of Cities, 1993.

Lee, Barrett, and Peter Wood. "Is Neighborhood Racial Succession Place-Specific?" *Demography* 28:1 (1991): 21-40.

Lemann, Nicholas. "The Myth of Community Development." *New York Times*, 9 January 1994.

Leonard, Henry. "Ethnic Cleavage and Industrial Conflict in Late 19th Century America: The Cleveland Rolling Mill Company Strikes, 1882 and 1885." *Labor History* (Fall 1979): 524-48.

Leonard, Paul A., Cushing N. Dolbeare, and Edward B. Lazere. *A Place to Call Home: The Crisis in Housing for the Poor*. Washington, DC: Center on Budget and Policy Priorities, 1989.

Leven, Charles L., James T. Little, Hugh O. Nourse, and R. B. Read. *Neighborhood Change: Lessons in the Dynamics of Urban Decay*. New York: Praeger Publishers, 1976.

Levine, Hillel, and Lawrence Harmon. *The Death of an American Jewish Community*. New York: Free Press, 1992.

Lewis, Sylvia. "Tough Love Works in Newark," *Planning* 59:10 (October 1993): 24–29.

———. "The Bank with a Heart." *Planning* 59:4 (1993): 23–28.

Liberty Hill Foundation. *Newsletter.* December 1992.

Lief, Beth J., and Susan Goering. "The Implementation of the Federal Mandate for Fair Housing." In *Divided Neighborhoods: Changing Patterns of Racial Segregation,* ed. Gary A. Tobin, 227–67. Newbury Park, CA: Sage Publications, 1987.

Lieske, Joel. "The Salvation of American Cities." In *Rebuilding America's Cities: Roads to Recovery,* ed. Paul Porter and David Sweet, 71–92. New Brunswick, NJ: Center for Urban Policy Research, 1984.

Lincoln, C. Eric. *Race, Religion, and the Continuing American Dilemma.* New York: Hill and Wang, 1984.

Linthicum, Robert C. *City of God, City of Satan: A Biblical Theology of the Urban Church.* Grand Rapids, MI: Zondervan Publishing, 1991.

Local Initiatives Support Corporation. *LISC Working Partnerships for Neighborhood Development 1991 Annual Report.* New York, 1992.

———. *1993 Annual Report.* New York, 1994.

Logan, John R., and Harvey Molotch. *Urban Fortunes: The Political Economy of Place.* Berkeley: University of California Press, 1987.

Logan, John, and Todd Swanstrom, eds. *Beyond the City Limits.* Philadelphia: Temple University Press, 1990.

Low Income Housing Information Service. *The Housing Poster.* Washington, DC, 1993.

Lukas, Anthony. *Common Ground: A Turbulent Decade in the Lives of Three American Families.* New York: Alfred A. Knopf, 1985.

Lupo, Alan. *Liberty's Chosen Home: The Politics of Violence in Boston.* Boston: Little, Brown, 1977.

McCarron, John. "Blue Collar Dream Skews City Policy." *Chicago Tribune,* 31 August, 1988. Fourth in the series "Chicago on Hold: Politics of Poverty."

Macauley, Fathia, and Reginald Chapple. *The Vernon Central Neighborhood Plan.* Presented by the residents and merchants of Vernon Central in conjunction with the Vernon Central Cluster of the Coalition of Neighborhood Developers. Report prepared for the Los Angeles Coalition of Neighborhood Developers, April 1994.

McDougall, Harold A. *Black Baltimore: A New Theory of Community.* Philadelphia: Temple University Press, 1993.

McKinney, Wade. "The Central Area." Text for a speech to the Cleveland City Club, 3 February, 1945. Manuscript at WRHS.

McTighe, Michael. "Babel and Babylon on the Cuyahoga: Religious Diversity in Cleveland." In *The Birth of Modern Cleveland, 1865–1930,* ed. Thomas Campbell and Edward Miggins, 231–69. Cleveland: Western Reserve Historical Society; London: Associated University Presses, 1988.

Maine, Gerry. "Housing Preservation Ordinance Celebrated." *Shelterforce* 10:9 (July/ August 1987): 9.

Malcolm X. *The Autobiography of Malcolm X,* with Alex Haley. New York: Ballentine, 1992.

Marcuse, Peter. "New York City's Community Boards: Neighborhood Policy and Its Results." In *Neighbourhood Policy and Programmes: Past and Present,* ed. Naomi Carmon, 145–63. New York: St. Martin's Press, 1990.

Marquez, Benjamin. "Mexican-American Community Development Corporations and the Limits of Directed Capitalism." *Economic Development Quarterly* 7 (1993): 287–95.

Martin, Phillip, et al. "Immigration to the United States: Journey to an Uncertain Destination." *Population Bulletin* 49 (September 1994).

Massey, Douglas S., and Nancy A. Denton. *American Apartheid: Segregation and the Making of the Underclass.* Cambridge: Harvard University Press, 1993.

———. "Trends in the Residential Segregation of Blacks, Hispanics, and Asians, 1970–1980." *American Sociological Review* 52 (1987): 802–25.

Mayer, Neil S. *Neighborhood Organizations and Community Development: Making Revitalization Work.* Washington, DC: Urban Institute Press, 1984.

———. "The Role of Nonprofits in Renewed Federal Housing Efforts." In *Building Foundations,* ed. Denise DiPasquale and Langley C. Keyes, 365–88. Philadelphia: University of Pennsylvania Press, 1990.

Medoff, Peter, and Holly Sklar. *Streets of Hope: The Fall and Rise of an Urban Neighborhood.* Boston: South End Press, 1994.

Meredith, Robyn. "Thrifts Set War Chest for Fight on Fair Lending." *American Banker,* 18 October 1994.

Michigan State University, Students of Urban Planning 485. "Fellowship Nonprofit Housing Corporation: A Bold Plan." December 1994.

Mid-City Planning Cluster of the Coalition of Neighborhood Developers. "A Plan for the Mid-City Community." Report prepared for the Los Angeles Coalition of Neighborhood Developers, March 1994.

Mier, Robert. *Social Justice and Local Development Policy.* Newbury Park, CA: Sage Publications, 1993.

———. "Some Observations on Race in Planning." *American Planning Association Journal* (Spring 1994): 57–63.

Mier, Robert, Kari Moe, and I. Sherr. "Strategic Planning and the Pursuit of Reform, Economic Development, and Equity." *Journal of the American Planning Association* 52:3 (1986): 299–309.

Mieszkowski, Peter M., and Edwin S. Mills. "The Causes of Metropolitan Suburbanization." *Journal of Economic Perspectives* 7:3 (Summer 1993): 135–47.

Miggins, Edward. "A City of Uplifting Influences: From Sweet Charity to Modern Social Welfare and Philanthropy." In *The Birth of Modern Cleveland, 1865–1930,* ed. Thomas Campbell and Edward Miggins, 104–40. Cleveland: Western Reserve Historical Society; London: Associated University Presses, 1988.

———. "Neighborhood Studies." In *A Guide to Studying Neighborhoods and Resources on Cleveland,* ed. Edward Miggins, 7–26. Cleveland: Cleveland Public Library, 1984.

———. "The Search for the One Best System: Cleveland Public Schools and Educational Reform, 1836–1920." In *Cleveland: A Tradition of Reform,* ed. David Van Tassel et al., 136–55. Kent, OH: Kent State University Press, 1986.

Miggins, Edward, et al. "The Ethnic Mosaic: The Settlement of Cleveland by the New Immigrants and Migrants." In *The Birth of Modern Cleveland, 1865–1930,* ed. Thomas Campbell and Edward Miggins. Cleveland: Western Reserve Historical Society; London: Associated University Presses, 1988.

Miller, Carol P., and Robert Wheeler. *Cleveland: A Concise History, 1796–1990.* Bloomington: Indiana University Press, 1990.

Miller, Mike. "Saul Alinsky and the Democratic Spirit." *Christianity and Crisis* 52 (25 May 1992).

Miller, William F., Michael Norman, and Richard Peery. "150 Years of Racial and Ethnic Heritage." *Plain Dealer Magazine,* 3 March 1991.

Mills, Edwin. "Urban Density Functions." *Urban Studies* 7:1 (February 1970): 5–20.

Milton S. Eisenhower Foundation. *Investing in Children and Youth, Reconstructing Our Cities, Doing What Works to Reverse the Betrayal of American Democracy.* Washington, DC, 1993.

Mingione, Enzo, ed. "The New Urban Poverty and the Underclass." *International Journal of Urban and Regional Research* 17:3 (1993): 324–26.

Moberg, David. "The Next Four Years: Neighborhood Agendas." *Neighborhood Works* 10:4 (May 1987): 1, 4–8.

Mollenkopf, John. *The Contested City.* Princeton: Princeton University Press, 1983.

———. *A Phoenix in the Ashes: The Rise and Fall of the Koch Coalition in New York Politics.* Princeton: Princeton University Press, 1991.

Molotch, Harvey Luskin. *Managed Integration: Dilemmas of Doing Good in the City.* Berkeley: University of California Press, 1972.

Morrison, Peter A., and Ira S. Lowry. "A Riot of Color: The Demographic Setting." In *The Los Angeles Riots: Lessons for the Urban Future,* ed. Mark Baldassare, 19–46. Boulder, CO: Westview Press, 1994.

Mortgage Bankers Association of America and U.S. Department of Housing and Urban Development. "Fair Lending—Best Practices Master Agreement." Unpublished document. Washington, DC, 14 September 1994.

Moynihan, Daniel P. *Maximum Feasible Misunderstanding: Community Action in the War on Poverty.* New York: Free Press, 1969.

Muhammad, Elijah. *Message to the Blackman in America.* Chicago: Muhammad Mosque of Islam no. 2, 1965.

Mu Kenga, Ida Rousseau. *The Black Church in Urban America.* Lanhorn, MD: University Press of America, n.d.

Munnell, Alicia H., Lynn E. Browned, James McEneaney, and Geoffrey M. B. Tootell. "Mortgage Lending in Boston: Interpreting HMDA Data." Working Paper Series, Federal Reserve Board of Boston. October 1992.

Nathan, Richard. *A New Agenda for Cities.* Columbus: Ohio Municipal League Educational and Research Fund, 1992.

National Community Reinvestment Coalition. *Catalogue and Directory of Community Reinvestment Agreements.* Washington, DC, 1994.

———. "CRA Dollar Commitments Since 1977." Washington, DC, 1995.

National Congress for Community Economic Development (NCCED). *Against All Odds: The Achievements of Community-Based Development Organizations.* Washington, DC, 1989.

———. *Tying It All Together: The Comprehensive Achievements of Community-Based Development Organizations.* Washington, DC, 1995.

Navarro, Carlos, and Rudolfo Acuna. "In Search of Community: A Comparative Essay on Mexicans in Los Angeles and San Antonio." In *20th Century Los Angeles: Power, Promotion, and Social Conflict,* ed. Norman M. Klein and Martin J. Schiesl, 195–226. Claremont, CA: Regina Books, 1990.

Needleman, Martin, and Caroline Needleman. *Guerrillas in the Bureaucracy: The Community Planning Experiment in the United States.* New York: Wiley, 1974.

"A Neighborhood Redeemed: Ravendale." Video. Public Broadcasting Service, circa 1991.

Neighborhood Reinvestment Corporation. *Transforming Lives, Transforming Neighborhoods: The Neighborhood Reinvestment Corporation 1993 Annual Report.* Washington, DC, 1994.

Nelson, Kathryn P. *Gentrification and Distressed Cities: An Assessment of Trends in Intrametropolitan Migration.* Madison: University of Wisconsin Press, 1988.

Nenno, Mary. *New Money and New Methods: A Catalog of State and Local Initiatives in Housing and Community Development.* Washington, DC: National Association of Housing and Redevelopment Officials, 1986.

Newman, Harvey. "Black Clergy and Urban Regimes: The Role of Atlanta's Concerned Black Clergy." *Journal of Urban Affairs* 8:1 (1994): 23–33.

Newman, M. W., and Lillian Williams. "People Power: Chicago's Real Clout." *Chicago Sun Times,* 6 April 1990.

Nickel, Denise. "The Progressive City? Urban Redevelopment in Minneapolis." *Urban Affairs Quarterly* 30 (January 1995): 355–77.

O'Connell, Mary. "Linking the Loop with Community Needs." *Neighborhood Works* 8:11 (November 1985): 1, 15–17.

O'Hare, William P. "America's Minorities: The Demographics of Diversity." *Population Bulletin* 47:4 (1992).

Olson, Mancur. *The Logic of Collective Action.* New York: Schocken, 1968.

OMG. *First Annual Assessment Report: Comprehensive Community Revitalization Program.* Philadelphia, 1994.

O'Rourke, Lawrence M. *Geno: The Life and Mission of Geno Baroni.* New York: Paulist Press, 1991.

Palen, John J., and Bruce London, eds. *Gentrification, Displacement, and Neighborhood Revitalization.* Albany: State University of New York Press, 1984.

Peirce, Neil R. *Citistates.* Washington, DC: Seven Locks Press, 1993.

Peirce, Neil R., and Carol F. Steinbach. *Corrective Capitalism: The Rise of America's Community Development Corporations.* New York: Ford Foundation, 1987.

————. *Enterprising Communities: Community-Based Development in America, 1990.* Washington, DC: Council for Community-Based Development, 1990.

Peterson, Paul. *City Limits.* Chicago: University of Chicago Press, 1981.

Piven, Frances Fox, and Richard A. Cloward. *Poor Peoples' Movements: Why They Succeed, How They Fail.* New York: Vintage Books, 1972.

Pogge, Jean. "Reinvestment in Chicago Neighborhoods: A Twenty Year Struggle." In *From Redlining to Reinvestment: Community Responses to Urban Disinvestment,* ed. Gregory D. Squires, 133–48. Philadelphia: Temple University Press, 1992.

Policy Statement on Discrimination in Lending. *Federal Register* 59:73 (1994): 18266–74.

Pool, Robert. "L.A. by Any Other Name." *Los Angeles Times Metro,* 28 January 1995.

Porter, Paul. *The Recovery of American Cities.* New York: Sun River Press, 1976.

Portes, Alejandro, and Alex Stepick III. *City on the Edge: The Transformation of Miami.* Berkeley: University of California Press, 1993.

Purdy, Matthew. "Left to Die, the South Bronx Rises from Decades of Decay." *New York Times,* 13 November 1994.

Quigley, John M. "What We Have Learned About Housing Markets." In *Current Issues in Urban Economics,* ed. Peter M. Mieszkowski and Mahlon R. Straszheim. Baltimore: Johns Hopkins, University Press, 1979.

Reed, Gregory, J. *Economic Empowerment Through the Church: A Blueprint for Progressive Community Development.* Grand Rapids, MI: Zondervan Publishing, 1994.

Regalado, James A. "Community Coalition-Building." In *The Los Angeles Riots: Lessons for the Future,* ed. Mark Baldassare, 205–35. Boulder, CO: Westview Press, 1994.

Rich, Michael James. "Congress, Bureaucracy, and the Cities: Distributive Politics and the Allocation of Federal Grants for Community and Economic Development." Ph.D. dissertation, Northwestern University, 1985.

Richmond, Henry R. "Rationale and Program Design." Washington, DC: National Land Use Policy Institute, 1994.

Ridley-Thomas, Mark. "Accountability." *Los Angeles Times,* 5 July, 1995.

Rivera, Robert. Lecture given at University of Houston, 18 April, 1991.

Rivlin, Gary. *Fire on the Plain.* New York: Henry Holt, 1992.

Robinson, Tony. "Gentrification and Grassroots Resistance in San Francisco's Tenderloin." *Urban Affairs Review* 30:4 (1995): 483–513.

Rogers, Mary Beth. *Cold Anger: A Story of Faith and Power Politics.* Denton: North Texas State University Press, 1990.

Rohe, William H., and Lauren B. Gates. *Planning with Neighborhoods.* Chapel Hill: University of North Carolina Press, 1985.

Roisman, Florence W., and Hilary Botein. "Housing Mobility and Life Opportunities." *Clearinghouse* 26:4 (1993).

Rooney, Jim. *Organizing the South Bronx.* Albany: State University of New York Press, 1995.

Rose, William G. *Cleveland: The Making of a City.* Cleveland: World Publishing,1950.

Rosenbaum, James E. "Changing the Geography of Opportunity by Expanding Residential Choice: Lessons from the Gautreaux Program." *Housing Policy Debate* 6:1 (1995): 231–70.

Rossi, Peter H., and Robert A. Dentler. *The Politics of Urban Renewal: The Chicago Findings.* New York: Free Press, 1961.

Rubenstein, Bruce. "The Trickle Around Theory." *City Pages* (Minneapolis/Saint Paul), 10 July 1991.

Rubin, Robert, Prado Cora Rodriguez, and Benetta Johnson. *Broadway/Manchester Community Plan.* Report prepared for the Los Angeles Coalition of Neighborhood Developers, 1994.

Rumbaut, Ruben G. "Passages to America: Perspectives on the New Immigrants." In *America at Century's End,* ed. Alan Wolfe, 208–44. Berkeley: University of California Press, 1991.

Rusk, David. *Cities Without Suburbs.* Washington, DC: Woodrow Wilson Press, 1993.

Saltman, Juliet. *A Fragile Movement: The Struggle for Neighborhood Stabilization.* Westport, CT: Greenwood Press, 1990.

Savitch, H. V., David Collins, Daniel Sanders, and John Markham. "Ties That Bind." *Economic Development Quarterly* (November 1993): 341–58.

Savitch, H. V., and John Clayton Thomas, eds. *Big City Politics in Transition.* Newbury Park, CA: Sage Publications, 1991.

Scavo, Carmine. "The Use of Participative Mechanisms in Large U.S. Cities." *Journal of Urban Affairs* 15:1 (1993): 93–109.

Scheie, David, et al. "Religious Institutions as Partners in Community Based Development: Findings from Year One of the Lilly Endowment Program." Indianapolis: Lilly Endowment, 1991.

Schill, Michael H., and Richard P. Nathan. *Revitalizing America's Cities: Neighborhood Reinvestment and Displacement.* Albany: State University of New York Press, 1983.

Schwada, John, and Paul Richter. "Mayor Snubs President over L.A. Loss of Grant." *Los Angeles Times,* 22 December 1994.

Scott, Mel. *Metropolitan Los Angeles: One Community.* Los Angeles: Haynes Foundation, 1949.

Sears, David O. "Urban Rioting in Los Angeles: A Comparison of 1965 with 1992." In *The Los Angeles Riots: Lessons for the Future,* ed. Mark Baldassare, 237–54. Boulder, CO: Westview Press, 1994.

"Seventeenth Annual Report of the Hiram House." Cleveland, 1913. Manuscript at WRHS.

Shabecoff, Alice. *Rebuilding Our Communities: How Churches Can Provide, Support, and Finance Quality Housing for Low Income Families.* Monrovia, CA: World Vision, 1992.

Shiffman, Ronald. "Remarks." Presented at the Association of Collegiate Schools of Planning, Columbus, Ohio, 31 October 1992.

Shiffman, Ronald, and Susan Motley. *Comprehensive and Integrative Planning for Community Development.* New York: Community Development Research Center, 1990.

Shlay, Anne B., and Robert Giloth. "Social Organization of a Land-Based Elite: The Case of the Failed 1992 Fair." *Journal of Urban Affairs* 9:4 (1987): 305–24.

Shlay, Anne B., Ira Goldstein, and David Bartelt. "Racial Barriers and Credit: Comment on Hula." *Urban Affairs Quarterly* 28:1 (1992): 126–40.

Simmons, Louise B. *Organizing in Hard Times: Labor and Neighborhoods in Hartford.* Philadelphia: Temple University Press, 1994.

Smith, Doug. "Quake Repairs Fall Behind in Poor, Old Neighborhoods." *Los Angeles Times,* n.d.

Smith, Neil, and Peter Williams, eds. *Gentrification of the City.* Boston: Allen and Unwin, 1986.

Smith, Richard A. "Creating Stable Racially Integrated Communities." *Journal of Urban Affairs* 15:2 (1993): 115–40.

Smith, T. Michael. "Becoming a Good and Competent Community." In *Rebuilding America's Cities: Roads to Recovery,* ed. Paul R. Porter and David C. Sweet, 123–42. New Brunswick, NJ: Center for Urban Policy Research, 1984.

Sonershein, Raphael J. "Los Angeles Coalition Politics." In *The Los Angeles Riots: Lessons for the Future,* ed. Mark Baldassare, 47–71. Boulder, CO: Westview Press, 1994.

Squires, Gregory D. *Capital and Communities in Black and White: The Intersections of Race, Class, and Uneven Development.* Albany: State University of New York Press, 1994.

———. "Community Reinvestment: An Emerging Social Movement." In *From Redlining to Reinvestment: Community Responses to Urban Disinvestment,* ed. G. D. Squires, 1–37. Philadelphia: Temple University Press, 1992.

———. *From Redlining to Reinvestment: Community Responses to Urban Disinvestment.* Philadelphia: Temple University Press, 1992.

———, ed. *Unequal Partnerships: The Political Economy of Urban Redevelopment in Postwar America.* New Brunswick, NJ: Rutgers University Press, 1989.

Squires, Gary, Larry Bennett, L. McCourt, and P. Nyden. *Chicago: Race, Class, and the Response to Urban Decline.* Philadelphia: Temple University Press, 1987.

Stegman, Michael A., and J. David Holden. *Nonfederal Housing Programs: How States and Localities Are Responding to Federal Cutbacks in Low-income Housing.* Washington, DC: Urban Land Institute, 1987.

Stoecker, Randy. *Defending Community: The Struggle for Alternative Development in Cedar-Riverside.* Philadelphia: Temple University Press, 1994.

Stone, Clarence. "Urban Regimes and the Capacity to Govern: A Political Economy Approach." *Journal of Urban Affairs* 15:1 (1993).

Stone, Clarence, and Heywood Sanders, eds. *The Politics of Urban Development.* Lawrence: University Press of Kansas, 1987.

Sullivan, Mercer L., and Elizabeth J. Mueller. "A Real Home or Just a Place to Stay? Outcomes of Community Development for Residents of Community-Based Housing Developments." Paper presented at Association for Public Policy Analysis and Management, Chicago, 27–29 October 1994.

Suttles, Gerald D. "Community Design." In *Metropolitan America in Contemporary Perspective,* ed. Amos H. Hawley and Vincent P. Rock, 235–97. New York: Sage, 1975.

Sviridoff, Mitchell. "The Seeds of Urban Revival." *Public Interest* 114 (Winter 1994): 82–103.

Swanstrom, Todd. *The Crisis of Growth Politics: Cleveland, Kucinich, and the Challenge of Urban Populism.* Philadelphia: Temple University Press, 1985.

Taub, Richard P. *Community Capitalism: Banking Strategies and Economic Development.* Boston: Harvard Business School Press, 1988.

Taub, Richard P., D. Garth Taylor, and Jan D. Durham. *Paths of Neighborhood Change.* Chicago: University of Chicago Press, 1984.

Teitz, Michael B. "Neighborhood Economics: Local Communities and Regional Markets." *Economic Development Quarterly* 3 (May 1989): 111–22.

Thomas, June. *Planning a Finer City: Redevelopment and Race in Postwar Detroit.* Baltimore: Johns Hopkins University Press, forthcoming.

Thomas, Kenneth. *Community Reinvestment Performance.* Chicago: Probus, 1993.

Tobin, Gary. *Divided Neighborhoods.* Newbury Park, CA: Sage Publications, 1987.

Trapp, Shel. "Dynamics of Organizing." *Disclosure* (March–April 1992).

Traynor, Bill. "Community Development and Community Organizing." *Shelterforce* 68 (March–April 1993): 4–7 .

Turner, Margery A., and John G. Edwards. "Affordable Rental Housing in Metropolitan Neighborhoods." In *Housing Markets and Residential Mobility,* ed. G. T. Kingsley and M. A. Turner, 125–60. Washington, DC: Urban Institute Press, 1993.

Turner, Margery A., Ray Struyk, and John Yinger. *Housing Discrimination Study: Synthesis.* Washington, DC: HUD, 1991.

U.S. Department of Housing and Urban Development. *The Dynamics of Neighborhood Change.* Washington, DC: Office of Policy Development and Research, 1975.

———. *Empowerment: A New Covenant with America's Communities.* Washington, DC, 1995.

———. *Housing in the Seventies.* Washington, DC, 1973.

U.S. Federal Housing Administration. *Underwriting Manual.* Washington, DC: U.S. Government Printing Office, 1938.

Urban Land Institute Advisory Services Panel. "Vermont Avenue Corridor, Los Angeles, California: Recommendations for the Revitalization of the Vermont Avenue Corridor in South Central Los Angeles." Report, 13 November 1992.

Vidal, Avis C. *Rebuilding Communities: A National Study of Urban Community Development Corporations.* New York: Community Development Research Center, Graduate School of Management and Urban Policy, New School for Social Research, 1992.

———. "Reintegrating Disadvantaged Communities into the Fabric of Urban Life: The Role of Community Development." Paper, New York, Community Development Research Center, New School for Social Research, 19 November 1994 and in *Housing Policy Debate* 6:1 (1995): 169–230.

Walker, Christopher. "Nonprofit Housing Development: Status, Trends, and Prospects." *Housing Policy Debate* 4:3 (1993): 361–414.

Walker, Judith. "Reforming the Role of Human Services in Government." In *Harold Washington and the Neighborhoods,* ed. Pierre Clavel and Wim Wiewel, 146–64. New Brunswick, NJ: Rutgers University Press, 1991.

Ward, David. *Cities and Immigrants: A Geography of Change in Nineteenth Century America.* New York: Oxford University Press, 1971.

Warren, Robert. "National Urban Policy and the Local State: Paradoxes of Meaning, Action, and Consequences." In *Exploring Urban America: An Introductory Reader,* ed. Roger Caves, 119–36. Thousand Oaks, CA: Sage Publications, 1995.

Weiner, Ronald, and Carol Beal. "The Sixth City: Cleveland in Three Stages of Urbanization." In *The Birth of Modern Cleveland, 1865–1930,* ed. Thomas Campbell and Edward Miggins, 19–23. Cleveland: Western Reserve Historical Society; London: Associated University Presses, 1988.

West, Cornel. *Prophetic Fragments: Illuminations of the Crisis in American Religion and Culture.* Grand Rapids, MI: William B. Eerdman's Publishing Company, 1993.

———. *Race Matters.* Vintage Books. New York: Random House, 1994.

Wetmore, Robert, and Helen L. Sause. "Striking a Public/Private Deal." *Urban Land* 54:1 (1995): 25–28.

Wheeler, Robert. "A Commercial Hamlet Is Founded: 1796–1824." In *Encyclopedia of Cleveland History,* ed. David Van Tassel and John Grabowski, xvii–xx. Bloomington: Indiana University Press, 1987.

Williams, Cecil, and Rebecca Laird. *No Hiding Place: Empowerment and Recovery for Our Troubled Communities.* New York: HarperCollins, 1992.

Wilson, William Julius. *The Truly Disadvantaged: The Inner City, the Underclass, and Public Policy.* Chicago: University of Chicago Press, 1987.

Winnick, Louis. *New People in Old Neighborhoods: The Role of New Immigrants in Rejuvenating New York's Communities.* New York: Russell Sage Foundation, 1990.

Winogrod, Mark. "The Riots—One Year After." *California Planner* (March–April 1993): 1, 7, 11.

Wood, Robert. "Model Cities: What Went Wrong—The Program or the Critics?" In *Neighborhood Policy and Programmes: Past and Present,* ed. Naomi Carmon, 61–73. New York: St. Martin's Press, 1990.

———. "People Versus Places: The Dream Will Never Die." In *Exploring Urban America: An Introductory Reader,* ed. Roger Caves, 137–43. Thousand Oaks, CA: Sage Publications, 1995.

Woodstock Institute. "Sound Loans for Communities: An Analysis of the Performance of Community Reinvestment Loans." Chicago: Woodstock Institute, 1993.

Wye, Christopher. "At the Leading Edge: The Movement for Black Civil Rights in Cleveland, 1830–1969." In *Cleveland: A Tradition of Reform,* ed. David Van Tassel et al., 113–35. Kent, OH: Kent State University Press, 1986.

Wylie, Jeanie. *Poletown: Community Betrayed.* Urbana: University of Illinois Press, 1989.

Yinger, John. "The Racial Dimension of Urban Housing Markets in the 1980s." In *Divided Neighborhoods,* ed. Gary Tobin, 64. Newbury Park, CA: Sage Publications, 1987.

Zdenek, Robert O. *Taking Hold: The Growth and Support of Community Development Corporations.* Washington, DC: National Congress for Community Economic Development, 1990.

The Contributors

REYNARD N. BLAKE, JR., has a master's degree in Resource Development/Urban Studies and is a Ph.D. candidate in the Urban Planning Program at Michigan State University. He has planned several Michigan State University conferences examining the role of faith-based institutions in community and economic development.

RACHEL G. BRATT received a Ph.D. in City and Regional Planning from MIT in 1976. Since then, she has been a professor in the Department of Urban and Environmental Policy at Tufts University. Bratt is the author of *Rebuilding a Low-Income Housing Policy* (1989) and a coeditor of *Critical Perspectives on Housing* (1986). She recently coauthored *Confronting the Management Challenge: Affordable Housing in the Nonprofit Sector* (1994). Her current work, funded by the Ford Foundation, involves developing models of self-sufficiency programs operated by nonprofit housing development organizations.

PETER DREIER is the E. P. Clapp Distinguished Professor of Politics and director of the Public Policy Program at Occidental College in Los Angeles. He received his Ph.D. from the University of Chicago. From 1984 to 1992 he served as director of Housing at the Boston Redevelopment Authority and as senior policy adviser to Boston mayor Ray Flynn. The Clinton administration appointed Dreier to the Advisory Board of the Resolution Trust Corporation. He has served as a consultant to HUD, the Connecticut Conference of Municipalities, the MacArthur Foundation in Chicago, ACORN, VISTA, and other government, community, and philanthropic organizations. He is a board member of the National Housing Institute and the National Low-Income Housing Coalition and was a founder of the Massachusetts Tenants' Organization in the early 1980s. Dreier writes widely on urban politics, housing policy, and community development. A regular contributor to *American Prospect* and the *Los Angeles Times,* his articles have appeared in the

Harvard Business Review, Social Policy, Urban Affairs Quarterly, Journal of the American Planning Association, Housing Policy Debate, National Civic Review, Nation, In These Times, New York Times, Boston Globe, and elsewhere.

SUSAN S. FAINSTEIN is Professor of Urban Planning and Policy Development at Rutgers University. She is coeditor of *Divided Cities: New York and London in the Contemporary World* (1992) and author of *The City Builders: Property, Planning, and Politics in London and New York* (1994). She has written extensively on issues of redevelopment, comparative public policy, and urban social movements.

ROBERT FISHER teaches social policy and community organization at the Graduate School of Social Work, University of Houston, where he is also chair of the program in Political Social Work. He is completing a book about doing public work in a private world. His books include *Let the People Decide: Neighborhood Organizing in America* (1994).

ROBERT GILOTH is senior associate at the Annie E. Casey Foundation and is initiative manager for the Annie E. Casey Foundation (AECF) Jobs Initiative. He formerly directed CDCs in Baltimore and Chicago that were engaged in employment training, adult education, economic development, housing, and community planning. From 1984 to 1987 he was deputy commissioner for Economic Development in the administration of Harold Washington. In this capacity, he directed the Research and Development Division in the Department of Economic Development that was responsible for a number of projects that attempted to link labor force development and economic development. Giloth has a Ph.D. in City and Regional Planning from Cornell University and is widely published on the topics of economic development and community development.

EDWARD GOETZ is associate professor in the Housing Program at the University of Minnesota. He is the author of *Shelter Burden: Local Politics and Progressive Housing Policy* (1993) and coeditor (with Susan E. Clarke) of *The New Localism: Comparative Local Politics in a Global Era* (1993). He has published several articles on local housing and economic development policy.

CLIFFORD HIRST is a Ph.D. candidate in urban planning at Rutgers University. He is writing his dissertation on citizen participation in Minneapolis and St. Paul.

W. DENNIS KEATING is Professor of Law and Urban Planning and associate dean of the Levin College of Urban Affairs at Cleveland State University. He has researched and published widely in the areas of urban planning and development, housing policy, housing and land-use law, and neighborhood development. His latest books are *Cleveland: A Metropolitan Reader* (1995, with Norman Krumholz and David Perry) and *The Suburban Racial Dilemma: Housing and Neighborhoods* (1994).

NORMAN KRUMHOLZ is a professor in the Levin College of Urban Affairs at Cleveland State University. He previously served as a planner in Buffalo, Pittsburgh, and Cleveland and was Cleveland's planning director from 1969 to 1979. He was a member of Pres. Jimmy Carter's National Commission on Neighborhoods. He is a past president of the American Planning Association (1987) and received the APA award for Distinguished Leadership (1990). He is the author of numerous articles and book chapters on planning practice, ethics, and theory. His most recent book (with Pierre Clavel) is *Reinventing Cities: Equity Planners Tell Their Stories* (1994).

JACQUELINE LEAVITT, a professor in the Department of Urban Planning in the UCLA School of Public Policy and Social Research, draws on qualitative research methods to focus on residents' involvement in community planning and housing policy. Her special interests concern the role of women in improving their environment, public housing, and housing as more than shelter. She is coauthor of *From Abandonment to Hope: Community-Households in Harlem* (1990) and coeditor of *The Hidden History of Low Income Cooperatives*.

EDWARD M. MIGGINS received a B.A. from Fairfield University in 1966, a Ph.D. from Case Western Reserve University in 1975, and a National Endowment for the Humanities (NEH) Fellowship at Columbia University in 1979. He has been employed at Cuyahoga Community College since 1972 and is currently a professor of history and urban studies and director of the Greater Cleveland Oral History and Community Studies Center at the college. Among other publications, he has edited and helped write *The Birth of Modern Cleveland: 1865–1930* (1988), *A Guide to Studying Neighborhoods and Resources on Cleveland* (1984), and *Responding to the Challenge: Cuyahoga Community College, 1963–1988* (1989). He is currently producing an oral history play on aging and has written another play, *Communities of Memory: Oral History, Ethnic Folklore, and Multicultural Education.*

JANET SMITH has a master's degree in Urban Planning from the University of Illinois at Urbana-Champaign and is a Ph.D. candidate in the Urban Studies Program at Cleveland State University. Her area of specialization is housing and community development, and current research includes racial diversity in urban neighborhoods and theories of neighborhood change.

GREGORY D. SQUIRES is Professor of Sociology and a member of the Urban Studies program faculty at the University of Wisconsin–Milwaukee. He recently spent two years working with HUD's Office of Fair Housing and Equal Opportunity on policy development pertaining to discrimination by financial institutions. Recent publications include "Does Anybody Who Works Here Look like Me? Mortgage Lending, Race, and Lender Employment," *Social Science Quarterly* (1995, with Sunwoong Kim) and *From Redlining to Reinvestment: Community Responses to Urban Disinvestment* (1992), which he edited.

PHILIP STAR, director of the Center for Neighborhood Development since 1988, joined the Urban Center after directing the Cleveland Tenants' Organization for ten years. He has been a consultant with the National Housing Institute and the Housing Law Reform Project at the University of Michigan. He received a master's degree from New York University and a law degree from Case Western Reserve University. He is admitted to practice in Ohio and New York. He is codirector of a HUD–designated Community Outreach Partnership Center (COPC) and has developed a neighborhood leadership development program.

JUNE MANNING THOMAS is an associate professor with a joint appointment in the Urban Planning and Urban Affairs programs at Michigan State University. She is author of *Seeking a Finer City: Redevelopment, Urban Planning, and Racial Change in Postwar Detroit* (forthcoming, 1996). During her sabbatical year, she worked as faculty coordinator in World Vision's training program for Detroit faith-based community development organizations.

AVIS C. VIDAL is director of the Community Development Research Center and associate professor of Urban Policy at the New School for Social Research. She has studied community-based development organizations extensively; her writings on their work include *Confronting the Management Challenge: Affordable Housing in the Nonprofit Sector* (1994) and *Rebuilding Communities: A National Study of Urban Community Development Corporations* (1993). She has recently placed the work of CDCs in a broader economic development and public policy context in "Reintegrating Disadvantaged Communities into the Fabric of Urban Life: The Role of Community Development" in *Housing Policy Debate*. Prior to joining the New School, she spent six years on the faculty of the Kennedy School of Government at Harvard University and two years on the Legislative and Urban Policy Staff at HUD, earning the Merit Award for Outstanding Service.

Index

ACORN. *See* Association of Community
  Organizations for Reform Now
Action for Grassroots Economic and
  Neighborhood Development Alternatives
  (AGENDA) (Los Angeles), 129(n11)
Adams, Charles G., 138
Addams, Jane, 19
Adult education, 17
Affordable Housing Act (1990), 55, 56(table)
AFL. *See* American Federation of Labor
African Americans, 4
  businesses, 19
  churches, 19, 61, 132–133, 135–136, 138,
    143(n1)
  church leaders, 133, 135, 136, 138, 141
  employment, 19, 20
  faith-based community development, 131,
    132, 134, 135–136, 137, 152, 202 (*see also*
    under Detroit)
  as fugitive slaves, 12
  in government, 20, 22, 52, 61, 78, 83, 124
  and home financing, 223–225, 226–227, 230
  housing, 19, 136, 137, 138
  and integration, 19
  neighborhoods, 19–22, 34, 61
  political activism, 41, 42
  political empowerment, 83
  population in cities (1960–1990), 207,
    212–213
  and property values, 223
  south-to-north migration, 7, 13, 18–19, 21
  and urban renewal, 30, 112
  women, 18, 19
  See also Racism; *under* Boston; Chicago;
    Cleveland; Detroit
African Methodist Episcopal (AME) church, 118
AGENDA. *See* Action for Grassroots Economic

and Neighborhood Development
  Alternatives
"Agenda for the '70s," 134
Agricultural land rights, 247
Akron (Ohio), 32
Alarcon, Richard, 127–128
Alinsky, Saul, 40(table), 41, 42, 46, 47, 84, 132
  tactics of, 225
  See also Trapp, Shel
Allegheny Conference (Pittsburgh), 153
Amalgamated Iron, Tin and Steel Workers
  Union, 15
AME. *See* African Methodist Episcopal church
American Bankers Association, 232, 233
American Family Insurance Company, 223–224
American Federation of Labor (AFL), 15
American Indians, 229
American Institute of Real Estate Appraisers, 223
Americanization classes, 17
Americanization Council (Cleveland), 18
American Muslim Mission, 133, 143(n5)
American Planning Association (APA), 114
American Shipbuilding Company, 12
American-Thai Education and Research Institute
  (ATI), 123
Antiblight Ordinance (Hartford), 173, 177
Anti-poverty programs, 4, 44, 246. *See also* War
  on Poverty
Antiurban bias, 207. *See also*
  Suburbs/suburbanization, and federal policy
APA. *See* American Planning Association
Appalachian groups, 23
Applebome, Peter, 46
Arizona, 46
Arson, 68
Asian Americans, 152. *See also* Immigrants,
  Asian

271

Star, Philip, 209
State government assistance to neighborhoods, 4, 145, 156, 173
Steel-rolling mills, 12, 15
Stokes, Carl, 22, 23
Student Non-Violent Coordinating Committee (SNCC), 40(table), 136
Students for a Democratic Society (SDS), 40(table)
Suburbs/suburbanization, 1, 4, 207, 211–212
 and auto, trolley, and train, 13, 211, 239
 churches, 142, 143
 -city economic disparities, 215
 and federal policy, 208, 238
 growth, 24, 207–208, 213
 growth restriction, 218, 247
 home financing, 51, 212, 223
 housing, 213
 housing starts, 208
 income, 214
 jobs, 165, 211, 213
 manufacturing sites, 211, 212
 move from, 22, 245
 politics, 237, 238
 and the poor, 5–6, 143, 212, 213
 race and class segregation, 207, 208, 212, 213
 taxes, 214, 247
 See also under Cleveland
Sullivan, Leon, 136, 202
 photo, 202
Sun-Belt, 165
Superior, Lake, 12
Sviridoff, Mitchell (Mike), 191, 203
 photo, 203
Swedna Foundation, 245
Systems of Survival (Jacobs), 196

Tax incentives, 55, 76, 157, 219, 238, 247
Tax-increment financing (TIF), 100, 102, 111(n3)
Tax Reform Act (1986), 55
Tax-sharing, 219
Taylor, John, 233
Technology, 15, 208, 239
Tenant organizations, 30, 40(table), 44
Tenants and Owners in Opposition to Redevelopment (TOOR) (San Francisco), 30
Tenants' rights law (Boston), 73–74
Tennessee, 46
Tenure, security of, 186
Texas, 46
Thomas, June Manning, 3, 61, 138
Thomson, Ken, 2
Thrift Supervision, Office of (OTS), 230, 233
TIF. See Tax-increment financing
Tipping point, 26–27, 29, 32
Title II. See Home Ownership Made Easy

Title VI, 181, 189(n1)
Tool lending library, 152
TOOR. See Tenants and Owners in Opposition to Redevelopment
Tourism, 2, 236
Transportation, 2, 11–12, 13
 gross national product (United States and Japan), 215
Trapp, Shel, 45
Traynor, Bill, 45
Treasury, Department of the, 230
Trickle-down economics, 3, 59
Trolley car, electric, 13, 18, 239
Turner, Bonnie, 129(n5)

UDAG. See Urban Development Action Grants
Ueberroth, Peter, 113–114, 129(n3)
ULI. See Urban Land Institute
Unemployment, 59, 68, 69–70
Union Bank (Los Angeles), 116
Union of Rumanian Societies in America, 18
Unions, 15, 43
 and African Americans, 20
 and community-based housing movement, 173–174, 226, 227
 for unskilled workers, 20
Unit conversion, 28
United Community Defense Services, 40(table)
United Neighborhoods Organization (UNO), 120
United Way, 40(table), 76
University of California, Los Angeles (UCLA) Urban Planning Program, 121
University of Illinois, 88
University of Minnesota, Hubert H. Humphrey Institute, 202
UNO. See United Neighborhoods Organization
Upon This Rock: The Miracles of a Black Church (Freedman), 137
Upper class, 40(table), 212
Uprooted, The: The Epic Story That Made the American People (Handlin), 9
Urban Development Action Grants (UDAG), 53, 54, 59, 216
Urban Fortunes (Logan and Molotch), 65
Urban growth machine, 2, 65
Urban Land Institute (ULI), 114, 129(n4)
"Urban mission" movement, 134
Urban neighborhoods
 categories, 236
 and CBD redevelopment, 3
 change patterns, 29–33
 change policy proposals, 246–248
 changes, 1, 10, 24, 27(fig.), 34–35, 37–38, 60, 236
 change theories, 25–29
 characteristics, 10, 24, 94
 community institutions, 1, 14, 16, 76, 217